THE **GREAT** NATIONAL PARKS

OF THE WORLD

THE GREAT NATIONAL PARKS
OF THE WORLD

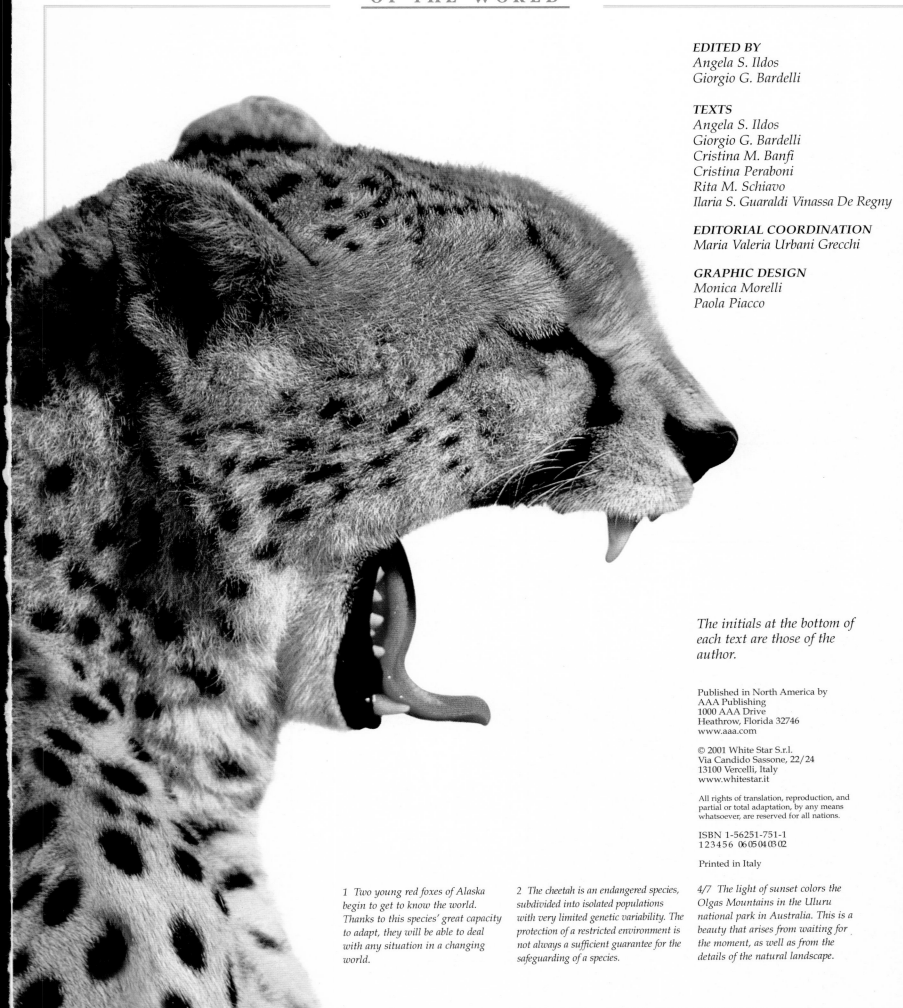

EDITED BY
Angela S. Ildos
Giorgio G. Bardelli

TEXTS
Angela S. Ildos
Giorgio G. Bardelli
Cristina M. Banfi
Cristina Peraboni
Rita M. Schiavo
Ilaria S. Guaraldi Vinassa De Regny

EDITORIAL COORDINATION
Maria Valeria Urbani Grecchi

GRAPHIC DESIGN
Monica Morelli
Paola Piacco

The initials at the bottom of each text are those of the author.

Published in North America by
AAA Publishing
1000 AAA Drive
Heathrow, Florida 32746
www.aaa.com

© 2001 White Star S.r.l.
Via Candido Sassone, 22/24
13100 Vercelli, Italy
www.whitestar.it

ISBN 1-56251-751-1
1 2 3 4 5 6   06 05 04 03 02

Printed in Italy

1 *Two young red foxes of Alaska begin to get to know the world. Thanks to this species' great capacity to adapt, they will be able to deal with any situation in a changing world.*

2 *The cheetah is an endangered species, subdivided into isolated populations with very limited genetic variability. The protection of a restricted environment is not always a sufficient guarantee for the safeguarding of a species.*

4/7 *The light of sunset colors the Olgas Mountains in the Uluru national park in Australia. This is a beauty that arises from waiting for the moment, as well as from the details of the natural landscape.*

CONTENTS

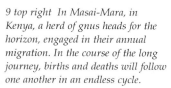

9 top right In Masai-Mara, in Kenya, a herd of gnus heads for the horizon, engaged in their annual migration. In the course of the long journey, births and deaths will follow one another in an endless cycle.

9 below Despite the fact the Atlantic Ocean is not far, the Namib National Park has a desert environment. The dunes of very fine sand gather together an unexpected variety of species, both animal and vegetable, many of which are exclusive to the place.

8 The mighty roar of the lion allows the male to affirm his supremacy over the territory, discouraging his rivals from approaching his pride. When his cry echoes in the savannah, everyone knows that he is its sovereign.

9 top left On the African plains of Serengeti, in Tanzania, the rising of the sun seems to set fire to the flattened comae of the acacia trees. A new day begins, but the night is not without its own events.

INTRODUCTION

The concept of "national parks," which started with Yellowstone in 1872, cannot be defined as a novelty by any means. And so, why publish a book today on this subject? There are many reasons.

For far too long, establishing a protected area meant sealing and delivering certain portions of land to the generations to come, while the entire surrounding countryside was exploited and defaced, often irreversibly. In this third millennium, mankind no longer thinks this way. Preserving means managing, enjoying, and restoring; not shoving into the attic the faded memory of how the world once was, but fully and constructively experiencing the incredible capacity—typical of our species—to act upon the environment.

There is still nature around the world. It is still possible to get lost in a rainforest, wander about a desert, climb the tallest mountains (which are still untouched) and swim over a pristine coral reef. Not because man has been unable to colonize every corner of the planet, but because he has realized that the irreplacable must be preserved and has dedicated certain areas of the world to do just that: national parks, natural reserves and protected areas of various types and levels of importance. It is equally true that often a national park is created for the main objective of safeguarding a particular aspect of a natural environment: a rare geological phenomenon, an animal species that risks extinction, or even just simply an exceptionally beautiful landscape. But each of these unique aspects cannot be considered apart from all the rest, so the importance of a protected area generally goes beyond what is found within its borders, which are often narrow. The reason behind their establishment differs each

time. What they have in common is the fact that those who created them spotted from the very beginning the biodiversity and uniqueness of that very place on earth; diversity that must have been preserved in the interaction with mankind. A forest, a river basin, a section of the coast or even mankind itself are not sealed compartments, each one existing independently of the others. A drop of water that is lifted by the sun as vapor, rising from the surface of the sea or a leaf on a tree, falls thousands of miles away as a snowflake, which in

INTRODUCTION

turn is imprisoned for centuries in an alpine glacier that melts to offer a drink to a roe deer hundreds of miles away, which in turn becomes the next meal of a lynx, which will then use part of its urine to mark its territory, wetting the base of a tree. This moisture can foster the growth of a mushroom that, after disseminating its spores, will quickly decompose and on and on, in an endless cycle that also involves our kitchen faucet. "Ecology," a word that is often misunderstood, is the name that science has been given to the relationships among all the parts of an ecosystem. It is a young science that has a long way to go, but one of its basic points is already clear: nothing exists independently of the rest.

In regions that are little populated by man or completely unpopulated, another value is added to the intrinsic value of the natural environment: the fact that there are regions in the world that can be defined as uncontaminated, wild and inviolate satisfies an inner need that is hard to express in words. We need to know that somewhere there still exist realities for which these terms have meaning, that not everything has been colonized, utilized or modified. That all the world is not enclosed within the scope of our daily experience.

Parks and reserves are not always found in uncontaminated areas. Indeed, quite often (and above all in Europe) in the immediate vicinity or even inside them there are human settlements and economic activities being performed. In many cases, the very structure of the park envisions not only an area of total protection in which its measures are valid, but also a partially protected buffer area. Within the latter, the attempt is made to reconcile environmental needs with man's activities, above all when

10 below Among the species that owe their survival exclusively to the creation of a national park, the Alpine ibex is a textbook case. The Italian park of Gran Paradiso has adopted it as its symbol.

10-11 A red fox patrols its snowy territory on a winter's day. Each individual, especially in the harshest environments, needs large spaces to move around in.

11 below The Tribulation Glacier, in Upper Valnontey, shows all its harsh grandeur. For the Gran Paradiso national park, one of the most important protected areas in Europe, the beauty of the Alpine landscape is a distinguishing feature.

10 top left Among the great predators that have been in danger of disappearing from Europe, the common lynx is one of the most beautiful but also most elusive species. Spotting it in its habitat is a privilege enjoyed by few, but its presence enriches us all.

10 top right The chamois can still run free, thanks to the protection accorded to mountain ungulates. Having previously vanished from many areas, the number of these large European herbivores has now been rising fast for many years.

they represent full-fledged local traditions. On the other hand, the mission of many parks is to support and valorize a local cultural heritage that also includes activities like raising livestock, which have made an important contribution to shaping the very appearance of the territory over the centuries, generally affecting the distribution and type of vegetation. Many protected areas are actually a small mosaic of reserves, each of which has the goal of safeguarding a particular environmental aspect, according to the characteristics of the territory.

Other elements that are by no means secondary can add value to a protected area. First of all are the tourism ramifications: an efficient park typically has structures designed to welcome visitors and give them information. It will also have accommodations from hotels to stark and simple refuges, trails or other ways of getting about in order to see the major points of interest, lookout points for fauna, botanical gardens, museums and personnel in charge of surveillance and accompanying tourists. In many countries with an old tradition of environmental protection, the yearly number of visitors to the national parks often exceeds the total population of the country. In Japan, for example, it is nearly tripled.

In the case of the best-known and most-frequented of protected areas, tourism and protection can also clash with each other. This is undoubtedly one of the problems that park managers are forced to face, and is confirmation that a well-managed protected area can become an opportunity for economic development. Part of the proceeds can also be used for protective measures.

Scientific research in a naturalistic framework, indispensable for understanding environmental dynamics, is another activity that can be carried out best in a territory that has been safeguarded. It is also an important source of data necessary to manage a protected area.

This book is essentially organized in chapters, each one dedicated to a specific continent or geographic area. Within these chapters the most representative of protected areas on the territory have been selected. However, considering the fact that the importance of the natural and cultural heritage transcends the boundaries of the individual countries, 150 member states of UNESCO (United Nations Educational, Scientific and Cultural Organization) in 1972 adopted a Convention for the Protection of the World Cultural and Natural Heritage, better known as the World Heritage Convention. The list includes the natural areas that bear exceptional witness to the particular phases of the history of the Earth, areas with major ecological and biological significance or that include unique natural phenomena, particularly beautiful places and environments that are especially significant for the conservation of biological diversity. Many of the areas protected by the national parks to which this book is dedicated are included on the list of assets that are part of the world's heritage.

The first step when it comes to falling in love always occurs through a glance, even a fleeting one. And so, to truly fall in love with planet Earth, we must let ourselves be enchanted by the splendid images of this book which represent the loveliest and most pristine places in the world. (I.S.G.V.D.R.)

14 bottom left A male ibex lets out his cry of challenge. Communication between animals is based on posture and sounds. The females emit a special signal to attract their young.

14 center The impala is the most widespread antelope in the vast savannah plains of east Africa. The photo shows a group of many females following a single male, distinguishable on account of his large horns.

14 right The Everglades National Park in Florida contains large marshy areas, with vegetation made up of trees such as pond cypresses, capable of living in flooded habitats. It is the dominion of the alligator.

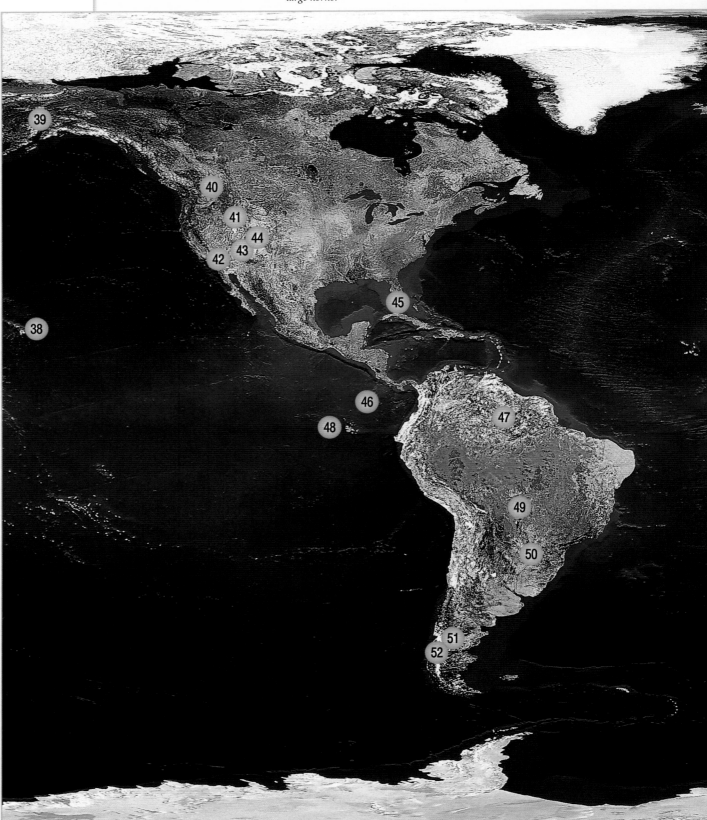

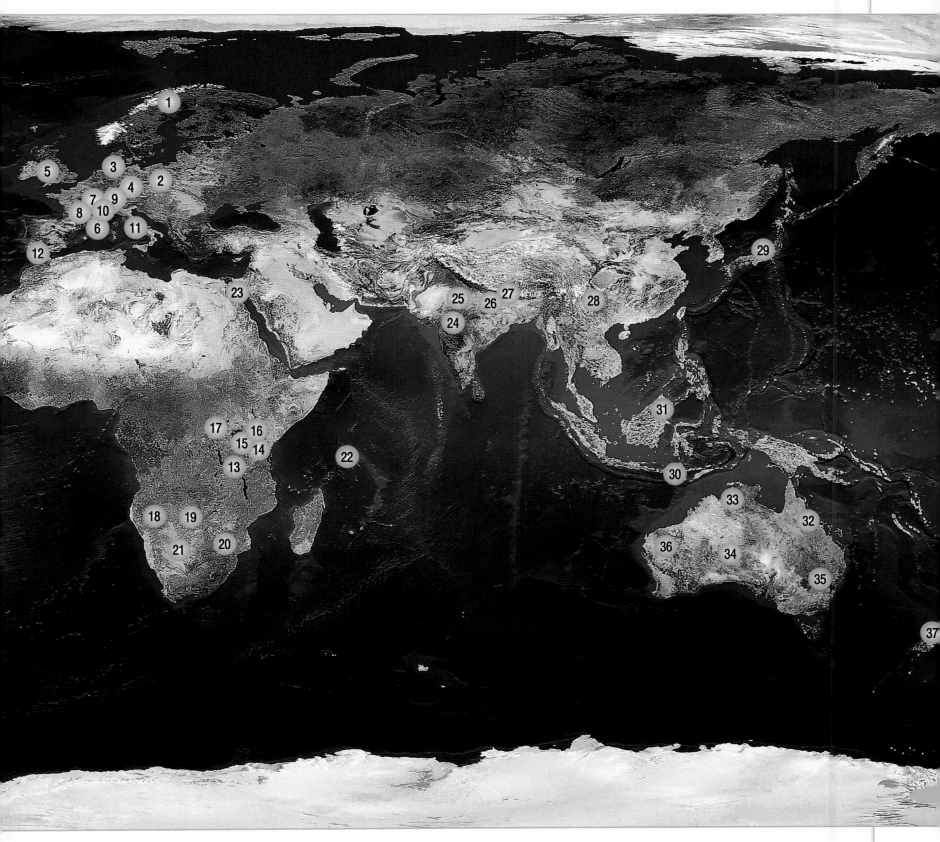

16-17 For African elephants water is an essential resource. During the dry season the herds move around continuously in search of drinking places, knowledge of which is passed down from one generation to the next.

18-19 In the Kings Canyon National Park a storm has just cleared the air. The sunset lights up the Evolution Peaks, along the famous trail named after John Muir, a pioneer of nature conservation in America.

20-21 Colored fish dance around gorgonia and alcyonaria, particular types of soft coral. For those who are keen on scuba diving, the protected areas of the tropical seas offer opportunities for observation, even at limited depth.

key

1 ABISKO	19 MOREMI AND CHOBE
2 TATRZANSKI	20 KRUGER
3 WATTENMEER	21 KGALAGADI
4 BAYERISCHER WALD	22 ALDABRA
5 LAKE DISTRICT	23 RAS MOHAMMED
6 PORT-CROS	24 RANTHAMBORE
7 VANOISE	25 CORBETT
8 CÉVENNES	26 CHITWAN
9 ENGADINA	27 SAGARMATHA
10 GRAN PARADISO	28 WOLONG
11 ABRUZZO	29 JOSHINETSU-KOGEN
12 DOÑANA	30 KOMODO
13 MAHALE	31 DANUM VALLEY
14 NGORONGORO	32 GREAT BARRIER REEF
15 SERENGETI AND MASAI MARA	33 KAKADU
16 TSAVO AND AMBOSELI	34 ULURU
17 VIRUNGA	35 LAMINGTON
18 ETOSHA	36 KARIJINI

37 MOUNT COOK
38 HAWAII VOLCANOES
39 DENALI
40 JASPER AND BANFF
41 YELLOWSTONE
42 YOSEMITE
43 GRAND CANYON
44 BRYCE CANYON
45 EVERGLADES
46 ISLA DEL COCO
47 CANAIMA
48 GALÁPAGOS
49 PANTANAL MATOGROSSENSE
50 IGNAZÚ
51 LOS GLACIARES
52 TORRES DEL PAINE

22 top left A young fox explores its world. Very common throughout the continent, the red fox adapts to the most disparate environments, often living in proximity to man without the latter realizing it.

22 top right A road borders Tarn Hows, in the Lake District National Park in England. A place that is anything but wild, but where a good balance has been struck between the natural environment and man's presence.

22 below The brown bear is among the species that have been most negatively affected by man's presence in Europe. It now survives in isolated residual populations, mostly within protected areas.

23 Valnontey, the Gran Paradiso National Park. The autumn colors of the larches are one of the most beautiful natural sights on the Alps and in northern Europe.

EUROPE
INTRODUCTION

"The Old World" is a very appropriate definition. This expression traditionally used to describe Europe underlines the main aspects of this continent: it's age. Nature's gift to Europe is a mild climate and fertile land that has made it a preferred colony for the human race, who founded major civilizations here. Those who travel through Europe usually concentrate on its artistic and historical treasures, yet this continent is home to a natural beauty that includes habitats that have no equal anywhere else in the world. Tales told by Europeans who visit distant countries always seem to communicate a vivid impression of immense exotic landscapes, whether they be Asian deserts, African savannas or American cordilleras. In Europe, however, everything seems to be pocket-sized. In just a few hundred miles we pass from the warmly scented Mediterranean to soaring Alpine slopes that exceed 13,000 feet in altitude, to coasts whipped

by Atlantic winds and sculpted by the force of its currents, to the energy of rolling inland plains, intensely farmed and dotted with cities rich in history. There are volcanoes in Iceland topped with snow and in the Mediterraneanthere are volcanoes topped with citrus trees. Earthquakes that are too close for comfort to remind us what a sprightly old lady Europe is, where the power of endogenous phenomena emerges with such liveliness that the territory is constantly evolving. Mountain chains born in the Cretaceous period are still growing, betraying their primitive seabed origins by spouting a fossil heritage of worldwide importance. Lakes of all sizes, fanned out or nestled amongst peaks remind us of when glaciers were far more extensive than they are now.

Europe's natural common denominator is, however, the sea: in a continent notched with a myriad of islands, peninsulas, isthmuses and fjords, no area is more than 370 miles from the sea. Certainly, the placid, warm Mediterranean has a different influence than the icy North Sea, and the Atlantic coasts touched by the Gulf currents show quite dissimilar flora and fauna from those that are not kissed by these currents. In any case, the mitigating, modeling effect of the sea ceases to be felt only in easternmost Europe, where it gives way to woods and continental steppe.

Europe is the cradle of countless civilizations, past and present, each characterized by a specific vision of the world and of nature. For Ancient Romans, nature was to be tamed and made to serve the human race, and even today we are astounded by the quality of civil engineering that was achieved for this purpose. For example, the spectacular Marmore Waterfall, the highest in Europe, is the result of a

24-25 Relatively inhospitable, the mountainous areas of Europe have preserved much of their nature intact. However, the careful observer can perceive the signs of man even here, such as the reduction of the woods in favor of grazing land. We are in the Valley of Rhêmes, in the Gran Paradiso complex.

24 below In spring, on the mountains still spotted with snow, a male black grouse exhibits itself and its fine physique in view of the reproductive season.

25 above The black grouse males, also known as mountain pheasants, face each other in special arenas with the aim of winning female favors. These areas, which are particularly important for these birds, should be carefully safeguarded.

25 below Always the symbol of power and determination, the royal eagle still flies in the European skies. It is possible to admire its impressive silhouette partly thanks to the protection measures carried out in its favor.

26-27 The Alps are the biggest mountain range in Europe, still rich in unspoiled areas. Two young male chamois chase each other in the snow, giving free rein to their exuberance.

deviation of the River Velino, ordered by the consul Curius Dentatus in the second century BC in order to recover and exploit for agriculture the precious land in Central Italy. The attitude of the northern Celts was quite different, for their Druid religion required perfect harmony with the forces of nature.

All these influences became part of modern Europe's "genetic heritage," and now the effects of thousands of years of environmental exploitation must be calculated, including the extensive and increasing concentration of inhabitants on a small but extremely diversified territory. Fortunately, the people of Europe realized some time ago that their surroundings had become very fragile. The first European national parks were founded as early as 1909, but even some time before this several areas of particular environmental importance were subjected to protective measures that in some ways could be called "private," since they were often royal estates or hunting reserves.

Nowadays this continent can boast one of the most longsighted and precise legislations of ecological politics. Environmental management in Europe must be articulated over several fronts: endangered species to be saved from extinction often co-exist with over-exploited species to be preserved, and kept under control. Most European habitats are in a state of degradation and must be recovered. The few areas that are still intact must be managed with great care as they are too small to survive alone, so it is vital they communicate and form an organized network of truly live landscapes so that a process of self-healing is triggered. The

chief instrument for intervening in a decisive way is to set up protected areas. In Europe such areas have a number of particular aspects; indeed, tourists are often surprised by the fact that European national parks allow farming, even quite large settlements, within their confines. The explanation for this lies in the history of this continent. It would be useless to pretend that vast sectors of territory could be kept intact with a concentration of 68 inhabitants per square mile. So it is far more effective to integrate humans in the preservation process, with their traditional activities and attachment to their homeland, with a true awareness of being part (and not antagonist) of the environment in which they live. Total protection measures may be applied where we find the most priceless treasures: species at risk like the otter, bear, lynx, or particularly vulnerable biotopes such as humid zones. This is when Europe's protection program involves truly wild areas, typical of mountain or island regions, but also coastal areas, urban outskirts, and wood-covered hills. The pages that follow are just a sample. (A.S.I.)

28 bottom left In the territory of the national park there are a number of water courses. The main one is the Abiscojåkka River, which in its upper course penetrates between levees of deeply hollowed rock.

28 bottom right "The gate of Lapland," Abisko stretches into the land of the midnight sun, is easily accessible and has first-rate tourist facilities: this photo shows it in all its peaceful splendor.

29 bottom The largest representative of the Mustelidae family is the wolverine. This creature is characterized by its remarkable ferocity and courage, to the extent that it engages in battle with carnivores many times its size.

28-29 Between Kiruna and Abisko stretches an area of semi-plain barren land, dotted here and there with supple birches. These trees struck the ancients on account of their tenacity and endurance, especially in relation to the slenderness of the trunk, so much so that they were attributed with magic powers.

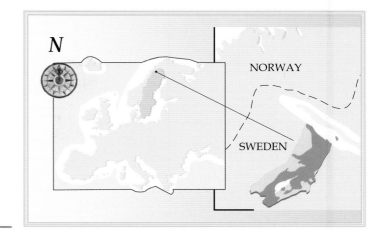

ABISKO
NATIONAL PARK

One morning toward the end of May, sunbeams penetrate the leaves of the birches and touch the waters of the countless lakes, but the evening sunset will never arrive: daytime will last until mid-July. This is what happens in the heart of Lapland—or perhaps we should call it the land of the "Sámi," as the native population prefers to be called. These people are now the ethnic minority here on the roof of Europe, but the Sámi once followed the rhythm of the seasons, leading a nomadic life seeking pastureland for their herds of reindeer and living in "lavvu," which look like the teepees of the American Indians. They would fish and make silver jewelry as the howling of the wolves accompanied the endless winters (breeding reindeer is no longer considered sufficient as a means of support). Among other activities, the young people now devote themselves to tourism, accompanying visitors as they explore this land of wide open spaces; or fish for prized species such as salmon and chars.

In 1909, a Swedish national park was founded here that remains one of the best-known to tourists: Abisko National Park, the first national park in Europe. Since it is easily accessible (as opposed to other parks in Lapland), it welcomes over ten thousand visitors a year. The basis for this project was the creation of a research station for scholars and students of natural science. This made it possible to save one of Sweden's most interesting areas from the dynamiting done in the numerous local iron mines, preserving it for naturalist studies of mountain areas.

Abisko is located on the southern shore of Lake Torneträsk and it is an important tourist destination, located along the Kiruna-Narvik road. Here, during the period of the "midnight sun," the ski resorts are fully open even after 10 p.m., when the shafts of sunlight make the outlines of the countryside even sharper. The park includes the Abiskojakka river valley and Mount Njulla, from the peak of which you can admire the entire lake below. The park also covers part of the shore of Lake Torneträsk, with the island of Abiskosuolo, for a total area of nineteen thousand acres. Just before its estuary, the river passes through a spectacular canyon surrounded by a vertical cliff about sixty-five feet, offering a hint of the geological history of these lands. The river delta is closed to visitors from May 1st to July 31st, to avoid disturbing the rich bird life, which nests during this period. About one-third of the area is bare rock: these are the peaks of the Scandinavian Alps (generally ranging in altitude from 3,960 to 4,950 feet above sea level). Just past the point where the crest begins to descend, lichens and moss,

dwarf willows, heather and alpine fields cover the ground, before giving way to the copses of birch trees.

The park is famous for its wild orchids—some of which are rare, while others are endemic, such as the *Epipogium aphyllum* and the platantera (*Platanthera oliganthe*). As you walk through this area, you'll certainly see lemmings chasing each other, or you may even see one of these small rodents being caught by a white fox. You may also catch the sight of the tracks of wolves, lynxes or the inquisitive wolverene (though the shy and generally nocturnal animals themselves prefer to remain hidden). The wolverene, a close relative of the martens and beech-marten, often approaches man-made items such as sack traps and hunting boxes, making itself quite unpopular among residents.

If you go near the lakes, you might see an imposing elk as it nibbles at mineral-rich aquatic plants, or the common loon "calling" as it swims. Or you might even see the now-rare snow partridge as it sits on its eggs amidst the beech trees. These are all minor details that help us understand how this park, with its colors, sounds and smells, can still impart a sense of peacefulness and magic, helping us forget that just past its boundaries, the howl of the wolf has now been replaced by the growl of snowmobiles. (R.M.S.)

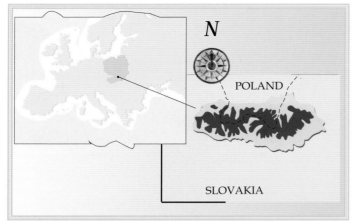

30 bottom The lakes are one of the characteristic features of the landscape, especially on the High Tatras. This portion of the mountain group is made up of impermeable rocks, which do not allow the development of karst phenomena.

30-31 Though it does not reach 8,200 feet in altitude, the Tatra mountain chain has a decidedly Alpine aspect, modeled by the ancient Quaternary glaciers.

TATRA
NATIONAL PARKS

The twin Tatra National Parks, located in Poland and the Slovakia, share a border of 40 miles. Together they form an outstanding attraction: an environment and a local culture whose importance was recognized by UNESCO in 1993, when it was already clear that this unique alpine environment was to be protected.

This is the site of lovely mountains, shaped by the glaciers of the Pleistocene. The Tatra mountain range is not very long, extending for only about thirty-seven miles and nine miles wide in the much larger complex of the central Carpathian mountains. However, it is a tall range that is divided into two separate parts distinguished first of all by their different geological nature. To the east, the High Tatras are composed

mostly of hard granitic rock that, through erosion, has been sharpened into rugged crests and towering peaks. This is a typical alpine landscape, with peaks reaching a maximum altitude of 8,707 feet with Mount Gerlach (Gerlachovsky stit), but they have a harsh beauty and majesty worthy of the Alps. The Western Tatras are formed of metamorphic and calcareous rocks, the latter having been dissolved and shaped by water. The mountains are not as tall, but they are a spectacular sight with their deep gorges and numerous caves, including the most developed one in the country, known as Wielka Sniezna. It is about twelve miles long and 2,670 feet deep. There are about 650 caves in the park, some of which can be visited by tourists.

Today, the Tatras are no longer marked by glaciers, but the presence of past glaciers can be detected by the U-shaped valleys, the moraines and the cirque glaciers that are often occupied by mountain lakes whose waters, which hold little life, are unusually clear. The torrents, lakes and waterfalls represent the main attraction of the territory, but they are plentiful above all next line in the High Tatras, where the crystalline rocks prevent the waterways from carving a riverbed hidden beneath the surface, as instead occurs in areas where calcareous rock prevails.

More than seventy percent of these national parks are marked by spruce forests, whose existence are mainly due to the age-old presence of man. For a long time, the forests were intensively exploited for wood, required for the mines of metallic ores that supplied the foundries in the area. Thus, today's woods have a different appearance from the ones in similar environments, the latter showing a uniform covering of spruce. Nevertheless, the landscape shows the typical vertical succession in bands characterized by different climates and vegetations. At an altitude of about 5,000 feet, the trees give way to twisted shrubs that withstand the harsh mountain climate. Located at even higher altitudes are alpine meadows, which precede the crests and rocky summits. Together, the grassy territories and bare rocks represent over one-fourth of

31 bottom left A deer proudly shows off its autumnal antlers. Scouring its territory it is ready to take on the challenge of any rivals in the love stakes.

31 bottom right Where any other creature would find itself in trouble, a chamois braves a steep rocky wall, giving proof to its extraordinary aptitude at moving around on rough terrain.

the surface area of the national parks. This is certainly not a desolate environment and indeed, it represents the main attraction for peace-lovers seeking a place for quiet meditation and broad horizons. It is not by chance that one of the people who came most frequently to the Polish Tatra Mountains was Karol Wojtyla, Pope John Paul II.

Even in the areas that are seemingly lifeless, the attentive visitor can see many of the more than 1,000 greater plant species that comprise the flora of the Tatra mountains: edelweiss (*Leontopodium alpinum*); and also the prestigious *Dryas octopetala*, the silent survivor of the glaciers of the Quaternary period, clinging to the calcareous rocks with tenacious woody stalks that trail along the ground, hidden by graceful leaves and embellished with numerous white flowers. These are places where you can also see the animal that symbolizes both national parks of the Tatra mountains, the chamois.

The fauna of these little Slovak-Polish Alps is mainly the type found traditionally in the European mountains, including the marmot, one of the mammals that attracts the attention of many hikers, thanks also to its loud whistles of alarm. Another species that is widespread at lower altitudes, and far less visible, is the wood grouse; viewing the exhibitionist parading of this animal is an experience that requires patience, attention, luck and a long silent wait in the dense pine forests. You can also get an idea of the naturalistic aspects of the Tatra Mountains by visiting the museums in Zakopane and Tatranska Lomnica, towns at the edges of the national parks. These museums are just one of the many facilities here, which include shelters, hostels and a network of 480 miles of marked trails, that welcome visitors to one of the loveliest areas in Europe. Poland and Slovakia, the countries for which tourism has become the leading economic resource, also maintain a local culture composed of unique architecture, traditions and customs that are marked by their strong tie to the land. (G.G.B.)

32 A young brown bear, curious about the world, has climbed up a fir tree. The adults, weighing from 450 up to 1,300 pounds, move around exclusively on the ground with their characteristic rolling gait.

33 top Peacefully stretched out on the rocky terrain so as to make the most of its warmth, this marmot looks as though it is yawning. This rodent digs deep lairs in the ground, where it spends the winter season in a deep sleep.

33 center The icy wind lifts up flurries of snow, beneath a threatening sky and in the presence of overhanging, dark rocky walls. This captures a highly atmospheric moment, for anyone who loves the mountains.

33 bottom Harsh and apparently eternal, the highest peaks of the Tatra mountains are without vegetation. Few environments lend themselves to meditation as much as the high peaks.

WATTENMEER
NATIONAL PARK

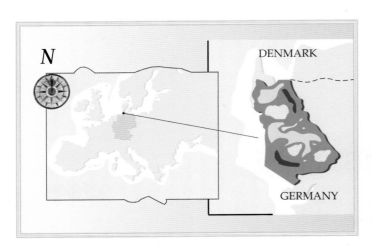

The Wattenmeer is a typical ecosystem of the North Sea, composed of a strip of low coastal waters and muddy tidal plains about six miles wide, stretching from Holland to Denmark and decorating the northern coast of Germany like the lace trim on a traditional costume. As is the case with all wetlands, only the attentive and trained observer can grasp its precious features at first glance. The less experienced ones instead see only mud, algae and few prospects for economic growth—reason enough to reclaim it! Perhaps we should thank the noisy royal seagulls (*Larus argentatus*) and the terns dancing in the windy skies, which nest here by the thousands, for having called the government's attention to this gem of sea ecology that is appropriately referred to as "the nursery of the North Sea," (given the predilection that also brings many prized fish species to reproduce in its water). The Wattenmeer has long been the object of safeguarding measures limited to single biotopes, such as Memmert Island in the archipelago of

34 bottom A pair of sea swallows take advantage of a brief moment of intimacy. Even in the crowded colony each individual always finds its partner, thanks to an elaborate dance of recognition.

the Eastern Frisian Islands, declared a reserve as early as 1907. Today, this unique landscape has finally been protected in the form of a national park, the largest in Germany, thanks to the farsightedness of the city of Hamburg and two other territories, Lower Saxony to the west and Schleswig-Holstein to the northeast. With independent administrative acts in 1985, these cities entrusted this heirloon to future generations.   In the early nineties, UNESCO ratified its specificity and the ecological importance of the different sections of the Wattenmeer, declaring them Reserves of the Biosphere, and since 1992 it has been listed among internationally important wetlands by the Ramsar Convention. In 1999 the park further increased its importance for environmental protection: the Parliament of Schleswig-Holstein moved to make the waters around the islands of Sylt and Amrum a marine reserve in order to safeguard small cetaceans, first and foremost the porpoise (*Phocoena phocoena*), which lives and reproduces along these coasts. This is the first true sanctuary in Europe dedicated to this purpose, with protective measures that ban motorboats, industrial fishing and all human activities that could disturb these cheerful but vulnerable cetaceans.

The Wattenmeer remains one of the most productive habitats on the planet; observing the incredible quantity of organisms that prosper here, despite the cold tides, will help convince us that shaping clay is enough to create life, just like in ancient mythology. Here, the tides of the North Sea welcome the waters of major rivers at constant flow, including the Elbe, the Weber and the Ems. This generates jagged coastlines, brackish fields, semi-submerged beaches and a wide variety of

34-35 The tidal plain of Wattenmeer stretches for more than 250 miles along the North Sea. It is not uncommon to find amber in the sand, the precious fossil resin sometimes enclosing insects that lived millions of years ago.

35 top The oyster catcher is a fairly large wading bird, but this does not limit its flying ability. It forms very large colonies on small islands on sand bars, and feeds off mollusks it extracts from the mud.

35 bottom A black-tailed godwit in flight lets out its cry, which to our ears sounds more or less like "rita-rita-rita.". It is another typical inhabitant of Wattenmeer.

36-37 Watchful, but generally relaxed, these common seals enjoy the warmth of a ray of sun on the shore uncovered by the low tide.

36 bottom The sea swallow is very agile in flight; to locate fish it assumes the characteristic "holy spirit" position, immobile in the windy sky, to measure the distance before taking a nosedive.

sandy islands that rise or disappear depending on the currents, creating a mosaic of protected environments that easily become a refuge for seals, cetaceans, crowded colonies of sea swallows, gossips, flovers and other sea and limicolous birds.

Here and there, as if to remind us that man no longer dominates this corner of nature, we find vestiges of long-gone eras; on the lush island of Neuwerk, at the mouth of the Elbe, you can still visit the medieval fortifications that protected the city of Hamburg against the incursions of pirates — perhaps using them as stations for bird-watching. A trek in a horse-drawn buggy will give you a chance to savor all the poetry and peace of this environment, although covering the beaches and tidal plains on foot make it easier to approach the bird colonies with discretion and — if you look closely — spy a piece of amber gleaming in the mud. (A.S.I.)

37 top The icy waters of the North Sea hold no fear for these sheldrake chicks, in Indian file behind their parents. We are near the homeland of Andersen, but we challenge you to point out an "ugly duckling" among these!

37 bottom Unlike most ducks, the sheldrake flies with slow beats of its wings, just as geese do. This is a male: it can be recognized by the red protuberance on its beak.

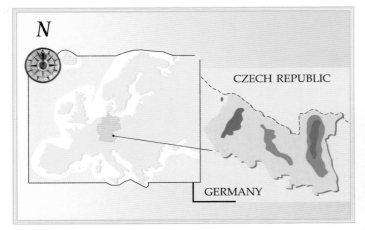

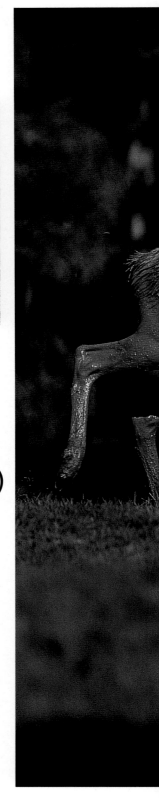

BAYERISCHER WALD
NATIONAL PARK

Near Munich, in the heart of a busy Europe that is crossed by traffic and highways, there is a hidden treasure. Only those who know the Bayerischer Wald will expect to come upon this surprise. It is an untouched strip of the ancient forests that covered the continent before human presence became so intense, a place where it is easy to forget the hullabaloo of civilization and instead imagine primitive ancestors as they hunt wild boars and deer. Today, only a few scanty sections survive of the various ecotypes of the original woods. One of these strips is protected by a national park, a vast 32,000 acres, and is part of the great Bohemian Forest that extends for 500,000 acres and even reaches over the border into the Czech Republic.

At first sight the Bayerischer Wald appears to be somewhat humdrum, but in reality it is a varied and ambient place that climbs to great altitudes, even as far as the Grosser Rachel Peak. In just a few miles it is possible to encounter climates and vegetation resembling those that we could otherwise meet only by taking a long trip from central Europe to the far north of the continent.

The park is managed, with the intention of safeguarding the most natural possible conditions for vegetation. So in the most precious forest areas, for instance near Lake Rachel, nobody has removed a tree trunk in almost a century. This is fundamentally important for the biological communities of the Bayerischer Wald, since the decomposition of the vegetation constitutes the basis for numerous food chains that guarantee the existence of the species that populate the park. Thus it is not uncommon to see dead trees, often slumped to the ground or still stubbornly stretching skywards. Hard, gray shelf-like fungus can often be seen on the trunks, which is partly responsible for the death of the plant. Far from being symptoms that the forest is suffering, these are actually signs of its constant rebirth. The soft, rotting wood provides nourishment for a variety of insect life, who in turn become food for animals such as woodpeckers. These birds peck holes into the trunks of ancient trees, not only in search of food, but also to create nests. When the woodpeckers abandon these

38 bottom The boreal owl is one of the elusive nocturnal inhabitants of the Bavarian Forest. It nests in the hollows of trees, but prefers the holes dug out and subsequently abandoned by the black woodpecker, the largest European woodpecker.

38-39 Two male deer face one another in a duel of strength and cunning, with the aim of forcing their rival to retreat and surrender. Generally, but not always, the damage done to the loser is not serious. The prize for the winner will be the right to reproduce.

39 bottom A stretch of trees as far as the eye can see, with tracts of it dotted with glades, mountains and water courses. This is the Bavarian Forest, one of the last wooded regions still intact in Europe, where man leaves nature to its own devices.

40 top left The mixed woods of needle-leaf and broad-leaf trees near Lake Rachel are among the best preserved in the Bavarian Forest. In autumn, the infinite shades of color delight all those who take pleasure in contemplating the beauty of nature.

40 top right A young female wild cat. This now-rare predator feeds mainly off small mammals (up to the size of a rabbit), and birds. A hunter of exceptional skill, it operates mainly at dusk.

MAGIC FOREST

hollows, they will be inhabited by other animals, including owls, who are not quite so well-equipped for excavating wood. The new tenants are not content to live in just any hollow, but they tend to choose those produced by particular kinds of woodpeckers, depending on their size and shape. For instance, Tengmalm's owl prefers holes dug by the great black woodpecker, the biggest of the European species.

Delicate carpets of mosses and curtains of lichens do much to create the fairytale atmosphere of these forests. In order to safeguard the integrity of the brushwood, the Bayerischer Wald can be explored only by following the specifically signposted paths. Otherwise, the countless visitors who crowd here each year would cause serious damage. On the other hand, however, 125 miles of footpaths are an excellent way of coming into close

contact with the forest. Excellent management has provided information panels, a library, play areas and theme walks for children, so that it really is possible to learn about an environment that is now rare in Europe, and to become fully aware of its importance.

Most of the territory is covered by an assortment of beeches, silver firs and spruces. Trees of all ages and sections of dense forest alternate with clearings—cushions of green moss in an infinity of hues, together with all kinds of undergrowth, such as lichens and mushrooms—to endow the wildest areas of the Bayerischer Wald with particular charm. It is a never-ending variety of guises and inspiration for further observation.

Amongst the most interesting park habitats are the peat-

40 bottom The brown bear has always evoked wonder and admiration on account of its strength and endurance. The widespread use of the bear as a heraldic symbol is proof of this.

40-41 Between the 19th and 20th centuries the lynx was almost exterminated in Europe, being wrongly considered to pose a danger. This, combined with the very retiring habits of this feline, make it difficult to spot.

42-43 In the Bavarian Forest it is common to come across split tree-trunks, whose decomposition provides new nourishment for the woodland. This is a slow cycle of renewal, which gives life to a habitat of magical beauty.

bogs, swampy zones where water stagnates and slows the decomposition of vegetable remains. Unique, mostly tiny, plant species live here, able to survive in the particularly acid soil.

Of the species that once abounded in these woods, and which survive nowadays only because of human intervention, we find the great predators: the wolf, the lynx and the bear. Despite protests and discordant opinion, it was decided to host Bayerischer Wald's large fauna in extensive enclosed areas, where animals are observed in conditions of semi-captivity so that tourists may see them, often with the use of binoculars.

This is a way of creating a tourist attraction which at the same time discourages visitors from trekking through the forest in the vain hope of an almost impossible sighting, and prevents the damage that would derive from such overcrowding. This

part of the Bayerischer Wald can also be visited in winter.

The forest is a mysterious place, and over the centuries it has inspired legends and stories that are further kindled by the peculiar morphology of the territory. Three heaps of flat stones lie at the top of Dreissel. They are the legendary thrones of the three kings of Bavaria, Bohemia and Austria, who defined this place as a point of convergence for the boundaries of their respective kingdoms. After all, the word "Dreissel" means "three chairs," and here the borders of Germany, Austria and the Czech Republic really do meet. And we may well imagine that the ancient kings, from the height of their thrones, are justifiably proud of how their descendants have protected the Bayerischer Wald from the corrupt invasion of "progress." (G.G.B.)

44-45 View of the Lake District from Blake Rigg. Crummock Water reflects the blue of the sky like the magic mirror of the fairies in Celtic myths.

44 bottom left Like a lord from the top of his castle, the peregrine falcon surveys his domain; it is unlikely that any prey will escape his lightning strike.

44 bottom right A highly active and playful creature, this otter prepares for a short rest before diving back into the water, the element in which it moves with greatest ease.

45 bottom A picture taken on the shores of Ullswater, the lake that Wordsworth preferred, believing it to be a paradigm of perfect equilibrium in terms of size and position.

N

ENGLAND

LAKE DISTRICT
NATIONAL PARK

What happens to those who wander among the gentle hills of the Lake District? It depends. The extraordinary variety of colors and scents of this romantic succession of meadows, rises, small lakes, farms from another age and white paths can arouse emotions ranging from serenity to euphoria.

The Lake District has been a national park since 1951, but the potential of the place was detected much, much earlier. As far back as 1500 B.C., the primitive Celtic peoples built one of their chief towns in the Lake District; here there was a flourishing production center of stone axes, which were then exported by sea to the Isle of Man. In Keswick it is still possible to see the remains of Castlerigg Stone, a stone circle 115 feet in diameter that recalls the more famous Stonehenge, and probably was also an important place of worship.

The past inhabitants of the Lake District were mostly shepherds. The hills are still dotted with white sheep and their lambs, but the wool industry has not prospered since the beginning of the twentieth century. On the shores of Windermere, the largest lake in the Lake District (10.5 miles long) and the most popular with tourists, the old woolen mill is now a museum of industrial archeology.

Slate quarrying has also contributed to the richness of the place: the gray-green roofs of the houses in the Lake District undoubtedly helped to create the timeless atmosphere that makes the place so unique. The ancient art of working slate has never been abandoned, even if today it is limited to the production of souvenirs.

It might seem strange that in a protected area such as this there is such a hubbub of human activity. In fact, the Lake District is a fairly unusual national park, in that the territory it consists of is almost all private property: a mosaic of farms and estates that since ancient times have preserved the magic of this land, albeit by exploiting its precious resources. Only a few bits of the primitive forest that in the Neolithic Age covered the entire area are now left; the trees have had to give way to grassland and meadows, which still today are the

principal feature of the landscape, and give the place a generally reassuring atmosphere. Immersed in the peaceful countryside dotted with lakes, it is possible to detect the magical presence of Mother Nature without the fear of coming across the fascinating but often lethal creatures that may populate other areas. For this reason, too, the Lake District offers an inviting prospect for all those who like walking in the countryside.

The more expert climber can brave Scafell Pike, the highest mountain in England at 3,200 feet, from whose peak on clear days there is a wonderful view of the whole Lake District and where it is even possible to make out Snowdon, the highest mountain in Wales. Those who are more mindful of traditions can spend their time running up and down the slopes (*fell running*, as it is known, the favorite sport of the ancient Celts). Less ambitious visitors can experience the thrill of riding a mountain goat.

The Mountain Goats are white minibuses that travel along every road in the park, driven by experienced drivers who,

without batting an eyelid, daily brave gradients of more than 25 percent.

The pleasantness of the place, combined with the cordiality and hospitality of the local people, easily explains the very high number of visitors who frequent this park, the largest in England with a surface area of more than 540 square miles: more than twelve million tourists a year!

The Lake District has had an exceptional sponsor: the outstanding poet William Wordsworth, who as early as 1835 edited *A Guide Through the District of Lakes*. This useful and accurate tourist guide is laden with such love for this area that it makes us feel sorry not to be "seated on a cloud between Scafell Pike and the Great Gable" to admire the radiating lakes, of every size and shape. Wordsworth's favorite was Ullswater, one of the long narrow lakes in the eastern area, which is surrounded by the Glencoyne forest and as a result particularly

adult. Her writer's imagination and a particular gift for drawing transformed the small wild animals of the park into fully-fledged characters (such as the famous and astute Peter Rabbit), protagonists of touching stories capable of enchanting generations of children. The first area of the national park consisted of the fifteen farms donated by Potter to the National Trust: an exceptional gesture, which makes us realize how much love this bewitching land can inspire.

It is rare in the world to find so much poetic beauty so easily accessible, so concentrated in limited dreamlike spaces. So, on your next trip to the Land of the Angles do not go without a visit to the Lake District National Park; it is assured that even the most aloof and hard-pressed businessman will spontaneously proclaim, along with William Wordsworth, "...and then my heart with pleasure fills / and dances with the daffodils." (A.S.I.)

THE POET'S PARK

atmospheric in autumn, when the red of the leaves of the trees tinges the waters with an unreal color. Wordsworth knew the Lake District extremely well, since it was here that he spent his youth and decided to settle with his family after his educational tours on the continent. And he was not alone: the poets Coleridge and De Quincey also lived at Rydal, not far from Dove Cottage, which was the first simple home of the Wordsworths. Here, the children's room is papered with newspaper and bears witness to a difficult period, the one that preceded the definitive consecration of Wordsworth as poet laureate. Herein lies the magic of the Lake District, the true muse of English Romanticism.

The nature in the Lake District has free-handedly lavished her gifts of beauty, peace and inspiration on writers, but it should also be said that the latter have repaid their dues in full. In fact, if today this enchanting area is protected and safeguarded from inevitable decay for future generations, we owe it most of all to the commitment of one writer: Beatrix Potter. Born in 1866 in the gray of London, the long holidays in the Lake District for the young Beatrix were real interludes of happiness, so much so as to prompt her to move there as an

46-47 Tarn Hows, set amidst the hills. The word tarn, meaning lake, derives from the ancient Celtic language, as do many other place names in the Lake District.

46 bottom left Mountains, meadows, lakes and a respectful and discreet human presence: this photo captures the whole spirit of the Lake District.

46 bottom right A rustling among the branches? The "culprit" may be a nimble red squirrel, busy collecting hazelnuts, acorns and other fruits.

47 Green meadows and rocky slopes come together on the peak of Causey Pike, one of the many possible destinations for excursions that will not fail to satisfy.

48 top left The typical Mediterranean landscape is precisely defined, creating a sharp contrast between the green of the maquis and the blue of the sea.

48 top right Small branches of red coral, from which project hundreds of polyps with tentacles reaching out in search of food, are now a rarity in the rest of the Mediterranean.

48 bottom The corals gradually create structures similar to old lace, so perfect it is almost hard to believe they could have a natural origin.

49 Similar to trees, dozens of specimens of Eunicella are strewn on a rocky wall. In a protected environment each little stone is always home to corals and sponges of various type.

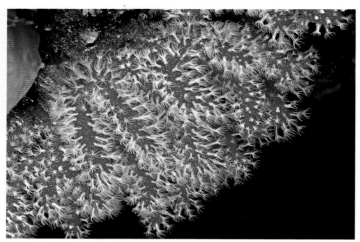

PORT-CROS
NATIONAL PARK

A small island in the Mediterranean very close to the French coast represents a natural environment that is still integral and untouched, and it gives us a good idea about what the coastal forests looked like in the past. We're talking about the island of Port Cros that—together with other islands, including Levant and Porquerolles—form the archipelago of Hyères, about six miles from the French Riviera. After the risk in the early-twentieth century of being transformed into an exclusive vacation spot for wealthy tourists—with hotels, buildings and sports facilities—its fate took a serendipitous and decisive turn in 1921 when part of the island was purchased by Marcel Henry, a well-to-do citizen who was also a botany and zoology enthusiast. He began and continued to manage the area with the objective of safeguarding the environment and preserving the preexisting natural conditions.

Upon his death, Henry's widow donated the property to the French government under the condition that it be made into a national park. The park was created in 1921 and today it covers about 4,700 acres, including Port Cros as well as the small island of Bagaud and an underwater area that is more than half of the total area. Visitors can enter the park year-long and can reach it by boat, embarking at the port of Levandou (Bagaud Island, on the other hand, is a total reserve and as such, no tourists are allowed to enter). Port Cros has just one small town and the remains of various fortifications that bear witness to the stormy past involving colonization and pirate raids. The island's vegetation is surprisingly lush and it thrives under the typical Mediterranean climate with mild winters and a sea breeze that keeps away the torrid summer heat.

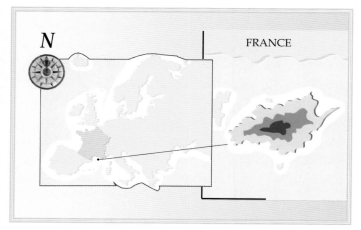

50-51 In the safety of its lair a
moray peeps out showing its thin
sharp teeth. This creature can
accidentally bite the hand of an
careless diver, confusing it with prey.
Its ugly appearance has inspired
many popular legends, but these
rarely correspond to the truth.

50 bottom The island of Port Cros
looks very lush due to the presence
of large forests of ilexes, which
uniformly cover its central part.

Following the numerous marked trails, you can cross the
various environments, which range from the coastal garrigue to
the maquis with myrtle and lentisk, to forests of ilexes and
Aleppo pines. The animal species that are present are also
noteworthy, first and foremost of which are the butterflies:
between the day and night varieties, over 220 species have been
observed.

During the route you'll undoubtedly have an opportunity
to see these butterflies when, with a delicate flutter of their
wings, they move from an arbutus to a clump of broom or
heather. But it is the birds that are the true lords of the island.
Here—in addition to herring-gulls, whose noisy presence will
not go unobserved by even the most distracted visitor—you
can also see two species that are now considered rare
throughout the Mediterranean: the greater and lesser
shearwater gather here in colonies to reproduce.

For sailors, the shearwaters, which love to fly over open
sea, are the sad warning of a storm when they fly in toward the
coast. As a result, for a long time they were persecuted; their
nests were destroyed and their young were killed under the
illusion that this would ward off bad luck among sailors.
Another illustrious guest on the island is the blue rock thrush;
if you look around, you can easily surprise this bird as it waits

patiently atop a rock for a passing insect to become its next meal. And if we look up, we can recognize the swift and elegant flight of the peregrine. The underwater environment protected by the park is also teeming with life and has been quite well-preserved from any impact of human activity.

A dive into these clear waters will open the doors to an unimaginable world. The rocky face slopes gently, covered with sponges and coral concretions with bizarre shapes. Here and there, you can see colorful spyrographs, with the feathery floating expansions ready to be withdrawn for protection into the animals' support tubs. Disorderly groups of *Helisates chromis* chase each other, ready to scatter in every direction at the first sign of danger, seeking shelter or hiding behind branches of red sea fans. In this kingdom, groupers reign supreme. Hidden in small caves and ravines, they look on

without moving, aware of being in a safe and inaccessible place. Timid and reserved, they are difficult to overtake in the open, particularly in their curious "candle" position. But a cavity can also be used as a hiding place for octopus, especially during their period of reproduction in the spring. It is hard to convince an octopus to come out and it will keep a sure grip with all the suckers on its tentacles; he's best off left alone! In the space where the bottom flattens out, fluttering fields of Neptune grass cover extensive areas, sheltering an incredible array of sea life, including lobsters and shrimp that, safe from fishermen, can grow to a substantial size. In the spots where the sandy bottom is visible, you may frequently encounter crinoids that, waving their arms rhythmically, look like they're dancing in a suggestive interplay of light and shadow on their exclusive and underwater stage. (C.B.)

52 top left This very young ibex, born at the end of the spring, is about to face its first winter. The cold season is particularly severe for these animals, allowing only for the survival of the hardiest individuals.

52 top right In its typical erect lookout position, a marmot observes, without distractions, the events going on around it. In case of danger, it will warn its companions with a sharp cry of alarm.

52-53 The Vanoise national park protects an area of high mountains in the French Alps. In the valley of Pralognan, a small inhabited center is almost overwhelmed by the imposing natural scenery.

53 bottom left An adult male is about to hurl himself with all his weight against his rival. The Alpine ibex is found in large numbers in the French park of Vanoise and in the neighboring park of Gran Paradiso.

53 bottom right The noise of an Alpine torrent enlivens the deep Pralognan valley. In the foreground, the pink flowers of Epilobium angustifolium, a common and striking colonizing plant, contrast with the dark background of the firs.

VANOISE
NATIONAL PARK

Aware of the length of its horns, a rock goat uses the tips to scratch its flanks, with all the imperturbability that can be inspired by the quiet dignity and silence of the alpine lakes that constitute its realm. It knows that here in Vanoise National Park, no one can threaten it.

The twin of Italy's Gran Paradiso Park with which it borders for several miles, the French park of Vanoise is a region of tall mountains that culminate in the 12,635 feet of the Grande Casse. This area of 330 square miles (together with the protected area in Italy) safeguards a total territory of approximately 485 square miles—a record for western Europe—in which animals can move about freely. This is also the first and most famous national park in France. Established in 1963, its founders had three objectives in mind: to protect a precious and beautiful alpine environment, to welcome and inform visitors, and to promote the development of economic activities compatible with the need for environmental protection. As a result, this protected territory has been subdivided into two main areas, a central one and a peripheral one. The former is marked by strict protection regulations. There are no roads or lift facilities, in order to protect these areas which are surrounded by over one hundred soaring peaks with altitudes of over 10,000 feet. In the peripheral area, human activity coexists with nature.

The complex natural history of these mountains is also documented by the fossil mollusks and fish contained in the rocks of many locations in the park. They bear witness to far-off times when the world was different from the one we know today, and they tell the tales of geological events that came long before the arrival of man, when these places were largely covered by the sea. Today, however, what welcomes the numerous visitors is the majestic mountain environment, abundant with evergreens: red firs, white firs, Scotch pines, larches, Swiss stone pines and mountain pines. They can be seen in sequence moving up in altitude in relation to the different climatic zones, until they give way to increasingly scrubbier shrubs, Alpine fields, rocks and glaciers. The harsh but lovely landscapes once hosted fauna that have now largely disappeared, but it is anticipated that the national park will foster their return. Not all of them were as lucky as the rock goat: gone are the wolf, lynx and wood grouse that were

present until about a century ago. The last bear was killed in 1921. The ossifrage, also known as the great bearded vulture, is one of the species that is currently being reintroduced.

Woodchucks, chamois and rock goats are well represented, but there are also more discreet inhabitants of the Alpine environment like the nutcracker. This crow with mottled feathers hides its reserves of food—composed in part of the seeds of the Swiss stone pines—in the ground, although it doesn't always remember exactly where. This lovely tree thus owes its existence as well as its extraordinary resistence not only to the harsh Alpine climate but also to the forgetfulness of the provident nutcracker. This is just one of the countless examples of the links between parts of an entire ecosystem; just as man cannot forget that splendor of unspoiled nature serves as a reminder that the beautiful, the untouched, and the natural still exist. And one of these places is the Vanoise National Park. (G.G.B.)

54-55 The fox is a rather unusual prey for the golden eagle. The great bird of prey usually prefers marmots or very young ungulates, which it kills with its powerful talons. The hooked beak serves primarily to tear off morsels of flesh.

54 bottom left A great climber but also a quick runner, the chamois sometimes goes into a mad gallop, often for no apparent reason. Maybe out of pure joie de vivre?

54 bottom right Although small in size, the ermine is one of the most voracious and determined predators. Tireless and very fast, its observation requires patience and an excellent knowledge of the terrain.

55 top In the deep Pralognan valley, the rocks show signs of erosion. Anything but unchangeable, the forms of the landscape are in constant renewal, according to cycles that are a good deal longer than human life.

55 center The golden eagle scours far and wide in search of prey, sustaining itself with just a few beats of its wings and skillful exploitation of the air currents. Spotting its imposing silhouette is less difficult than is generally believed.

CÉVENNES
NATIONAL PARK

Just a few miles from Montpellier and the Mediterranean Coast, the Massif Central reaches its southernmost point, where a landscape of gentle green slopes contrasts with arid rocky calcareous tablelands dramatically ridged by deep gullies. This is the territory under the protection of *Parc National des Cevennes*—the Cevennes National Park. There are no vertiginous peaks: the tallest mountain is Lozère, which barely skims 5,500 feet. The park's central area is comprised of mainly calcareous plateaus, called Causses, that reaches of 3,300—4,000 feet in altitude. No one lives here or comes this far up during the freezing winter months, but in summer shepherds bring flocks of thousands of sheep to feed on the luxuriant pastures.

The delicious ewes' milk produces Roquefort, a cheese that has become famous over the centuries for its excellence. Extensive coniferous, beech and oak forests flourish on the granitic terrain and constitute another important economic resource for local inhabitants who are employed as forestry workers. But the park's real treasure is the wealth of flora that blooms everywhere and has often been christened with fairytale names. In spring every nook becomes a virtual carnival of color: in the clearings there is a prevalence of the great pink flowers of the Turk's-cap lily, also called "lady's ringlets;" the golden yellow pheasant's-eye or *Adonis veronalis* (named after the lovely Adonis of Greek mythology); the citrus yellow orchid known as lady's-slipper, whose blossom resembles this type of footwear. On the plateaus there are violet-tinged pasque-flowers, with their bell-shaped corolla, and off in the distance the feather grass trembles in the wind, as if dancing to some secret and enchanted music. (C.B.)

56 top Following the general abandonment of traditional sheep-farming, the griffon vulture has become rare in much of Europe. Various projects to reintroduce it are in progress, returning this great vulture to the skies.

56 bottom The mist allows a glimpse of the rounded undulations of Mount Aigoual, covered with a cloak of vegetation, much of which is grass and is suitable for grazing. It is one of the highest places in Cevenne, just a little more than 5,250 feet in altitude.

56-57 The griffon vultures, like all similar species, scavenge off the carcasses of dead animals. Among their prey are the cattle who occasionally fall into the gorges.

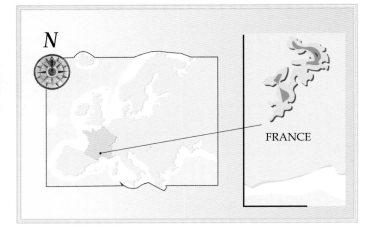

N

FRANCE

AN ENCHANTED GARDEN

57 bottom left The calcareous walls overhanging the gorges, the projecting cliffs and the fissures in the rocks are ideal sites for the griffon vulture to build its nest. In the most suitable spots there can be several nests, forming colonies.

57 bottom right The wing span of the griffon vulture reaches almost nine feet, giving it an impressive silhouette. Its large wings support it for a long time without it having to beat them, aided by the upward air currents.

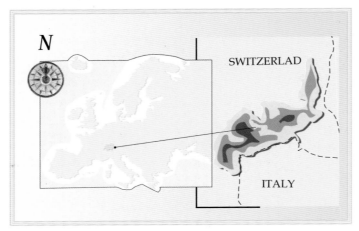

ENGADINA
NATIONAL PARK

Anyone visiting the Engadina, the valley of the Inn River, should be prepared to find it leaves at least three different impressions. The first impression is undoubtedly one of a typically Alpine landscape, with soaring peaks of changing color from dawn to dusk, verdant pastures and impervious forests, and lively bubbling brooks whose daily action shapes the terrain. Secondly, if we follow the course of this water, we find ourselves further distanced from the Alps. The Inn, in fact, rises in the Bernina massif, on the Italian border, but flows into the Danube. All of the Engadina is part of the hydrographic basin of Vienna's great river, and the typical central-European atmosphere can be experienced up here.

But let's wait before abandoning ourselves to the waltz and face the third impression: we are in the Canton of Grisons, which within the Swiss Confederation is a world apart. Its people proudly speak a language, called Ladin, which does not exist anywhere else in Europe. The many influences of the neighboring peoples have been merged into an absolutely unique culture, which permeates every aspect of life here.

The westernmost point of Switzerland is the Val Monastero, a tributary of the Engadina. There is another interesting feature here: the presence of the only Swiss national park, established in 1914 and only 105 square miles in size. Many think that such a limited expanse does not make it possible to completly safeguard the biological diversity found in the area, and that this, in fact, thwarted the attempts made in the past to increase it.

Between 1920 and 1924, the ibex was reintroduced into the park territory, and the red deer, which had once vanished, is now at the repopulation stage. In 1961, an ambitious project led to the reintroduction of the lammergeyer, the great vulture that specializes in feeding off bone marrow and, in order to procure this delicacy, drops the bones from a great height so that they break on the rocks below. Other inhabitants of the park are the chamois, squirrels, woodpeckers and the great ravens.

Another inhabitant of the park is the capercaillie, who each spring enters into competition with other males to win the attention of the female capercaillie, actually demarcating arenas in which they challenge each other to singing contests, heedless of the foxes waiting in ambush.

On the screes at an altitude of over 6,500 feet the marmot is

58 center The edelweiss, symbol of mountain flora, is often thought to live on inaccessible rocky cliffs. In reality its most typical habitat is that of the Alpine pastures.

58 bottom In order to attract the attention of the few pollinating insects high up in the mountains, the Gentiana verna shows off its bright blue color, in such a way as to be even more visible.

58-59 In the presence of the Engadina mountains, sweeping Alpine meadows characterize the Swiss National Park, with views that extend as far as the eye can see, in the cool of the wind.

59 top The delicacy of Scheuchzer's campanula, which takes its name from a famous 18th-century Swiss naturalist, contrasts with the harshness of the rocky places in which it can grow.

59 bottom left In a view from Munt la Schera, the artificial basin of the Lago del Gallo colors with blue the Livigno valley. Its waters flow into the Inn river, which crosses the Lower Engadina.

59 bottom right For centuries the Alpine meadows have been used for grazing livestock. This has helped to give the landscape its present-day appearance, by lowering the upper limit of the woods.

A SMALL ALPINE
JEWEL

queen: what we can observe of her on the surface, and which very often consists of a series of whistles followed by a rapid escape, does not give any idea of the complexity of the life of this adorable rodent in the subsoil. That is why at Zernez, in the park's highly informative Visitors' Center, a model marmot's lair that you can walk in has been laid out.

From the geological point of view the park territory is completely lacking in crystalline rocks such as granite and gneiss: two hundred million years ago there was a warm tropical sea here; the calcareous and dolomitic sediments that made up its bed have corrugated to form what are now

mountains up to 10,380 feet in altitude. On this base the vegetation is diversified into altitudinal bands, with Alpine prairies that are home to more than 650 plant species, shrub land in which the scented mugo pine covers a good 10 square miles of the park, and forests of Scotch pine, spruce, larch and stone pine at the lower levels.

Within its confines, the Swiss national park contains everything that characterizes the Alps, and more. Indeed, there is no point worrying about its small size; in fact, the Swiss park borders onto the Italian Stelvio Park, which in its turn joins up with the Adamello Park, comprising one of the largest, most varied, effective and modern protected areas in all of Europe. It is of little importance that a state border runs through the middle of it; the golden eagle, when it effortlessly traces majestic arcs in the clear Alpine skies, certainly does not care. (A.S.I.)

60 top left The tall stems of fescue, the typical grass of the Alpine meadows, are the favorite food of the ibex. The winter will have much less to offer, so it is best to make the most of it.

60 bottom left A very common inhabitant of the meadows and the stony ground, the marmot is one of the easiest Alpine animals to spot.

60 right At the end of the summer, when the magnificent horns of the deer have completely developed, the males let out great bellows. These act as a cry of challenge to their rivals in mating.

60-61 A male deer leads its herd, made up of several females and their fawns. Its grandeur and strength is combined with the grace and elegance typical of this animal.

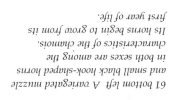

61 bottom left A variegated muzzle
and small black hook-shaped horns
in both sexes are among the
characteristics of the chamois.
Its horns begin to grow from its
first year of life.

61 bottom right It is not easy to spot
a golden eagle posed just a short
distance away. It can usually be
admired whilst it hovers at great
heights, scouring far and wide in
search of prey.

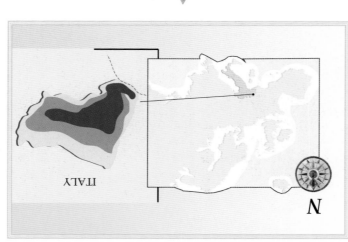

GRAN PARADISO NATIONAL PARK

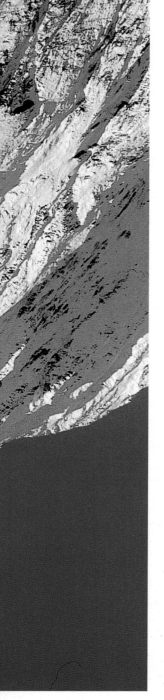

I n the cold winter air, at high altitude among snow-covered mountains, the sharp sounds of energetic banging can be heard. This noise is neither the consequence of falling boulders, nor the effect of an avalanche. It is the clash of horns, over the right to reproduce, of two rival male ibexes. The large mountain goat rises up on its back hooves, lowers its head, thrusting forward its heavy dueling weapons and lets itself fall forward, striking firmly and exploiting its full weight, which can reach over 200 pounds.

The ibex (*Capra ibex*) is the best-known inhabitant of the Gran Paradiso National Park, its symbol and the very reason for its existence. Between the end of the 18th century and the beginning of the 19th, this goat with the large scimitar-shaped horns was already in danger of extinction as a result of hunting. The last herds survived only on the Gran Paradiso. Joseph Zumstein, a forest inspector from the Italian village of Gressoney, requested a measure of protection, and the Kingdom of Piedmont issued a ban on hunting. It was the first step towards safeguarding this extraordinary herbivore, without which the Alps would not be the same.

In 1856, King Victor Emanuel II declared a portion of the present-day territory of the park to be a Royal Hunting Reserve, even setting up a specialized corps of guards for its surveillance. In 1920, the King of Italy, Victor Emanuel III, donated the reserve to the state, a vast 5,190 acres, for the establishment of a national park. This came into being at the end of 1922, and was the first Italian national park. Today this protected area, among the principal ones in Europe, extends for more than 177,840 acres between the regions of Valle d'Aosta and Piemonte, as a continuation of the French national park of Vanoise, with which it has been paired since 1972.

Valleys shaped by glaciers and tumultuous torrents, as well as mountains partially covered with glaciers culminate in the 13,320 feet of Gran Paradiso. This is the environment protected by the park. The valleys and slopes are covered with forests of firs, larches and stone pines, but these are not the main attraction of an area whose altitude is almost too high to foster dense woodland. Furthermore, in the past the woods have been cut back by man in order to extend the land available for pasture. The human presence is itself an important part of the Alpine environment, whose features mankind has shaped throughout history.

One of the purposes of the park is to hand down and enhance a cultural heritage typical of peoples who for centuries have lived in comparative isolation, especially in relation to the peoples on the plain. It is a cultural heritage that can, for example, be seen in the mountain huts typically built in stone along the Piedmont side, and in stone and wood in the Valle d'Aosta. However, the principal attractions of Gran Paradiso are sought chiefly in the beauty of the Alpine landscape and in the

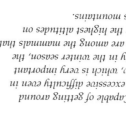

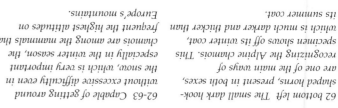

62 bottom left The small dark hook-shaped horns, present in both sexes, are one of the main ways of recognizing the Alpine chamois. This specimen shows off its winter coat, which is much darker and thicker than its summer coat.

62-63 Capable of getting around without excessive difficulty even in the snow, which is very important especially in the winter season, the chamois are among the mammals that frequent the highest altitudes on Europe's mountains.

63 bottom left The red fox is not a typical species of the high mountains, but its ability to adapt to the most varied situations enables it to survive even in difficult conditions, such as those of the Alpine winter.

63 bottom right The Alpine hare also owes its survival to the particular characteristics of its fur. Brown in color during the summer, it becomes white in winter, concealing the animal's presence on the blanket of snow.

64 *Two adult ibex males engaging in the winter clash of horns. Thanks to Gran Paradiso, the mountain goat has been saved from extinction.*

65 top left *Two curious young ibexes observe the photographer. The photo reveals the extent of the particular confidence with which these animals confront the void of the precipices.*

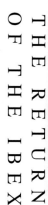

65 top right *The horns of the ibex, which are much more developed in the male than in the female, allow us to estimate the age of the animal, which generally does not exceed fifteen years.*

65 center *The horns of no less than three males are locked in combat. However, this summer behavior is only a timid try-out for the far more serious winter conflicts, when the right to reproduction will be the prize at stake.*

65 bottom *In upper Valnontey, a clear dawn floods the glacier of Tribulation with golden light. The present-day glaciers, although smaller than those that modeled the Alps in the past, are one of the characteristic features of the Gran Paradiso landscape.*

ease with which it is possible to admire closely the fauna and flora. The meadows, rocks, screes and glacial moraines are home to a flora that in the course of its evolution has devised a variety of refined strategies to survive in extreme conditions.

During the severe Alpine winter, this place becomes a kingdom of ice, covered with many feet of snow; during the summer the same landscape becomes an arid area of stony ground made red-hot by the blinding sun. Yet life endures, even if often it is reduced to hard crusts of lichen welded to the rocks. Brightly colored flowers, often of minute size, seem to spring directly from the rocks, compensating for their minuteness by grouping in large pink, blue and yellow bushes. The intensity of colors has the effect of attracting the attention of the few pollinating insects, but also that of the most casual tourist. Among the most elegant plants of the mountain flora, the mountain lily (*Paradisea liliastrum*), with it's snow-white funnel-shaped corollas, has been chosen as the symbol of the Paradisia botanical garden. This prestigious scientific and didactic institution is based in Valnontey, near Cogne, in one of the best-known and most popular valleys in the park. Visiting it is the best way to begin to get to know the plant species of Gran Paradiso.

In fact, Valnontey is home to one of the routes most used by the numerous walkers who tread the paths of this Alpine park, in the vicinity of the Vittorio Sella refuge, it is unlikely that the ibexes will fail to appear. Continuing towards the chalets of the Herbetet, a route that requires caution, you will be able to make out the glaciers at the valley head. Despite their often imposing and treacherous appearance caused by crevasses and seracs, the present-day glaciers are only a tiny reminder of those that in a

far-off past gave shape to the valleys and mountains, not only in Gran Paradiso but along the whole Alpine arc. There are about fifty glaciers today in the national park, constantly shrinking year after year. The gradual reduction of the extension and volume of the glaciers does not, however, eliminate the characteristic signs of their presence: the "U" shape of the valleys, the distinctive boulders known as moraines, and the tiny lakes. All these elements, to the careful observer, tell the story of every single slope and every valley. From the highest peaks five major valleys begin, two of which are in Piemonte (Valle dell'Orco and Val Soana), and three in Valle d'Aosta; these are larger and much more popular and include Valle di Rhemes, Valsavaranche and Valnontey.

The Valsavaranche, by way of the Vittorio Emanuele II refuge and the Chabod refuge, provides the principal access to the summit that gives its name to the whole massif as well as to the national park. However, it is not essential to venture among the glaciers to appreciate the characteristics of this Alpine environment, which is still substantially intact. The Ciarforon peak, surmounted by a hanging glacier in the form of a snow-white hood, the cracked trunk of an age-old larch, the sharp cry of alarm of a marmot, the rapid and carefree flight of a flock of alpine choughs with their black plumage and yellow beaks, are among the sights that everyone can enjoy.

Much is still being done to restore to the Gran Paradiso environment all the features that were present originally, especially in terms of the fauna. Indeed, not all the animals have been as lucky as the ibex. The painstaking reintroduction after its extinction in 1912, of the lammergeyer, a vulture with a wing span of more than eight feet and a characteristic black beard, is now legendary. Its impressive size makes it look like a small glider, but its habits are no less unusual. The lammergeyer does in fact feed off bones, which it can break by lifting them up in flight and letting them fall on the rock. This extraordinary species is making its return to the Alps thanks to human effort, just as in recent years the ibexes, increasingly numerous in the Gran Paradiso National Park, have been recorded on almost all of the Alpine arc from which they had disappeared. But this is not all: the great predators, the wolf and the lynx, are also returning entirely on their own accord. (G.G.B.)

66 top A female ibex stares at us, half curious and half concerned. In the Gran Paradiso National Park it is possible to approach these ungulates with great ease, but this fact should not make us disrespectful towards them.

66 bottom With its altitude of 13,320 feet, the summit of Gran Paradiso is the highest elevation in the territory of the park. From the top, which is battered by a ceaseless wind, there is a sweeping view of countless Alpine peaks.

67 On a freezing winter's day, a solitary fox roams the snowy slope, amidst rocky walls encrusted with ice. An inhospitable environment puts those animals that do not hibernate to a severe test.

ABRUZZO
NATIONAL PARK

Twenty thousand years ago, ancient hunters would climb the Marsican mountains in search of prey. During the summer, they would begin their trek from a plateau that is now known as Piana del Fucino, in central Italy. Back then, the place names were probably different, but even today people still climb these slopes to find the most beautiful chamois in the world, the Abruzzo chamois.

Now, men settle for just a glimpse, perhaps because they aren't as hungry as they once were. Or maybe they hunger for something else: for woods, the wind whistling through the trees, harsh yet sweet mountainsides, flowers that don't need gardeners, or the yearning for a fleeting encounter with wild animals. The land of Abruzzo can satisfy this kind of hunger, because it is still a land of trees, mountains, flowers, chamois, wolves and bears.

Yellowstone National Park was founded in 1872 and it was the first (and probably most famous) in the world. But this was also the year that a royal hunting reserve was created in the mountains of Camosciara to protect the chamois and the Marsican brown bear. In 1923, the reserve became the heart of the new Abruzzo National Park, which then covered 45,000 acres. Today it has an area of 123,500 hectares, plus 247,000 in an adjacent external area.

Over the years, the difficult work done in the park was rewarded with international recognition, including the "European diploma for the conservation of nature," granted by the European Council in 1977.

Its mountains are also ancient; not very tall, they have been shaped by time through various natural phenomena that have given them an appearance that is gentle in some areas and

N

ITALY

68 top left In the mountainous massif of the Camosciara rise peaks that, though they may not be high in altitude, often look inaccessible. This is the result of their geological nature: erosion moulds the calcareous rocks into steep sheer walls.

68 top right The wolf, twhich is among one of the greatest European predators, is a discreet creature. It is not easy to spot one, though they are starting to repopulate many of the areas from which they had disappeared.

68 bottom A young chamois of Abruzzo curiously explores its world. It one of the most typical creatures found in the Abruzzo National Park, and is a different species from the Alpine chamois, but has similarities with the Pyrenean type.

68-69 A group of chamois of Abruzzo rest on a cliff, negotiated without particular difficulty, thanks to their climbing aptitude. Highly skilled in moving around on rough terrain, they often travel in large herds.

70 bottom right A large part of the Camosciara Mountains is constituted by rocks that are impermeable to water. This allows for streams to flow at surface level.

71 A Marsican bear in his favorite habitat. This sub-species (about 100 elements) is one of the most important European populations.

70-71 The rocky landscapes are the most typical of the inner core of Abruzzo. At higher levels the woods give way to stony ground, and only isolated trees attempt to colonize an environment that is no longer suited for them.

70 bottom left The silhouette of Mount Marsicano, viewed here from Pescasseroli, singles out one of the principal rises in the Abruzzo National Park. With its curtain of woods, it is the habitat of the Abruzzo brown bear.

rugged in others. This alternation of landscapes is one of the biggest attractions of this protected area nestled among the regions of Abruzzi, Latium and Molise.

Vast beech forests, which are some of the largest in Italy, contain age-old tree specimens whose wood, softened by time, yields easily to the beak of the Lilford woodpecker as it carves holes into it to make its nest and look for larvae and invertebrates for food. But above all, these woods are the home of a large mammal that is the pride of the Abruzzo Park.

The tracks it leaves are as large as a man's, but the deep grooves cut into the ground by its sharp claws are what makes them distinctive. Tree trunks that are visibly scratched and rocks that have been overturned to find insects are other characteristic signs of its presence. This is no ordinary bear, but the Marsican brown bear, a separate sub-species of the European brown bear. It is one of the few remaining populations of the western European bear and it is carefully protected here, with probably about one hundred specimens. It is difficult to catch a glimpse of this lazy and solitary animal, which may even climb to the highest altitudes in search of food, preferring a diet of berries or other fruit, insects, roots and, every so often, large prey. Its activities slow down during the winter, but the cold season is precisely the period in which the bears give birth, mainly in January.

Stretching beyond the upper boundaries of the beech forests are the mountain meadows and stone quarries that are partially colonized by the dwarf mountain pine (*pinus mugo*), which is quite rare in the Apennines. Climbing past the woods going up the Camosciara or the other mountains, you may encounter another local celebrity, which owes its survival to the protected area. Slender, dark hook-shaped horns in both males and females and daytime habits are the characteristics of the herbivorous Abruzzo chamois. It is now considered to be a separate species that is different from the chamois of the Alps and is more similar to the Pyrenees type.

There are many other animals that populate the park, some of which have disappeared in many other areas because they have traditionally been considered "inconvenient" in places where man dominates the territory. These include the wolf and lynx in particular, but deer and roe deer have also returned. While sighting animals may take a bit of hard work and a stroke of good luck, the national park can be visited all year long, thanks to the mild climate of central Italy. Each season has its own attractions, but it is between spring and summer that every corner of the area becomes most enjoyable, and visitors can climb the highest peaks and penetrate the most solitary valleys. The flowers, chirping birds, green countryside and animal spoor are never banal, especially with the wide range of information available at the Park Center, which organizes year-round activities for visitors of all ages. While the park might be crowded during pleasant weather, the silent explosion of autumn colors can be enjoyed in peace and quiet. This is also ensured by the fact that automobiles are only allowed on the roads linking the local towns. The other roads can be covered on foot, bicycle or horseback. In wintertime the lacy embroidery of frost and ice as well as animal tracks in the snow are also enjoyed by tourists on one of the park's skiing excursions.

Man is the park's other "inhabitant," living in the area's medieval towns. One of the keys to the success of the park is the

LAND OF CHAMOIS, WOLVES AND BEARS

division of the area into different zones safeguarded with different levels of protection (complete reserve, general reserve and protected area), in order to meet the diverse needs of the natural environment and of the specific population. The "complete reserve" areas can only be accessed on foot, along specific trails. This is naturally the most interesting part from an environmental standpoint. In the "general reserve," where man and nature meet, activities typical of the local tradition, such as sheepfarming, are allowed. The environment of the "protected area" instead shows the decisive influence of man, especially through agriculture. Lastly, the towns, many of which have been restored, offer tourist accommodation facilities. Nevertheless, it is in the full reserve that nature flaunts its finest features, which are even more precious if we consider that it is in the middle of one of Europe's most densely populated countries. Abruzzo National Park has been so successful that it is considered a point of reference and a model for the other protected areas.

While Italy is most famous for its cities and its artistic heritage, we must also remember that between late May and early June, you can climb the Abruzzo mountains to admire the velvety purple flowers of the Marsican iris (*Iris marsica*), which exists nowhere else in the world. And this is just one example of all the marvels that are protected by a national park whose emblem is not just any bear, but the Marsican brown bear. (G.G.B.)

72-73 A touching photo of the chamois of Abruzzo. In this species mating takes place between the end of October and *the month of December and births between May and June. The young remain with their mothers for about a year.*

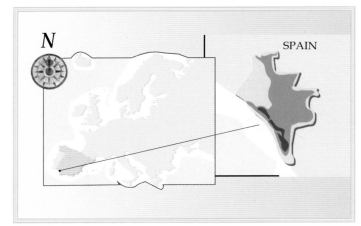

DOÑANA
NATIONAL PARK

W hen beautiful Doñana, Duchess of Medinasidonia, was lost in the forest along the lower course of the Guadalquivir, no Prince Charming came to save her. So our unfortunate heroine wept so hard that (as the legend goes) her tears created one of the world's most precious natural areas.

A national park founded in 1969 (as well as being a Biosphere Reserve, Special Birdlife Protection Area, Heritage of Mankind), this is the southeast extremity of Huelva province, in Andalusia, not far from such great cultural cities as Seville and Cadiz. Doñana National Park extends for over 123,500

acres across the Guadalquivir Delta, with a further 133,400 acres of natural park that create an invaluable area for safeguarding species that are at risk for extinction. Until 1960 this marshy zone could be reached only on horseback and with some difficulty.

Nowadays a number of asphalt roads have made it more easily accessible, so that the annual number of visitors has risen greatly. Such interest is due greatly to the fact that Doñana is a true international birdwatchers' paradise, with over 360 species that nest here or simply take advantage of the peaceful lagoons to rest a while during migration. Spain is justifiably jealous of

this treasure; visitors are welcome, but only guided tours are allowed around the most precious part of the Park. The reserve's expert personnel accompany visitors along the extensive trails and these tours have to be booked at least a month in advance. It is worth the effort, however. Few other areas display such a hybrid and changing landscape, a manifest example of the harmony that exists between the forces of nature. Doñana, in fact, is the result of the mingling of sweet and savory, wind and earth, sand and greenery; not in conflict, but rather in a passionately Mediterranean embrace.

The park territory is quite recent in terms of geological origin, and was almost entirely constituted by the sediments transported seawards by the Guadalquivir river, filling an ancient sea gulf that until just a few centuries ago reached as far as Seville. Here, the western tides of the Atlantic have molded the earth to form a sort of peninsula that ends at Punta de Malandar, the park's southernmost point. One of the park's most interesting and spectacular entrances is actually on that coast, heading south from the town of Matalascañas. To reach it we travel along the famous Coto de Doñana, where the slow and unpredictable movement of the dunes, created by the sea and modeled by the wind, offer a new landscape every day.

Inland, the dunes are replaced by the salt marshes or *marismas*, colonized by those particular vegetable species that apparently do not realize how salty the soil is or how the winter floods alternate with the summer drought. The chief examples are saltwort, *Arthrocnemum glaucum*, and *limonastrium*. These brackish soils also have other aficionados: it is not unusual to see flocks of geese eating the sand as they winter in Doñana. Apparently this strange habit helps them digest the hard horse chestnuts that are their only source of food throughout the winter.

The borderline between Coto de Doñana and the rest of the park is a strip of woodland that has grown stubbornly on the sandy dunes, barely consolidated by maritime mugwort, sedge-grass and hooded matweeds. Depending on soil

74 center After a lavish meal based on aquatic invertebrates, a flock of pink flamingoes abandons the marisma, alarmed by a noise perhaps or by the arrival of a predator.

74-75 The sands of the Atlantic and the vegetation of Iberia unite to create this undulating stretch of dunes, sculpted by the wind and trodden by few: the Coto de Doñana.

75 bottom left In the cool of twilight a fallow deer nibbles on the tender grasses at the edge of the pine forest. This cervid, originally from the Middle East, probably owes its diffusion in the Mediterranean basin to the ancient Romans.

75 bottom right The ocean wind tousles the manes of this small herd of horses, but does not seem to bother the colt, nor limit its healthy appetite.

characteristics, the parasol pine may prevail, replaced by cork oak, or eucalyptus, while to the north there are extensive heaths and shrubby plains. One of the park's few buildings, Palacio de Doñana, is found here: formerly a hunting lodge and now a research station.

The birdlife is undoubtedly Doñana's greatest asset, for it hosts rare species of great interest, most notably the imperial eagle. Of the world's surviving 125 couples, 15 nest here. Winter months are the best for bird watching, since the greatest number of winged visitors are seen between November and January. Nevertheless, it would be a serious oversight to forget that Doñana is the home of large herbivorous mammals such as fallow deer, bucks, wild boars, and, of course, predators such as the Iberian lynx. There are several varieties of this species, but all are quite rare because their wooded habitat is progressively disappearing.

Aficionados of cold-blooded species will find several interesting

76 top Wherever the dunes have become established, there is a stretch of pine forest, home to the domestic pine; it gives shelter to some of the most typical species of Doñana, such as the lynx and the fallow deer.

76-77 A mosaic of colors, as in an impressionist painting; even from an aerial view the marismas of Doñana Park immediately give a sense of the huge variety of this habitat.

THE WORLD IN A FLUTTERING OF WINGS

77 top left A reed bowed by the wind? The brown striated plumage and total immobility of the bittern are able to deceive both predators and prey.

77 top right The family grows, the house is rebuilt: an elegant stork makes ready to organize its enormous nest, under the somewhat disappointed gaze of its young. Usually that long beak signals the arrival of their food!

reptiles, such as the ocellated lizard and the spur-thighed tortoise, as well as amphibians and fish, not to mention this territory's wealth of microhabitats, whose populations are worthy of a separate volume.

Doñana's flora and fauna are extraordinary, but they are also quite fragile. On April 25, 1998 an accident in a lead and zinc mine near Seville leaked toxic waste equal to the volume of 1,500 Olympic swimming pools into the waters of a tributary of the Rìo Guardiamar, which flows into the Park. The ensuing large-scale devastation of fish and other aquatic creatures was the first signal of environmental pollution that is even today, difficult to evaluate. Human progress cannot be halted but prudence is the first rule, especially when the impact of our actions may jeopardize the integrity of an entire heritage for humanity. For Doñana is a complex and rare system of interaction, links and equilibrium, to be found nowhere else on earth. (A.S.I.)

77 bottom With an icy stare, which makes us glad we are not leverets, a spotted lynx shows off its splendid fur. This feline, endemic to the Iberian peninsula, finds one of its last refuges in the park.

78 top left Constant rainfall during every month of the year and sufficiently high temperatures enable the constant growth of equatorial rain forest; this is a perfectly balanced ecosystem.

78 top right The dry season looms: plants, animals and humans prepare to face the long months of drought in Ruaha National Park.

AFRICA
INTRODUCTION

I t is certainly out of fashion to begin a description of Africa using the word "exploration." Outdated figures come to mind with the images of men in safari suits and pith helmets followed by an entourage of native bearers loaded with baggage and equipment, off to seek great rivers teeming with crocodiles. The deserts, the lakes, the forests, the cascades, the mountains, the coast, the savanna, the rivers are all now known and the era of David Livingstone and H. M. Stanley has almost been forgotten.

After Christopher Columbus' first voyage in 1942, another five years passed before Vasco de Gama completed his circumnavigation of the African continent to reach the Indian Ocean. After this exploit, another three centuries passed before explorers penetrated the center of Africa, when America and Asia (or at least their main features), were already known to Europeans.

Even though the most outstanding of ancient civilizations, ancient Egypt, flourished in Africa (despite the fact northern Africa was a part of the Roman Empire, and despite the widespread diffusion of Arab culture during the Middle Ages), a large part of the continent was cut off from contact with the rest of the world until relatively recent times. Why?

The answer lies in the physical characteristics of a territory that exceeds 11,600,000 square miles, 4,960 miles from north to south and 4,650 miles from east to west; it the second largest continent. Just below the slim Mediterranean strip we find the world's biggest desert, the Sahara, an almost insufferable red-hot area. Even the southwest coasts were not easy to negotiate since another great desert, the Kalahari, slithers down to the Atlantic. The Equatorial region is hot and humid, and the intricate green tangle of rain-forest is even more of a hurdle. Once the desert was tamed, the forest became a second enormous obstacle that

78 bottom The serval's enormous ears enable it to pick up the rustling of its habitual prey, small rodents. It can stand for ten minutes with its eyes closed, listening for noises. Then it will fall on its prey using its powerful paws to strike the animal.

79 Even an implacable predator like the leopard is capable of great tenderness towards its offspring: this cub knows that for the first two years of its life its mother will keep close watch. After that, however, it will be on its own amongst the perils of the savanna.

80 bottom right as if in answer to some silent command, all the flamingos of the flock take flight in the same direction, a magnificent choreography illuminates Nakuru National Park.

81 left The immense savanna of Serengeti National Park unfolds beneath our gaze and seems to embrace the horizon.
The enormous distances to be crossed may not be frightening but nevertheless, the herds that migrate habitually follow the traces of what little water is available.

80-81 Thousands of lesser flamingos tinged with pink line Kenya's Lake Bogoria. They feed by dipping their heads in water and filtering the shoal mud with their gilled beaks, using their tongues as a piston.

80 bottom left Mating season has arrived for the flamingos of Lake Bogoria: thousand of males take part in a collective mating parade before the females, marching with heads held high and necks stretched out.

also shut off much of the Equatorial coast. The very rivers were not convenient navigation channels for penetrating inland; they are a mass of rapids, waterfalls and cataracts, created by the structure of the highlands that forced to a halt all those who tried to navigate upriver. When sea journeys were at the mercy of a breath of wind, the Equatorial calm discouraged navigators from proceeding towards the southern Atlantic for fear of interminable flat calm.

The romantic epics of 19th century explorers gradually filled in the gaps of knowledge, but with great effort. Names of places often inspired by reigning monarchs and European nobility began to fill the white spaces on maps that used to read "hic sunt leones," or, "here are lions." Much water has flowed under the proverbial bridge since then, and much has changed. There are still lions, but they scare nobody.

National parks are now an important economic resource for many African countries, who understand how environmental protection can also be a source of income (or, in other words, tourism). Above all, however, the great African parks preserve a natural heritage without which the world would be much poorer.

Unlike other continents, Africa has no great mountain chains. The only exception is the Atlas range in the far northwest, but they have quite a European appearance. The great flat tablelands, rolled out by erosion that took an incalculable length of time, are broken, however, by isolated mountain groups or great fractures in the earth's crust. The highest mountains are usually of recent volcanic origin, such as Kilimanjaro, which is Africa's highest peak at 19,000 feet. Eastern Africa has a number of volcanoes including Oldoinyo Lengai, sacred to the Masai.

The volcanoes are lined up along the Rift Valley, a great rift in the terrestrial crust that for millions of years has been cracking the continent in half, from Sinai to Mozambique. If all goes as geologists predict, in a future millions of years ahead, eastern Africa will be separated from central western Africa by a new ocean of which the Red Sea is but an embryo. For the time being, the Rift Valley retains its unified appearance, dotted with great deep lakes, and its elongated form. Many of the lakes are rich in salts of volcanic origin, to the point that their waters are inhabited only by special life forms. The most spectacular of these forms is undoubtedly the flamingo, with flocks of millions of these pink specimens.

Another feature of Africa is its massive gathering of animals, especially in the savanna, where immense flocks of antelopes, zebras, buffaloes and elephants are shifting constantly in search of pasture and in pursuit of rainfall. One third of the continent is covered by grass, and whose most important and spectacular sectors are protected by several of the globe's most famous and popular national parks. The savanna that spreads mainly through eastern Africa gives way to tropical rain forests moving westwards. Intricate, impenetrable, unpredictable and swarming with species still largely undiscovered, these are also one of the most endangered habitats on the planet, threatened by intense deforestation. This is also the home of some of our closest relatives, such as the gorilla. The great columns of hot damp air that rise from the Equator are brought about by the sunrays and unleash intense rains that nourish the forest.

The masses of dry air, deprived of all water vapor, slip north and south and give rise to another typical element of the African landscape: the desert. It may seem paradoxical that such desolate territories require protection, for they offer only rock, sand and aridity. Yet these extreme habitats are the home of a multitude of species that have adapted to life in limited conditions, whose existence contributes a great deal to Africa's biological wealth. Nor should it be forgotten that the unique charisma of many places on this continent is purely visual: gigantic Victoria Falls, the great deserts of rolling sand dunes as far as the eye can see, the sudden appearance of an impressive mountain of savanna, the green blanket of tropical rain forest.

Despite enormous problems, which are almost always triggered or aggravated by humanity, Africa has always managed to safeguard its best parts with an extensive network of protected areas, which are often the most efficient and frequented in the world. The hope that this is a sign of rebirth and redemption is well founded: it was right here—the continent at the center of the world—that the human race emerged. (G.G.B.)

81 bottom right The flamingo's peculiar beak filters pond water. The lesser flamingo feeds on miniscule algae, but the common flamingo prefers small shellfish, and this type of nutrition explains its pink plumage.

82-83 United by their mutual need to seek prey, two young lions charge fast at the first light of dawn. When they become lords of their own territory, they will no longer tolerate the presence of other males, and the delicate task of hunting will be entrusted to the lioness of the flock.

MAHALE MOUNTAINS
NATIONAL PARK

The national parks of Kenya and Tanzania can satisfy visitors with completely different expectations. For some, everything is highly organized, with hotel facilities that seem European and can accomodate a large crowd of tourists. This "easy Africa" — where the scenery, undoubtedly some of the most magnificent and unique in the world, acts as a backdrop to a large number of animals that virtually pose for our camera lenses — doesn't always satisfy our hunger for adventure. But for those with a taste for adventure, there is also the opportunity to follow in the footsteps of the first explorers to reach these lands. For example, very few tourists decide to visit the region of the Makari Mountains on the Tanzanian shore of Lake Tanganiyka. Boat is the only way to reach this special area, which was declared a national park in 1985. There are no logistical infrastructures, nor are there any roads; this is the only African park that can be visited strictly on foot.

The Mahale Mountains National Park, which covers a little over 5,250 square feet, with altitudes from 2,625 to about 8,200 feet, offers enchanting landscapes with numerous spurting waterfalls

84 bottom left The rainforest overlooks Lake Tanganyika, one of the basins that originated following the great tectonic rift of the Great Rift Valley.

84-85 The light that filters between the branches plays in the hair of a male chimpanzee while he is enjoying the delicious berries of the Harungana madascariensis.

85 bottom right Ancient trunks covered with lianas and other epiphytes accompany anyone penetrating the forest of the park.

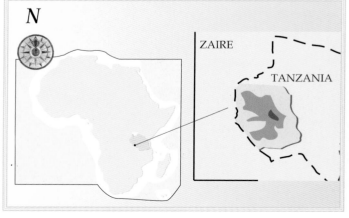

86-87 A young male yawns, showing his long canines. The chimpanzees' diet is predominantly vegetarian, and sometimes they actually organize hunts.

86 bottom All primates love to groom each other to reinforce social relations; it is thought that this behavior gave rise to the kiss!

amidst bamboo, albizia, kite trees, tall podocarps and numerous other plant species, and just as many animals living among their foliage. It is truly stirring to look up between the branches and catch a glimpse of a partially covered home: this is the unmistakable sign that there may be a family of chimpanzees nearby.

With its gait at times on two feet, a result of front limbs that are as long as its hind limbs (as opposed to other anthropomorphic animals, like the gorilla, which has much longer "arms"), the chimpanzee is the monkey most closely resembling humans. It is also the only one that can make tools for a specific goal without being instructed how. Nowadays, the chimps only live here and in the nearby national park of the Gombe River, home of famous researcher Jane Goodall. The chimpanzees of Mahale are also the object of many in-depth studies.

Since 1961, chimpanzees have been monitored by a team of Japanese researchers. To establish initial contact, three methods were tested in different areas: habit, imposition (in this case, a young orphaned animal that could demonstrate trust in humans was adopted) or the supply of food. Only the latter solution led to regular relations, which are ongoing even today, with over a hundred chimps, divided into families with numbers varying from five to thirty specimens.

Also residing in both the forest and on the miombo savannah, where the umbrella thorn and whistling-thorn acacias prevail, are rather rare mammals such as the giant squirrel, the black and white Angola colobo and the Shape grysbok, a small antelope similar to the dik-dik and prevalently a nocturnal animal. And then there are elephants, buffaloes, lions, leopards and many other types of monkeys. Bird-lovers will find interesting fowl in every environment: the red-collar widow bird amidst rushes and small ponds; in the palm groves the striped mouse-bird, so called because of its agility in climbing trunks. The crowned eagle, colorful bee-eater and jays can be seen on the mountaintops. In the rainforest, you can hear the melodious song of the red-breasted thrush and be amazed by the shades of blue, purple and yellow shown off by the Ross's turaco.

Lastly, let's not forget that the park includes part of the bank of the Tanganiyka, where there are countless hippopotamuses and crocodiles. There are over 220 species of fish here; particularly interesting for scholars of evolution is the family of Cichlids, small fish with showy colors and very pronounced territorial instincts that have managed to adapt to the different microenvironments, creating a very large number of endemic species. (R.M.S.)

TRUE AFRICA

87 center The scientific name of the chimpanzee is Pan (Pan troglodytes), like the mythological god of the woods; though this female in her daytime refuge is certainly more reminiscent of a lazy elf.

87 bottom The chimpanzees have a hierarchical social structure: here the alpha and beta males relax from the wearying work of leading the troop.

88 bottom right The round blue lake
of Empakaai, surrounded by steep
shores, clearly shows its volcanic
origin. From the edge of the crater
one can see over Ngorongoro and
Serengeti, all the way to Kilimanjaro.

88-89 The edge of the volcanic caldera,
1,970 feet high in relation to its inner
plain, defines a composite environment
on the horizon, which in addition to a
great wealth of fauna includes
savannah, scrubland and wet regions.

88 bottom left A herd of gnus grazes
amidst the acacias, in the setting of
the steep wall that marks the
boundary of the Ngorongoro crater.
The gnu is one of the most common
antelopes.

NGORONGORO
CONSERVATION AREA

You travel down a long trail, bumping along in a jeep surrounded by the smell of Africa, until you get to Lake Makadi, which is enormous when it rains but is divided into three ponds during the dry spells. Various herbivores come to its shores to drink and an enormous variety of birds can be seen: these include larger and smaller flamingos, saddle-bill storks, tantaluses, and stilt-plovers. Marabous stroll on the slender and seemingly fragile legs, while ibises and glossy ibises with their long crescent-shaped beaks look for invertebrates.

Visitors to this region of Tanzania can see an amazing variety of animals, but to reach this body of water, located at an altitude of about 5,575 feet, you need to descend a good 1,970 feet. In fact, the lake is in the crater of the famous Ngorongoro, the "big hole" in the Maa language. About eight million years ago, the volcano spewed out an immense quantity of magma and then its cone, emptied at this point, fell in on itself to form the current crater — or rather caldera — that extends for a diameter of 10 miles. Around this better-known volcano there are also other volcanoes such as Ol Doinyo Lengai, which is still active and last erupted in 1983.

89 top left Small volcanic cones pepper the main crater of Ol Doinyo Lengai. Gray flows of boiling alkaline mud furrow its slopes. The site of truly spectacular phenomena, it is no surprise that its Masai name means "mountain of God."

89 top right The Ngorongoro region owes its present-day state to the volcanic phenomena that affect much of east Africa. The presence of volcanoes is in turn connected to the existence of the Rift Valley, a great rift that runs through Africa from Sinai to Mozambique.

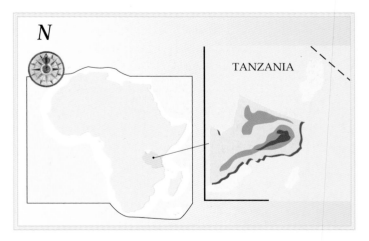

All these cones, which extend for over 3,100 square miles, are part of what is commonly known as Ngorongoro National Park, although from a legal standpoint the Tanzanian government considers the actual national park to be only the crater of Ngorongoro (about 100 square miles). No one is allowed to live here and the Masai cannot bring their herds here to graze. The rest of the territory is managed as a conservation area.

South of the lake is a lovely and intricate fever-acacia forest known as the Lerai forest; it is the crowded reign of yellow baboons, cercopiths and multicolored birds. Hanging from the tree branches are the intricate nests of the golden weaver birds and spekes, and if you listen carefully, you'll be lucky enough to hear the violent sound of grass being tugged up from the dense vegetation. This indicates the presence of an elephant, whose passage along the escarpments of the crater is often marked by uprooted shrubs and signs of digging with its tusks in search of mineral salts.

As we continue our travel through the park, the environment changes completely: in the eastern area water-bucks, zebras, gnus, hartebeests, warthogs, and Thomson and Grant gazelles graze and plunge into the Gorigor marsh, which is fed by a spring. Giraffes are all that's missing from the crater, but this is hard to notice in this well-populated natural zoo. We can keep going — being careful not to crush the herbaceous vegetation under our feet and never leaving the trails, which were marked after careful study to isolate fires, which are common and even essential to life on the savannah.

An immense grassy plain opens out before us, broken up only by a few areas with bushes that may host a black rhinoceros or a herd of buffalo. If crowned cranes, plovers or bustards suddenly fly off, you'll need to become more mindful because lions or hyenas could be hunting. The former are so numerous here (over 100) that they leave no leftovers for the jackals and

90 bottom A young zebra follows its herd, made up of females led by a dominant stallion.

91 The black rhinoceros is a seriously threatened species. Places such as Ngorongoro are of

fundamental importance for the safeguarding of these mammals.

92-93 The photograph shows the great caldera of Ngorongoro, which originated from the depression of the land following an impressive volcanic eruption.

90 top left Two black rhinoceroses roam the prairies of Ngorongoro.

90 top right Submerged during the day to protect themselves from the sun, the hippopotamuses leave the water only in the cooler hours to graze on the grass along the banks.

INSIDE THE VOLCANO

hyenas, which are thus forced to hunt actively, even in broad daylight. Our complete tour ends with a look at the northernmost pond of Mandusi, where herons and nycticoraxes heedlessly seem to observe the sleepy hippopotamuses, whose eyes, ears, and nostrils are all that stick up from the surface of the water.

Anyone who arrives at the volcano early in the morning may find a cloudy sky and caldera surrounded by fog—almost making the thousand voices of the savannah even more evocative—but within a short time the sun will come out. At first, the overall view of the caldera, with its crown extraordinarily intact, is surprising. Wherever you turn, you can't help but be amazed by this splendid jewel of nature, which is so dazzlingly bright throughout the year that its scenery has few rivals in the world. This is also the gravesite of Professor Bernhard Grzimek (1909-1987), an illustrious German zoologist and naturalist, and the author of an enormous encyclopedia on animals, and his son, who died here after an airplane accident with a vulture while filming a documentary.

The outside of the crater presents a lush vegetation, composed mainly of nuxias, albizia gummifera, twisted junipers and arboreal crotons, with yellow podocarps and cassipurea sticking out, or pillar trees completely covered with lichens. Monkeys of all types can be discerned in its branches and it is easy to stop and admire their behavior for hours at a time. The adults from a group of green cercopiths who shout and grunt, showing their teeth, excited by the arrival of intruders. Soon

after, however, they begin their normal activities again, looking for delicacies—an insect, a lizard or an egg adds to their main diet of seeds, fruit and leaves. If one of them should approach, the position of its tail will indicate its mood; if it is horizontal this means fear, and if it gradually folds up its back this is a sign of confidence. The baboons are also excellent climbers, and they find food and particularly night shelter amidst the branches. Some of them have learned that tourists are a good source of food and they can sometimes become inquisitive or even aggressive in order to steal some food after its rightful owners have moved off.

Going north toward the Serengeti, past the dunes, we come to Olduvai Gorge. A German entomologist stumbled onto it by chance in 1911 to chase a butterfly. Inside this deep canyon (31 miles long and 295 feet deep) that connects Ndutu Lake to the Ol Balbal pool, he found fossil bones later attributed to a horse that was long extinct. Twenty years later, the archeologist Louis Leakey and his wife, residents of Nairobi, decided to start doing research there. First they discovered stone tools and then in 1959, they found the skull of what would be called *Australopithecus boisei*, a primate that lived about 1,700,000 years ago. The research has continued and the current direct of the Nairobi Museum (Kenya) is none other than the Leakeys' son.

From the lookout point, it is easy to see the five geological layers that have been identified so far; under the current layer is the one dating to the erosion of the gorge by the river. Beds four and three were marked by *Homo erectus*, the second one held *Australopithecus boisei* and *Homo habilis*, and the last lava layer, dating to 1,900,000 years ago, is now being studied. The museum is definitely worth a visit. It is well organized and has numerous artifacts on exhibit from Olduvai, the vulgarization of "oldupai," an agave whose fleshy leaves the Masai use as bats for a game popular among these people.

A few miles away is an even more evocative site: the oldest hominid footprints were found at Laetoli. Over three and a half million years ago, during the Pliocene epoch, a group of *Australopithecines* walked—in a definitely upright position—over the ashes of a volcano. Once these ashes solidified, they preserved the traces of this passage, alongside the imprints of hyenas, gazelles, elephants and rhinoceroses. Who knows, perhaps even then Ngorongoro charmed our ancestors. (R.M.S.)

SERENGETI
NATIONAL PARK
MASAI MARA
GAME PARK

The landscape begins to take shape as the golden light of the sunrise mixes with the blue sky of a fresh and milky dawn; on a baobab, a leopard is still enjoying its freshly killed prey and birds are chirping everywhere. The grass crunches under the hooves of antelopes that start to graze, while a lioness drinks at a well with her pups. It's a new day on the Serengeti, the endless "great plains" in the Maa language, extending between the Ngorongoro plateau, Lake Victoria and the Reserve of the Masai Mara in Kenya. Dominating it along the horizon is the superb mass of Kilimanjaro, soaring to an altitude of nearly 19,680 feet. Initially a hunting reserve and then a natural reserve created through the work of the famous zoologist and naturalist Grzimek, the current Serengeti National Park covers an area of nearly 5,800 square miles. Although this vast territory may initially appear to show little variety, the different types of savannah—from the grasslands to the forested area—the dense

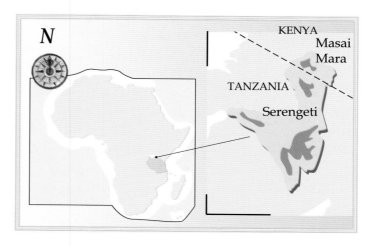

95 left Along the banks of the river Mbalageti stretches a forest, dense but limited to the immediate vicinity of the water. It is a typical tunnel forest, a characteristic ecosystem of the rivers that cross the savannah.

95 right The river Mara crosses a vast plain, which in the dry season turns yellow, dusty and parched. The turbid waters of the river do not look very inviting. Many animals have migrated towards more favorable areas.

94 Crossing an expanse of very high grass, a group of elephants heads for the river Mbalageti to drink and take their bath. Such refreshment is necessary in the great heat of Serengeti.

acacia groves and the wooded plains along the rivers flowing into Lake Victoria host fauna typical of the specific habitat, sometimes only at particular times of the year. This area, the outlying Ngorongoro Park, the nearby Tarangire Park and the Masai Mara reserve are all included in the immense protected ecosystem of the Serengeti, which has been declared a "natural reserves of the terrestrial biosphere."

The surface area of the park generally presents itself as a sea of waving grass that appears to be either ocher or green in color, depending on the season. It is dotted with various species of acacia, candle-shaped euphorbia and commifora, and is interrupted by trails, lush vegetation edging the waterways and kopjes, and colossal piles of granitic rock. The latter constitute unique microhabitats; these circumscribed formations offer shelter to numerous reptiles and agile mongooses, as well as shy klipspringers and friendly rock rabbits. Here you are likely to find a pair of dik-diks, tiny antelopes that are just over a foot tall and with a long and mobile nose, intent on nibbling at aloe and acacia bushes—sometimes rising on their hind legs. Every so often, the male leaves odorous secretions from its tear glands on the vegetation in order to mark it territory.

The Moru kopje, located in the southern part of the park, is extremely suggestive and interesting. Amidst magnificent aloe plants, some of which are up to thirteen feet tall, you can admire the rock paintings of the Masai, perhaps under the watchful eye of an agama or gecko. Here too, you hear the cry of alarm of the rock rabbits, generally territorial males that also act as sentinels. Given their resemblance to woodchucks, it seems impossible that they could be related to elephants from an evolutionary standpoint. Their main enemy is undoubtedly the Verreaux eagle, with its distinctive white back and yellow claws. Leopards, caracals and jackals are the other predators typical of the kopjes. It is fantastic to stand on high ground and gaze as far as the eye can see across the vast prairie, the home of elephants,

96 bottom Crossing the river Mara is a delicate enterprise, in which the gnus run grave risks. Many of them die by drowning, others are preyed on by crocodiles.

96-97 In a disorderly mass of bodies, dangerous for the animals themselves, countless gnus cross the river Mara to undertake their annual migration through the grazing lands.

97 bottom left Having reached the banks of the river, the gnus hesitate for a long time before crossing. When the most enterprising dare to take the plunge the others follow en masse, in one of the most spectacular and dramatic annual events in Africa.

97 bottom right After crossing the river Mara, the gnus find themselves having to climb up the steep bank. Many do not succeed, remaining trapped in the mud, trodden underfoot by the rest of the herd and at the mercy of the crocodiles.

blesbocks, hartebeests, zebras and ostriches, warthogs and long-eared foxes.

Among the wild animals that can be seen are the herds of cattle belonging to the Masai, the most famous ethnic population of these lands, today considered to belong to the Maa language of the Nilotic group. They came from Ethiopia in the seventeenth century and, until 1850, they were warriors feared by all the other tribes. Toward the end of the nineteenth century, however, bovine plagues, drought, famine and pox decimated the population, which split up into two warring factions. The losers had to give their cattle to the winners and devote themselves to agriculture. The Masai are still tied to a semi-nomadic life of raising livestock and a milk-based diet. The cattle are also bled so the people can nourish themselves on their blood, while sheep and goats, whose milk is considered to be women's food, are commonly eaten, as are buffaloes and elands—the only wild animals. But be careful, before you can take a picture of the Masai you need to agree on a price!

In order to approach a large number of animals, the guides often accompany visitors close to the water, preferably in the central area of the park where the arboreal savannah gradually turns into dense acacia groves mixed with sycamores, ficuses

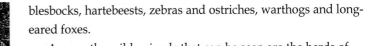

and sausage trees. The sausages are obviously the particular fruit of this tree, which exceeds thirty-two feet in height, despite the fact that its trunk is rather small. Up to 3 feet long and weighing up to 8 pounds, they are poisonous to man but are considered a delicacy by monkeys and boars. If you notice a terrible stench nearby, one of the sausage trees might be in bloom; it relies on flies for pollination! On the riverbanks, you can see numerous traces of the animals that come there to drink; the long narrow hoof prints of giraffes, the large round ones of buffaloes, and the prints of hyenas, porcupines and

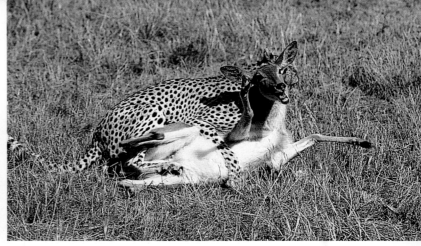

98 The future of the cheetah is not guaranteed by his sixty mile-an-hour sprint. The reduction of suitable habitats and the very limited genetic variability of the existing specimens are the principal threats to this species.

99 top left In what to our eyes looks like a cruel game, two young cheetahs are in training for their future hunting activity. Their mother deliberately procures for them easy live prey, with which to practice.

99 top right After a very quick chase, the cheetah has caught an antelope. Death will be fairly slow, because the weak jaws and short teeth of the predator are incapable of a devastating bite like that of the lion.

99 bottom left The cheetah seems to be specially built for speed, with a small head, slim muscular body and very long feet. Its non-retractable claws guarantee it a constant grip on the ground.

99 bottom right The very young cheetahs have a long white mane, which falls out with age, extending from the head to the base of the tail. This makes them similar to the honey-badger, an aggressive and formidable creature, which few predators dare to attack.

100 top left Among the lions the role of the male, which is imposing and strong, is mainly to protect the territory and the pride. With his cubs, however, he can be tender, putting up patiently with their rowdy games.

100 center left In young lions there are evident spots on the coat similar to those of the leopard, which later become a uniform color in the adult.

Perhaps this is evidence of the descent of the lion from very ancient spotted ancestors.

100 bottom left A cub would like to play, but his mother is sleeping. The adult lions spend a lot of time in an absolute state of rest, while the vivacity and curiosity of the cubs allow them to discover what the world is like.

rhinoceroses. All you need to do is wait, and you won't be disappointed. At a certain point, you'll hear some rustling: an impala leaves the brush to scout the area. It long ears are outstretched to listen, it takes a few steps and then stops hesitantly until it reaches the shore. Behind it is a sitatunga, the only long-haired antelope that seems to be escorted by a group of baboons looking for the seeds of aquatic plants, mainly water lilies. Lastly, agile, supple and circumspect is a giraffe that timidly spreads its front legs and licks at the water. The bird life amidst the reed thickets of the rivers is very rich, given that the Serengeti boasts of over 350 species of birds.

The masters in the areas where the river is calmer are the hippopotamuses, which can stay underwater for up to twenty minutes, nibbling at the plants on the riverbed. Where the water flows faster, crocodiles float immobile, resembling tree trunks. The annual cycle of the Serengeti is also marked by the appearance of zebras, striped gnus and gazelles that migrate clockwise along the edges of the park, seeking food and water.

100 right Three lionesses set off hunting, during which the movements of each individual will be perfectly coordinated. It is one of the key moments in the life of the lions, the only felines that display true social behavior.

101 A lioness transports a cub of about two weeks to take him to safety away from one of the fires that periodically devastate the savannah. The attention the lionesses pay to their cubs is devoted and kind.

*102 top left Although able to move
with a certain speed on its robust
feet, the African crocodile is truly at
ease only in the water, where it takes
refuge when it is disturbed.*

*102 top right The Grumeti River,
richly surrounded by vegetation, is
an ideal place in Serengeti to observe
animals with aquatic habits, such as
hippopotamuses and crocodiles.*

*102 bottom When hatched, the baby
crocodiles are around 12 inches long.
The mother, delicately using her
powerful jaws, transports them to the
water where they are relatively safe.*

Starting in December, the first rains regenerate the grass of the plains. In the borderline area between the Serengeti and Ngorongoro parks, the herds share a vast territory and mating occurs during the same season that most of the zebras give birth. The foals, which have brown stripes, start to trot near their mothers, while the stallions kick and, above all, bite each other. Meanwhile, the gnus are more phlegmatic; these "chatty" antelopes pretend to attack each other, horns locked on the ground, in simulated combat. They prefer ostentation to action and thus rarely wound each other. Most of the gnus are born around February and the great southern plain feeds about two million of these antelopes, in addition to 300,000 zebras, gazelles elands and blesboks. The intense March rains then transform the entire protected area into a green sea and the herds gradually head north through the "western corridor," where they follow the waterways and cross the wooded areas, lining up in columns that can extend for miles.

The rainy season ends in June and under the broiling sun, the plains soon turn yellow and ocher, the numerous species of acacias show off only their thorns and the wells dry up. For herbivores, the fated day has arrived: the so-called "great migration" that will bring them to perennial rivers. The land shakes under the hooves of the galloping animals, and amidst the immense cloud of dust the grunting and lowing covers the voices of the young. In just three or four days, they will cover over 124 miles, and only the strong will succeed in this undertaking. The weaker ones serve as food to the crocodiles waiting in the Grumeti River. The reptiles capture as much prey as possible, drowning the animals and then eating them once things calm down again. Hyenas, jackals and vultures spend the

102-103 *The terrible jaws of a crocodile clamp the head of a Thomson gazelle. The reptile preys on large mammals by waiting in ambush underwater and then taking advantage when the latter come to drink.*

103 bottom *Grasped by the throat while drinking on the bank, a zebra has been dragged into the river, where it has no escape. It will probably not be devoured immediately, but left to rot in the water.*

104 Hippopotamuses can be very aggressive, especially when the males are fighting their rivals in defense of their females. A hippo shows his tusks as an act of intimidation.

105 left The hippopotamuses spend only the coolest hours of the day or night on dry land, where they go to graze. Each of them devours 80 pounds of vegetation every day, before returning to the water.

105 top right A family of hippopotamuses in the muddy waters of the Grumeti River. These animals could not do without water, in which they spend the day protecting their bare skin from the sun's rays.

105 right center top The savannah visible from the Itonjo hills, dotted with acacia trees, is crossed by large herds of African buffalo. They are constantly on the move, traveling even dozens of miles a day, in search of grazing land.

night vying for victims, while many mothers go back and forth across the river trying to find their lost young. The route through the northern territory can slow down at this point, so that from August to October (the driest period for the Serengeti), the animals can exploit the Masai Mara Reserve in Kenya, where water is always available.

Founded in 1961 in the territory in which the Masai were interned in 1889, this destination encloses a hilly area crossed by a rich network of waterways. The Mara is the main one and its fords are the preferred destination of migrating herbivores. Here, lions, leopards and cheetahs wait for just the right moment to carry out their fundamental roles in the selection process; prey every two or three days will give them proper nourishment. In November, the sensitive nostrils of the herbivores start to perceive the arrival of the first rains and the plants begin to bud slowly. Taking different routes, the various groups of antelopes return south, where they will nibble on the first blades of fresh grass and start a new cycle. (R.M.S.)

105 right center bottom The enormous size, large horns and irascible temperament make the African buffalo a very dangerous animal. It is also a difficult prey for the lions, who when they attack it must resort to a group strategy.

105 bottom right The auricles of the African elephant, with their large surface, help to dissipate body heat — an important adaptation for life in the sunny savannah.

106-107 With the rising of the sun a new day is about to begin in Serengeti. A lioness looks as though she is admiring the dawn with us, in a place of full evocative beauty but also of daily dramas.

108 top left Mount Kilimanjaro, an unmistakable point of reference for all those who move through the savanna, is a volcano. Its peak at an altitude of almost 20,000 feet conceals erupting craters amidst snow and ice.

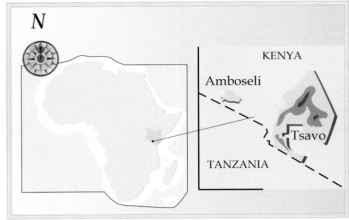

TSAVO AND AMBOSELI
NATIONAL PARKS

An endless golden stretch with thousands of straw-colored tones—yellow, ocher, siena—gradually shade into the orange and red of the sky, where the clouds, indigo and violet, accompany the enormous fiery disk of the sun as it descends. The day is about to end and soon the little bush babies, like big-eyed elves, will start jumping on the branches of the acacia in search of insects. An owl will softly fly from the termite hill on which it stopped to rest, the leopard will pad softly in search of prey; all the animals on the savannah prepare for another night. The parks of southeastern Kenya are well equipped, with lodges that have little to envy of European hotels, and their vicinity to the capital city of Nairobi has given rise to an influx of many—perhaps too many—who dream of "wild Africa."

After bouncing over the holes on the trails, getting overheated in the closed cars but happy to have a chance to photograph a watering hole or a predator on the hunt, visitors feel like they've become the stars of a film or documentary. This is what happens in the great Kenyan park of Tsavo, which was founded in 1948 and split up for administrative reasons into Tsavo East and Tsavo West National Parks. Its name comes from the river that crosses it and means "slaughter" in the language of the WaKamba, the Bantu ethnic

108 center top There are a number of species of zebra on the East African plains but the most common is Burchell's zebra. It lives in small family groups comprising a dominant stallion and several females, whom the male defends from rivals.

108 bottom center The crowned crane or pavonian crane is one of the most beautiful African birds. Characterized by its crest of long fine feathers, it lives on the bushy banks of rivers or marshes, feeding with small animals and seeds.

108 bottom Waterbucks bound to the presence of water as they need to drink every day and for this reason they are never too far away from a water source.

109 Two giants: Kilimanjaro's unmistakable silhouette, the highest mountain on this continent at over 19,000 feet, forms a backdrop for a giraffe, a species whose males often exceed sixteen feet in height.

110 top left Noisy trumpeting and menacing stance for two male African elephants as they confront one another. For adults it is a competition for mating rights, for the young it is a game; but it is also an apprenticeship for how to behave as adults.

110 top right On the Amboseli Plain an elephant serenely tears at the grass with its trunk. The cattle egrets take advantage to unearth some small animal usually hidden by the vegetation.

110 bottom The young elephant, surrounded by adults, has nothing to fear. Elephants have an extremely developed sense of parental care in the animal world and each cub enjoys a high chance of survival.

AT THE EDGE OF NIGHT

group that has reached this land, probably from the Kilimanjaro. First shepherds and then hunters, then merchants and markers on hunting expeditions, today they devote their time to producing ethnic jewelry and wooden sculptures.

The protected territory, with two national parks and the adjoining reserves, covers an area of more than 8,880 square miles, offering a significant variety of habitats. The grassy plains alternate with the savannah with its trees and shrubs, as well as the acacia groves, the baobab woods, tamarinds, borassus and dom palms and the lush canopy forest.

About two-thirds of the eastern Tsavo is closed to tourism and is reserved for scientific research, but the area that is available for visits is nevertheless vast. Of particular interest are the frothy Lugard Falls, a series of rapids on the Galana River against the backdrop of the Yatta plateau, an ancient and immense lava stream that stretches toward Nairobi. Here, at any time of the year you can observe numerous mammals, reptiles and about a hundred bird species. Another lookout point is the rock formation of Mudanda, a gigantic granitic kopje that is over a mile long, with a dam at its base.

The constant presence of water and the fresh breezes demand that some wild animal always stops here to drink. Also of interest in the western Tsavo are the Mzima Springs, with an enormous quantity of crystal-clear water under the shade of dom palms and wild ficuses. It is also exciting to descend to special windows that afford an underwater view of the river: tilapias, barbels and catfish swim before the visitors' eyes, a few hippopotamuses walk on the bottom, crocodiles swim slowly and some pelomedusas, the helmeted

turtles typical of the African swamps, bask in the sun on the riverbanks.

The park's main attractions are the large herds of elephants (up to 700 specimens) and buffaloes (up to 1,000 head), now unique throughout the world. It is around the colossal baobabs, the gigantic African trees whose trunks can reach a circumference of 130 feet, that the signs left by the elephants can be seen; during dry spells, they dig into the trunks with their tusks to suck out the sap. The trees survive in spite of this, and the oldest specimens reach the age of three thousand years. Elephants, buffaloes, rhinoceroses, lions and leopards—the so-called "Big Five" of the savannah—also live in the nearby Amboseli National Park, reduced in 1974 to 150 square miles, as opposed to more than 1,200 in the previous reserve. The herds of the Masai can no longer enter here to drink and wells have been made for them outside the reserve. This was done to prevent a situation that occurred in the 1970s when during a prolonged dry spell, the herds were

110-111 A herd of elephants wanders through the Eastern Tsavo National Park. These animals require enormous expanses of territory where they rove in search of water and pasture. If they are confined in areas that are too small they must scourge for vegetation, depriving themselves of necessary sustenance.

111 In the dry season, even a small pool of muddy water attracts Tsavo fauna. The low vegetation shows clearly the tracks cut by the animals making their way to the watering-place.

led to the ponds that were constantly fed by underground springs. Afraid of these herds, the wild animals left the area and most of them died of thirst.

Amidst acacia groves and canopy forests there is an incredible variety of fauna, but the most spectacular aspect of this little park is experienced at sunrise; as the first rays cut through the short silence that lies between the voices of the night and the greeting of the new day, the two peaks of Kilimanjaro can be briefly seen: the volcanic crown of Kibo and the jagged tip of Mawenzi, and in just a short time they will be enveloped by the clouds. (R.M.S.)

112-113 The hyena-dog is one of the African savanna's most efficient predators, thanks to the perfect coordination between members of the pack. Despite this, the hyena-dog is one of Africa's most endangered mammals — only a few thousand animals survive in the entire African continent.

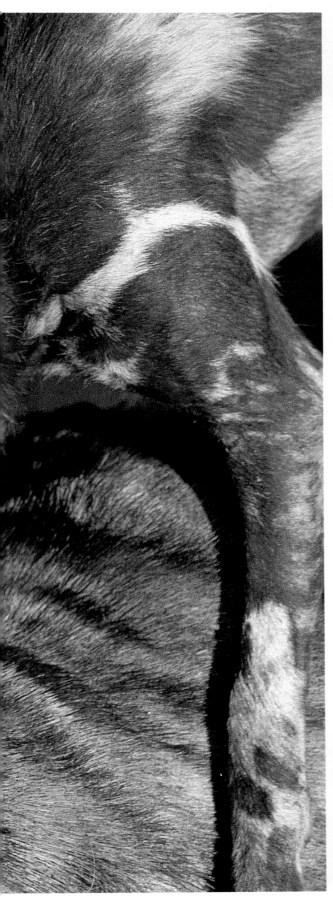

113 top Three hyena-dog cubs fight over a piece of meat that an adult has just regurgitated for them. This image clearly illustrates how hard life is in the savanna, but also how closely the cubs and adults of a species bond.

113 center The spotted hyena clings tightly to what remains of a warthog head. Even the latter's long fangs were not enough to save it. Hyenas have exceptionally strong teeth that can break even the toughest bone.

113 bottom The lappet-faced vulture (Torgos tracheliotus) is one of the first to arrive when an animal carcass becomes available, sighted from miles away. Its dimensions mean that it towers over other vultures and forces them to get in line.

VIRUNGA
NATIONAL PARK

At last, from the dense milky fog, a rustling sound can be heard and a huge male with silver-grey shoulders appears. For a moment, the gaze of the small and hairless man meets that of the calm and slow moving gorilla, his enormous relative. In the excitement of the moment, the arduous journey becomes a thing of the past; the long and difficult trip is instantly forgotten. Despite the muddy trails, the rain that seems to penetrate right through to your bones, the clouds of annoying insects… everything is just fantastic.

Mountain gorillas, larger and with longer fur than their cousins in the plains, live only here in the forests of the Virunga Mountains: a chain of volcanoes, many of them active, with the highest peak, Volcan Karisimbi, reaching up to more than 14,760 feet. These mountains in central east Africa form a natural border between three countries, Rwanda, Democratic Republic of the Congo and Uganda. Virunga National Park of

the same name, actually consists of a strip of land approximately 25 miles by 9 miles between Rwanda and Congo, but its borders are frequently changed.

In Uganda there is another protected area which is small and unfortunately quite remote. Above 9850 feet in altitude, day and night temperature ranges are extreme: it is not an exageration to say that each day brings the summer and each night the winter. In fact, temperatures vary more in 24 hours than from one half of the year to the other. The vegetation consists of huge bamboo forests, which at higher elevations give way to moor land with heather, moss, lichens and above all typical Seneca plants with fantastic shapes, as well as giant Lobelia plants that can reach a height of more than 13 feet.

Unlike chimpanzees, gorillas are exclusively vegetarian and eat 50 different kinds of plants, though their preference is for bamboo and they will eat 44-66 pounds of it each day

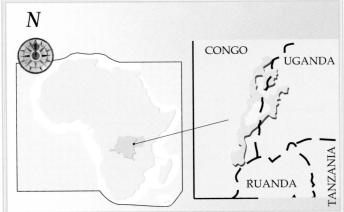

114-115 The dense forest that covers Africa's Virunga Mountains is the home of the world's last mountain gorilla population. The apparent impenetrability of their habitat does not appear to have discouraged poachers.

115 bottom right The unmistakable silhouette of the volcano Sabinyo looms over Virunga Park. The forest seems interminable and conceals swampy clearings and deep slumps.

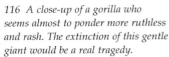

116 *A close-up of a gorilla who seems almost to ponder more ruthless and rash. The extinction of this gentle giant would be a real tragedy.*

(a tendency to overeat gives them their protruding bellies and often causes digestive problems). They just have to reach out a 'hand' and food is available: it's almost like sitting in a huge salad bowl. The groups of gorillas often move from place to place so as not to ruin the vegetation, which in any case will grow again quickly.

The days are monotonous for these gorilla giants, who can weigh up to 440 pounds. A rain shower or a ray of sunshine through the mist is a special moment, when greater socializing or simple observation of other forest inhabitants takes place. A female gorilla stops to contemplate a small chameleon: how strange, this creature with a slow, solemn gait, claws with opposable articulations and prehensile tail, as it advances along the branches, scrutinizing his observer, first with one eye and then another. A little way ahead, a large male has discovered a nest of soldier ants; ready to hunt any prey, they build temporary nests when the larvae are ready to transform into pupae. These ants are an excellent source of animal protein, but are also able to make their way through even the thickest of furs to inflict a painful bite. The only chance for the gorilla to enjoy their delicious flavor is to grab a handful and run away.

Not so easy to observe are tree coneys or plantain-eaters. Only by visiting the park can you begin to understand the famous scholar Diane Fossey who spent most of her life in these forests. She lived here from 1967 until she was murdered in 1985. She now rests in a cemetery that she created for her 'friends.'

There are still a thousand problems to be solved concerning the protection of this area, which is home to several species of animals. The local people have few resources and want to use the parklands for timber felling, grazing and antelope hunting as well as for agricultural use, given that the volcanic soil is very fertile. In fact, a multinational company has made substantial investments for the creation of chrysanthemum plantations. Many of the local inhabitants have never seen a gorilla and do not understand their importance; that's why it is fundamental, alongside a team of game wardens, to have a program of education and sensitisation for the indigenous people.

Naturalistic tourism is promoted within well-defined limits (only 1 hour is allowed with the gorillas, at a distance of not less than 16 feet, as a precaution against the transmission of disease), to raise funds for the park. It is feared that mountain gorillas will become extinct within a century of their discovery; the risk of seeing these, less than 400 primates for only a few more years, is great. Research continues in the meantime, not only regarding the ecology of the gorilla species, but also that of local animals. Herbivores in general, and in particular the cercopith monkey, which is commonly found in the Virunga Mountains and surrounding forests, are also living from a diet mainly of bamboo shoots, and therefore compete with gorillas in the search for food. Another risk imposed upon the inhabitants of this environment is the fact that the area is volcanic, an unpredictable factor; volcanoes can destroy parts of the forest but they can also discourage human habitation and actually increase the amount of space for gorillas. Will we succeed in assuring the dignified survival of this fascinating relative of ours? (R.M.S.)

117 bottom right In the twilight a dominant male, called a silverback because of the silver gray color of its back, betrays its powerful muscles, in seeming contrast with the peaceful nature of these cousins of the human race.

116-117 When a gorilla meets an adversary it will attempt to intimidate it with frightful expressions, screams and displays of its extreme strength. It is rare, however, that a gorilla attacks a retreating enemy.

117 bottom left The cheeky face of a young gorilla caught by the camera while immersed in its games. Gorillas grow fast: at four months they are fast runners, at seven they are agile tree-climbers. Mothers take care of their young for at least three years.

ETOSHA
NATIONAL PARK

Nature-lovers still hoping to observe animals in the wild will, without doubt, need to look in Namibia. This young nation, known until just a short while ago by the name of Southwest Africa, gained its independence from South Africa in 1990 and today is one of the African countries with the highest standard of living. Moreover, it possesses an enormous wealth of natural beauty, which the government has wisely and providently thought to preserve by founding a series of parks on national territory, whose aim is to safeguard the environment and protect the flora and fauna that exists here. The economic return from the great number

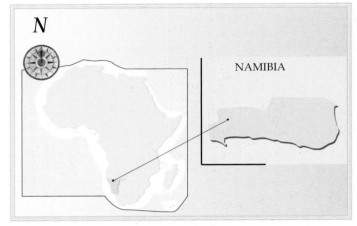

118 center left The leopard as a predator is not well equipped for long chases. It prefers to lay unexpected ambushes for its prey, taking advantage of the numerous hiding places offered by a habitat rich in rocky recesses and trees.

118 center right The springbok is primarily known for the spectacular bounds it makes in case of danger, with its feet together and in rapid succession. Their purpose is not only to alert his fellow creatures but also to discourage predators.

of tourists that visit these still uncontaminated areas every year vastly repays this policy of environmental protection.

Namibia actually possesses one of the oldest and certainly one of Africa's most important national parks—Etosha. With over 8,500 square miles of surface area, it is a unique park, both for the quantity of animals that it hosts and for its peculiar ecosystem, which may still be considered untainted by human intervention. It is to be found in the northern part of the state, not far from the Angolan border, in a territory where savannahs and grasslands roll together into timeless space. In 1907, this area became part of the hunting reserve (over 38,500 square miles) that Von Lindequist, governor of the German colony at that time, instituted to protect wildlife that was being systematically decimated at that time. This contributed to maintaining the state of the whole area and increasing interest in nature. In 1958, a real national park was created with the construction of more than 496 miles of fencing to define the borders that were established in 1970 and remain to this day.

Almost at the center of the park is the spectacular Etosha

Salt Pan that extends for almost 1,950 square miles. In the language of the Ovambo, one of the region's greatest ethnic groups, the name means "great white depression". It represents the last vestiges of an ancient lake, of gigantic dimensions, which nowadays will only hold water in certain seasons. In the dry season, from May to October, it appears as a slightly surreal white desert surrounded by savannah. In fact, as the water evaporates it deposits a white salt crust over

the entire plain, accompanied by tinges of color produced by various algae and minerals.

Under the scorching rays of the midday sun it is not unusual to be deceived by mirages and nonexistent images outlined against the horizon. Etosha Pan offers a spellbinding show each day at sunset, when a sheet of fire seems to engulf the plain in one of the most fascinating sunsets on Earth. On the side south of the pan, where the underlying strata emerge, there are pools of water and small lakes everywhere, a vital lure for all the animals living in the park. In fact, these water reserves are a real aggregation center, especially in the dry season, when the great thirsty herbivores assemble, often side-by-side with their predators.

Those who wish to sight Etosha Pan animals will have to get up early! Zebra, kudu, oryx, and gazelles are more likely to gather in the early morning hours and are intent on drinking as lions and leopards stroll serenely past, almost as if there were a tacit agreement that hostilities be put aside for the brief moment of watering. Later the roles of prey and predator are resumed in the continuous and inevitable fight

118-119 The extraordinary plants of Aloe dichotoma dominate in the arid plain, mostly covered with shrubs. Noted particularly for their spectacular fauna, the African parks can be just as attractive for the flora which they are home to.

119 bottom The proportions of the giraffe force it to adopt an uncomfortable position when it is drinking. Its large size and the presence of the group reduce the danger of predators at a relatively awkward moment.

for survival. There is a precise hierarchy applied for approaching the water; first of all the lions, who clearly show they are "king" here, and the other predators follow: leopards, cheetahs, hyenas. The second shift sees the arrival of the herbivores, who crowd to the shore in more numerous and unruly groups.

There is one animal that reveals its disrespect of rules of precedence, the elephant. They arrive in single file, lifting great clouds of dust with their heavy legs while leaving no doubt as to whom will drink first. During the rainy season, from November to February, it is more difficult to sight animals; in fact the abundance of water scatters fauna throughout the park. It is the moment when the vegetation is green and luxuriant, and watercourses often invade trails and make moving inside the park very difficult. But it is also the moment in which the Pan is flooded, attracting large numbers of birds such as pelicans and flamingos, who find food here. It is always an experience to see them take flight like a team of perfectly synchronized acrobatic flyers; a collision appears inevitable but never occurs in the pink whirlwind of thousands of pulsating wings. The park offers tourist facilities where board and lodging are available. The most charming are without doubt Namutoni, in the eastern part of the park, obtained from an old fort built by German troops in the early twentieth century, during the war against the Wambo tribe.

On the opposite side there is Okaukeujo camp, where the park has its head offices. A nearby well is illuminated at night so that sighting animals is even easier. It is not rare to get within 35 feet of black rhinos. These great pachyderms are now a rarity throughout Africa, but thanks to a program of protected reproduction, the park contains nearly 400 of them. This territory is also the last shelter for Kirk's dik-dik; at 16 inches in height and 13 pounds in weight, it is the world's smallest antelope.

Those who wish to visit the park with their own cars may

THE SALT PLAIN

do so, provided they do not disturb the animals and respect some simple rules, dictated mostly by common sense; nor should they put themselves senselessly at risk—this park remains an untamed environment. There is a 37 per mile/hour speed limit, and it is forbidden to leave the car if there are animals nearby, even if they appear harmless. A few simple precautions will make the safari more enjoyable. With a little attention we will soon discover happy, hopping guenon monkeys hiding amongst the branches of a mopane tree or spot tall giraffes who move agile on their long legs from one acacia to the other, or recognize the silhouette of a solitary leopard scrutinizing the territory from the height of a termite-mound.

The greatest risk we run is that of wanting to linger one more day, then another and another, attracted by the irresistible lure of nature. (C.B.)

121 bottom left There are not many places for the Etosha elephants to find sufficient quantities of water. However, the largest specimens of the African elephant are in fact those found in the driest areas.

121 bottom right In the desolate plains of Etosha, thirst is one of the greatest problems. Every time an opportunity presents itself, those animals most in need of water, such as zebras, take a long drink and even defy the predators lying in ambush.

120 bottom The ostrich compensates for its lack of flying skills with a great aptitude for running. The ease with which it moves allows it to cover large distances in search of the most favorable places. It generally moves in groups.

120-121 Two oryxes roam in their inhospitable desert habitat. It is incredible how these large antelopes can survive with very limited quantities of liquid, thanks to their refined physiological adaptations.

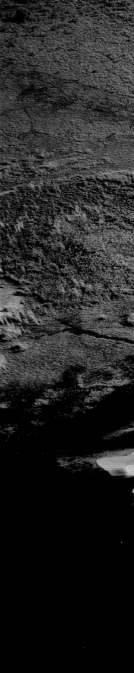

MOREMI
GAME RESERVE
CHOBE
NATIONAL PARK

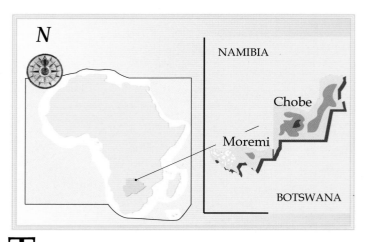

Two million years ago, in present-day Botswana, there was a lake that no one had ever given a name, perhaps because there was no one there to give it one. It was probably the largest African lake of that time, fed by great rivers coming from far-off mountain regions. Then movements of the earth's crust shifted the course of its eastern influents. One of these, that today we call Chobe, began to run east, throwing itself into the Zambesi, which in turn flows into the Indian Ocean. The amount of water in the lake was, thus, diminished, causing the climate to become drier. The great basin dried up, leaving a vast and inhospitable extent of sand and salty earth, the former Lake Makgadikgadi, in the northern part of the Kalahari desert. Today this river has a name, Okavango, but as it wanders between the desert and the savanna, it no longer finds its lake. It begins in the mountains of Angola, not far from the Atlantic Ocean. But it obstinately insists on flowing east, trying to reach the Indian Ocean that is too far away. Its waters are, thus, lost in the desert, forming a gigantic internal delta, as large as 7,700 square miles, one of the most spectacular environments in all of Africa. The river flows among thousands of islands, islets, tortuous canals and meanders that create extents of reeds and papyrus that slow its flow and make its course extremely long. Its flood stage takes five months to flow from the mouth of the delta to its edges, following a path of 187 miles, with only a difference of 197 miles in its level.

This periodic advance and retreat of the waters gives life to a very intricate and endless combination of environments, characterized by a great biological diversity and protected, in its northeastern part, by the Moremi nature preserve. This latter, located north of Maun, provides the best opportunity to admire the richness of the delta fauna. Usually, tourists reach the preserve from Maun by flying in small airplanes. Few of the preserve's equipped campsites are actually reachable by road and the option of travelling by land is, in any case, not very convenient. Flying over the delta

and observing it from above is, moreover, the best way to become fully aware of its complexity, its relationship with the surrounding desert and its exceptional beauty.

The Okavango forms thousands of islands, often very small and dotted with palms, whose green differs from that of the reeds and papyrus at the bottom of the flooded sections, visible because of the transparency of the water (which is drinkable). Around the islands one finds white beaches, together with intense blue borders where the color of the sky is reflected. The presence of animals is evidenced by the network of paths in the emergent portions, but hundreds of species are directly visible by visiting the multi-formed environments of the delta. More than 400 species of birds live here; among those better adapted to life in the swamps there is the African Jacana or water pheasant. This bird of modest dimensions

has disproportionately long fingers on its claws, with which it moves by walking on the floating vegetation. Among the most spectacular is the African Saddle-Beak, a large stork with a bizarrely colored beak that is often seen together with other species. And herons, fisher martins, storks, geese, ducks, ibis, spoonbills, cormorants and darters, also called "snake birds" because of their long, flexible necks, an effective weapon for harpooning fish. As for mammals, there are elephants and hippopotamus and even water antelope and an

122-123 A branch of the Okavango Delta pours its sediment rich waters into the Xigera Lagoon. Only aerial observation will make it possible to fully appreciate the overall characteristics of such a composite environment.

123 bottom left Wallowing in water and mud is a very important activity for elephants, who thus protect their hides from dehydration and parasites.

The young, of course, have the most fun here.

123 bottom right The carmine bee-eater (Merops nubicoides) builds its nest in specially dug tunnels in the earth walls and thus colonizes the various areas suitable for this purpose. This colored assembly of birds is one of tropical Africa's most kaleidoscopic spectacles.

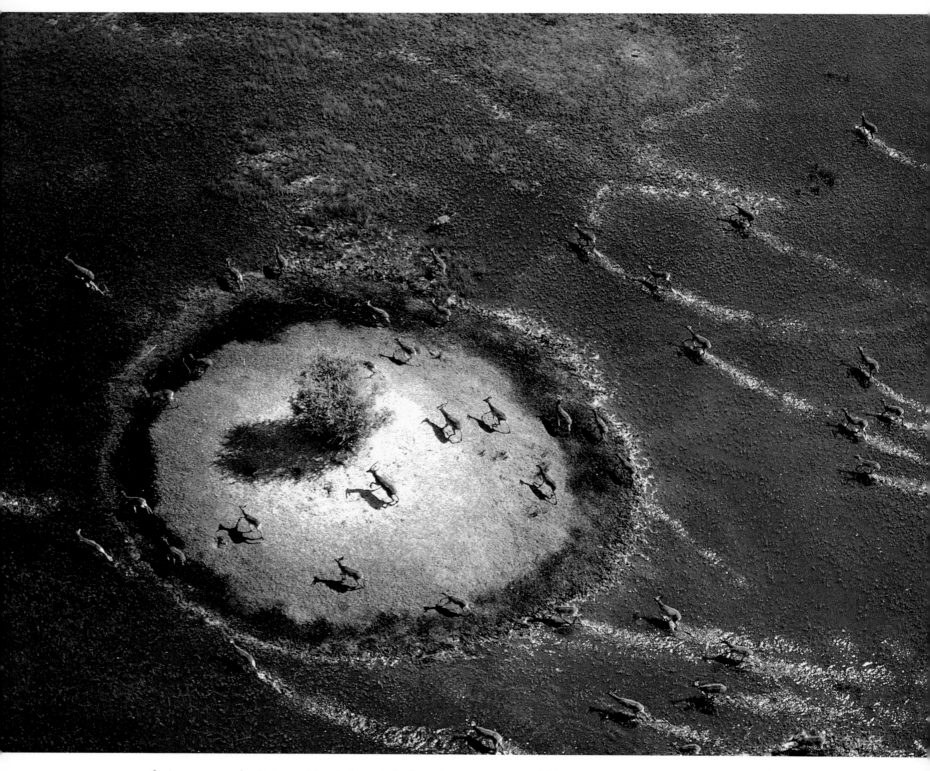

elusive presence, the sitatunga (*Tragelaphus spekei*). This unique antelope is characterized by its strong legs and very long hoofs that, thanks to their particular structure, provide the animal with stable support even on muddy ground. The sitatunga can also remain immersed in the water for long periods, in addition to hiding in the vegetation, leaving only part of its muzzle on the surface to breathe. In this way it easily escapes any land predator, but not the crocodile.

The most extensive of the delta islands, Chief's Island, is found inside the Moremi nature preserve. In over a 387 square miles, the savanna and the swamp mix in an explosion of bio-diversity. One of the best ways to visit this extraordinary environment is to use a "mokoro," a canoe typical in this part of Africa, carved from the trunk of a particular species of ebony, Diospyros mespiliformis, whose wood resists both termites and water. A standing man pushes it using a pole made from strong and flexible mogonano

wood (*Terminalia sericea*). In this way, its slides through water lilies and clear water, between cane reeds and papyrus.

The best time of year to visit is winter in the southern hemisphere, when the sun shines and the air is dry without the oppressive heat of summer. There are no mosquitoes and, in dealing with the dry season, the animals tend to concentrate in the areas of remaining moisture. (Because of the heat and the tormenting mosquitoes at this time, the summer season is a less than ideal time for visiting the great Okavango delta.)

From the Moremi nature preserve, a road leads northeast towards the Chobe national park, crossing a vast scrubland. The national park is found in the extreme north of Botswana, on the border with Namibia and Zimbabwe, reaching about fifty miles from Victoria Falls. It is a protected area that includes a multiplicity of environments and forms of life, so much so that few parks in the world can compete with Chobe. The zebra migration takes place in the southwestern part of the national park, dominated by the Mababe Depression.

The Moremi and the Chobe national parks are two of the most important protected areas in Botswana, placing this country in the forefront of the dark continent for protection of the environment. In northern Botswana, where the rainy season is a little more generous, there are extensive grassy savannas and woods of mopane trees with leaves shaped like butterflies. The animals make great use of it, appearing in surprising herds of herbivores, whose presence cheers the hearts of tourists, lions, leopards and hyenas. From November to April, when the rains bathe the savanna, the herds disperse in all directions. But the rain is difficult: it falls in one area and not another, forcing the animals into a nomadic life.

During the dry season, the fauna concentrate along the permanent waterways: the Chobe river, the Linyanti swamps, the Okavango delta and, in years when the sky is more generous, the Boteti river. The evening visit to the water is the most suitable time to observe the animals. Impalas, black antelope, buffalo, elephants and zebra, all hesitating to lower their heads, fearful of not noticing the presence of predators. Because, in the savanna, hunger and thirst are serious things. The elephants have less to worry about. As big as mountains, no carnivore with any sense would dare to attack them. They also make out much better in the search for water: they are perfectly familiar with the location of every well, and only at the beginning of the dry season do they decide to go to the Chobe. Perhaps they go because thirst forces them to leave their mopane woods behind, whose leaves, by now yellow, are always pleasant and nutritious. But in the end, the attraction of the Chobe prevails.

(G.G.B.)

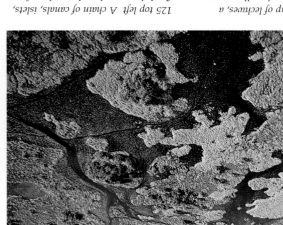

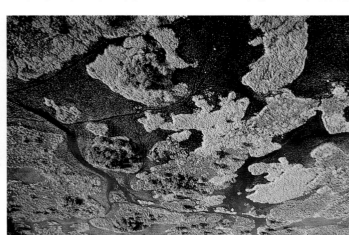

124-125 A group of lechwes, a species of waterbuck, gallops across one of the countless islets dotted across the Okavango Delta. The rich fauna and the varied habitats make this region one of the most spectacular natural attractions of the entire African continent.

125 top left A chain of canals, islets, flooded savannah and stretches of papyrus are the essence of the Okavango Delta. This vast alternation of habitats, each of which has very limited extension, favors the presence of countless forms of animal and plant life.

125 top right A solitary lechwe (Kobus lechwe) trots across the flooded plain. It is one of many species of waterbuck that concentrate only where there is an abundance of water, as it cannot survive without drinking even for brief periods.

125 bottom The tranquillity of the swamp is animated by water sprayed by galloping animals. This is no game, however, but a territorial dispute between lechwe males (Kobus lechwe) as the mating period approaches.

KRUGER NATIONAL PARK

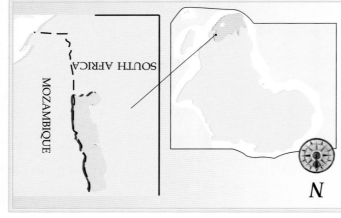

There was a time when elephants had short noses. One of these, who was young and inexperienced, refused to listen to the advice of his elders. They had told him to avoid the muddy waters of the Limpopo river, because the crocodile hid there. Whatever could a crocodile be, he wondered? Driven by curiosity, the little elephant went to the river banks and there was nothing particularly frightening there. The water was so cloudy that he could not see below the surface. He put his head under, and that is when the trouble started! The crocodile sank its teeth into his nose, but the little elephant was quick to react and managed to stop himself being dragged into the water. He tried desperately to get free and trumpeted loudly, but no one could hear him. As the crocodile pulled him towards the water, he dug his feet in and put up a fight. All of a sudden the crocodile slackened his grip and the little elephant was freed. The tugging on his nose had stretched it out of all proportion and he was not brave enough to show his face to his companions. What would he have told them? From that day forth the elephant has had a long nose, is a wise creature and never loses sight of its young.

This is just one of the many stories that are told, full of that magic that is so often transformed into mal d'Afrique. However, the muddy waters of the Limpopo River really do flow, at the border between the South African Republic and Mozambique, marking the boundary of one of the oldest parks in Africa.

Kruger National Park is named after Stephanus Johannes Paulus Kruger, former president of South Africa as well as commander in the war against the English between 1899 and 1902. As early as 1884, this statesman proposed to establish a reserve to protect the fauna endangered by the hunting that had been unleashed during the course of the gold rush, which had begun fifteen years earlier. The reserve became operative many years later and constituted the first nucleus of the Kruger National Park, founded in 1926. It consists of an area of almost 7,700 square miles, extending for 217 miles from north to south and for 37 miles from west to east, where the Lebombo Mountains run along the edge of the Mozambique border. The territory, characterized by a particular climate and vegetation, is a savannah rich in trees and bushes called "Lowveld." The landscape lies on the plain and has few hills, with a maximum altitude of around 2,600 feet; but in terms of the wealth of its vegetable and animal species relative to its size, there are few places in the world that compare with it. Every now and again, islands of rock called "koppies" emerge from the sea of vegetation, characterized by particular flora and fauna, different from those in the savannah. It is one of the most interesting ecosystems in the park, whose inhabitants live in relative isolation compared with creatures similar to them.

Besides the rivers Limpopo and Crocodile, at the northern and southern borders, respectively, the Kruger National Park is crossed by other waterways, some of these, such as the Sisha and the Timbavati, exists only when the southern summer rains – from October to February – brings them back to life. The winter, from June to August, is the dry season. In this period it

MOZAMBIQUE

SOUTH AFRICA

N

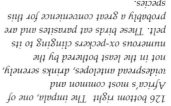

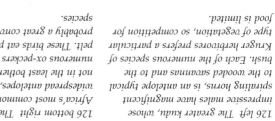

126 left The greater kudu, whose impressive males have magnificent spiraling horns, is an antelope typical to the wooded savannas and to the bush. Each of the numerous species of Kruger herbivores prefers a particular type of vegetation, so competition for food is limited.

126 bottom right The impala, one of Africa's most common and widespread antelopes, drinks serenely, not in the least bothered by the numerous ox-peckers clinging to its pelt. These birds eat parasites and are probably a great convenience for this species.

127 bottom left The characteristic profile of a hartebeest, caught as it runs, proves the athletic abilities that this antelope requires to ensure of animal and plant life.

127 bottom right A moment's rest for the giraffe, but never letting its guard drop. The seated position makes it vulnerable since its weight and long hooves make it great effort to return to a standing position.

126-127 The Sable River is one of the chief water courses that crosses Kruger National Park. Dense bush is the home for an exceptional variety of animal and plant life.

its survival in a habitat that is rich in resources but is not lacking predators.

is possible to witness, around the same well of muddy water, the most diverse animals drinking. In fact, the antelopes alone, recorded in the park, belong to around twenty different species, from the small duikers to the omnipresent impala (*Aepyceros melampus*) and to the giant eland or common eland (*Taurotragus oryx*), which weigh to 1,760 pounds. The numerous species of herbivores satisfy their appetite by each dedicating themselves to the search for set types of vegetation, whose diversification is among the reasons for the variety of fauna. The giraffe, the common eland, the impala and the two species of African rhinoceros, both present in the Kruger National Park, have distinctive feeding habits. The assortment of herbivores is naturally a source of supply for the classic African predators: lions, leopards, cheetahs, hyenas and the rare African hunting dog (*Lycaon pictus*). The latter, similar to a multi-colored dog, is one of the African animals most at risk for extinction. The wealth of vegetation is also a source of life for the cercopithecids. These monkeys feed mainly off fruit, seeds, leaves and flowers.

It might seem that such a paradise of fauna would not require particular maintenance, but this is not the case. Before the presence of man, natural fires represented one of the phenomena regulating the Lowveld environment. Each year, therefore, several areas of the park are deliberately set fire to in order to recreate the renewal cycles for its vegetation. In this way, an attempt is made to preserve the exceptional biodiversity of Kruger National Park, which consists of nearly 140 species of mammals, 500 species of birds, more than 100 species of reptiles, 50 species of fish and 33 types of amphibians. Sometimes unusual presences are noted, such as when, in 1950, a bull shark was spotted having come up from the sea along a stretch of the Limpopo River's muddy waters. In this instance, however, it does not seem to have grabbed anyone's nose. (G.G.B.)

128 The stretching leopard is enough to strike fear. Every culture that has had contact with this terrible feline has emphasized its shrewdness and its ferocity; for the ancient Egyptians it was an animal sacred to Seth, god of evil.

129 top left The egg found on the ground is not only a pleasant snack for this ground hornbill, it is also a small trophy to be exhibited when preening in a dominant stance for the benefit of a rival.

129 bottom left The Olifants River brings some water and a little relief to a habitat comprising mainly arid savannas alternating with bush. This is the most typical habitat found in the protected territory of Kruger National Park.

129 bottom right A caudate roller shows off its lilac breast plumage from its isolated perch. These birds are voracious insect eaters and the first to arrive when a fire wreaks havoc in the habitat of their tiny prey.

129 top right The Cape weaver bird (Ploceus capensis) is an extraordinary architect and perfect builder of spherical nests solidly attached to vegetation. For its work it uses mainly blades of grass and ensures that the interior of the nest is soft and comfortable.

130-131 This contorted trunk has won an infinite number of battles against the aridity of the Kalahari. It is a living reminder that the law of natural selection is pitiless, but the cloudy sky offers tenuous promises of rainfall to the thirsty herds.

130 bottom left Once they are weaned, young lions abandon the pack in fear of being eaten by adult males. Solitary or in small groups they spend their early years learning the secrets of the Kalahari. But is it a good idea to bother a couple of porcupines?

130 bottom right The piercing glance of the suricate misses little, not even an expert nature photographer. The animal stands so still it comes across as a stone statue and surprises observers with fast reflexes at the first scent of danger.

131 bottom A male oryx, stately as a Zulu warrior, looms against the clear blue sky. Justifiably proud of its horns, even lions are in awe of this beast; but strangely enough, it is the female that has the longest horns, sometimes reaching 5 feet.

KGALAGADI
TRANSFRONTIER PARK

The herds of antelopes that migrate and roam in great numbers throughout this arid territory probably never ponder over the meaning of an array of white stones that stretches for miles and miles; they must concentrate instead on seeking water and food. The stones in question represent the border between two countries, the Republic of South Africa and Botswana.

In this case, the bipeds who dominate the planet wanted to give top priority to the needs of this harsh yet vulnerable environment and its fauna, who are forced to migrate periodically in order to survive. This is the reason that Kgalagadi Transfrontier Park was established in 1998, the new name given to the protected area composed of the Kalahari National Park at the northwestern end of the Republic of South Africa and of its twin in Botswana, Gemsbok National Park. The area totals 14,000 square miles that are now rightly managed as a single entity.

The Kalahari Desert is part of the broad sandy basin that stretches from the Orange River north to Angola, touching Namibia to the west and Zimbabwe to the east. The soft rock that constitutes its base was eroded and shaped by the wind, creating a stretch of sandy dunes with a characteristic orange color. They stretch parallel to each other as far as the eye can see and, as opposed to what can be observed in Namibia, this is not quicksand. The "red desert" is the nickname given to the Kalahari, even though it is not actually a desert. The annual rainfall, concentrated in the period from January to April, amounts to about 8 inches—too much for the conventional definition of "desert." However, there are often years in which only 4 inches of rain falls, perhaps in the form of a single and devastating rainstorm. The dusty earth does not hold moisture well and the high summer temperatures, which exceed 104°F, quickly turn the few puddles that have formed during the rainy season into vapor. Thus, it may not be a true desert, but try telling this to the creatures that live there!

Antelopes abound among the mammals; one of the most characteristic is the springbok, or leaping antelope (*Antidorcas marsupialis*), which owes its scientific name to the fold of skin that extends longitudinally in the rear part of its back. The fur in this "pocket" is lighter in color; when it is in danger, the animal extends its hide to raise the light fur and make it visible. By reflecting light, it acts as a signal to the entire pack. Flight follows, and it can even reach 55 miles/hour, an impressive sight because the animals show off with leaps that can reach 12 feet in order to discourage predators.

With horns as sharp as scimitars, reaching a length of up to 5 feet, and stripes along its hide that look like Indian war paint, the oryx or gemsbok (*Oryx gazella*) is easy to pick out. The king of carnivores is the majestic lion of the Kalahari, with its dark

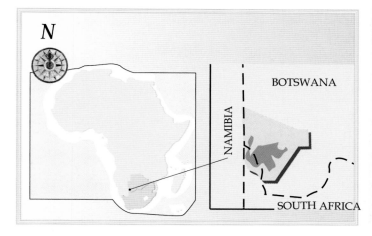

mane. Despite its noble appearance, it does not disdain feeding on carrion, especially when it is forced to go without water for months at a time. Many carnivores in the park have "garbage-collector" habits; the availability of prey is too unreliable for them to survive on hunting alone. As red as the dunes that offer it a home, the brown hyena wins the prize when it comes to adapting to this hostile environment. It can nourish itself even by gnawing at the oldest bones left scattered across the spare clumps of dry grass. At night, you may come across porcupines, the largest African rodents; they are over three feet tall when they straighten their pens. If you wait with infinite patience, you may be lucky enough to see the shy suricate standing straight up

DON'T CALL IT DESERT!

on its hind legs, like whimsical puppets but disappearing as fast as lightning at the first sign of alarm.

In the Kalahari, beauty also dons feathers; over 200 bird species have been recorded here. The weavers nest in the branches of acacia trees, joining forces to build "condominiums" with a diameter of seven feet that surely will not go unnoticed. The clear sky also makes it easy to sight birds of prey, which are often present in the park. The Kalahari became a national park in 1931, in order to hinder the poaching that was exterminating both herbivores and carnivores. Today, it is one of the easiest places to see and photograph African fauna, largely due to the particularly barren landscape.

The Kgalagadi Transfrontier Park requires a certain spirit of adaptability from visitors, but this is bound to be rewarded. Every time of the year reveals different aspects of the magical red desert. The most favorable in terms of climate is the fresh and dry season from April to September, but anyone who wants to observe lions is best off facing the height of January and February, and if you want to be enchanted by the wild galloping of thousands of antelopes, you'll have to take advantage of the end of the rainy season and visit the Kalahari in March-April.

The two main routes of communication in the park run along the dry beds of the Nossob and Auob Rivers; which serves as unpaved and dusty roads that travel for hours before reaching the next welcome center. Along the river there are wells supplied by characteristic wind pumps, which attract many herds, especially during the early morning hours and late afternoon, followed by their predators. Transit in the park is forbidden after sunset; at this point visitors are forced to relax and enjoy the starry southern sky, accompanied by the hoarse barking of the geckos. (A.S.I.)

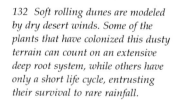

133 top right In the Kalahari, where the drought reaps many victims, it is opportune to opt for necrophagy rather than be a predator; so the scavengers prosper, like this saddleback jackal, intent on quenching its thirst.

133 center right In the twilight tranquillity springboks seek grass and bushes. This symbol of the Republic of South Africa has been decimated by hunters; at one time herds would be as many as a million examples.

133 bottom right Summer rain has brought the flamboyant flowering of a Boophane disticha, which now awaits pollinating insects. Its succulent bulb is toxic.

132 Soft rolling dunes are modeled by dry desert winds. Some of the plants that have colonized this dusty terrain can count on an extensive deep root system, while others have only a short life cycle, entrusting their survival to rare rainfall.

133 top left A spotted hyena quenches its thirst at a temporary pool. This heavily muscled animal has jaws strong enough to grind bones effortlessly and is unjustly unpopular; in reality its social behavior is complex and it is especially affectionate with its young.

134 bottom right White as a powder puff, this very young gannet waits for its parents in the nest, sheltered amidst the vegetation. On their arrival, thanks to a series of ritualized signals, it will manage to feed off part of the fish caught by the adults.

135 top left Wearied by the extreme heat of the tropical sun, a giant tortoise relaxes in the shade of the palms. With a life expectancy of 100-150 years, this species certainly does not need to hurry!

134-135 An aerial view of the atoll, at the border between sky and sea, makes Aldabra resemble a precious ring. The crystal clear waters of the internal lake, which is relatively shallow, stand out here on account of their bright turquoise color, and are home to a fauna that may even include large sharks, "captured" by the sea currents.

134 bottom left Group photo of a family of red-footed gannets. The young, who can be recognized because of their brown plumage, share a crowded perch with the adults, waiting to master the secret of flight and defy the ocean.

ALDHABRA
ATOLL

A trip to the Seychelles, in the middle of the Indian Ocean, north to Madagascar? Images spring to mind of white beaches, lazy, florid palms bending to see their reflection in an ocean of astounding blue. There we are: relaxed, happy, convinced that the afterlife could offer a no more pleasing paradise. A corner of the Seychelles, comprised of ninety-two volcanic islands directly east of Zanzibar, is actually Aldabra, the loveliest part of this fairytale archipelago. To discover Aldabra we have to go south, about 620 miles from the capital Mahé. It is an Arabic word—Al Khadra, "the green one," "the garden," explained by the thick tangle of mangrove forest. It became possible to visit this pearl of the Indian Ocean only in 1999 and it really can be called "tiptoe" tourism. The research station can house only twelve people at a time and it is takes at

135 right The mushroom-shaped islands cut out by the erosion of the daily tides and thickly covered mangroves are used as roosts by the birds that live in the archipelago.

The noisy frigate birds attract the attention of visitors and cause rarities such as the sacred ibis of Aldabra to pass by unobserved.

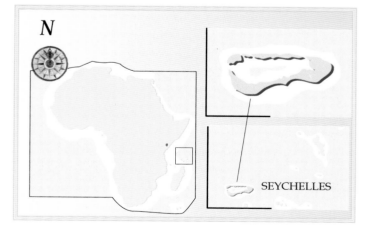

SEYCHELLES

least five hours from Mahé, travelling both by air and by boat.

The atoll of Aldabra embraces a central lagoon of 105 square miles, the largest in existence, and it could easily hold all of Mahé. The lagoon empties twice a day as result of the tides; there are four principal passages in which the strong tide thrusts forward a wall of water that can reach 10 feet in height, at a speed of 19 feet/sec. Numerous aquatic creatures ride or suffer from these regular movements; even devilfish and sharks

tiger may be sucked into the lagoon. The tidal channels split the atoll in four main calcareous islands. Two main terraces exist, respectively 13 and 26 feet above sea level, and they correspond to the two separate phases of coral growth and subsequent erosion, with rocks that can be razor sharp. Here and there emerge the so-called "mushrooms": rocky formations that sea erosion has modeled to a mushroom shape, colonized by green mangroves and a refuge for birds and other small animals.

Aldabra's fauna is incomparable and the undisputed center of attention is the giant turtle (*Geochelone gigantea*). There are over 200,000 here, five times more than in the Galapagos. They are concentrated in the southeast corner of the atoll, Grande Terre, where an assemblage of over 1,700 turtles per square mile come to resemble rush hour traffic! These sovereigns of the reptile worlds, which are over a 3 feet in length, live a lazy existence that becomes animated only in the mating period. They adore being cleaned of parasites and their chief assistant in this activity is also a true rarity: the white-throated rail (*Dryolimnas cuvieri aldabranus*), the last species of flightless bird now found throughout the Indian Ocean. Other characteristic birds are the dimorphous egret (*Egretta gularis dimorpha*), whose plumage varies from white to black as it gets older, the sacred blue-eyed ibis (*Threskiornis aethiopica abbotti*), and various species of hurricane bird, tropic bird and gannet. This enormous biodiversity is explained by the abundance and variety offered by 198 different species of vegetation of which nineteen are endemic. A triumph of color awaits us underwater: coral,

136 top left A shoal of bluestripe snappers (Lutjanus kasmira) *dazzle with their gaudy colors.*

136 top right A shoal of thumbprint emperors (Letherinus harak) *is immortalized here as it swims among the mangroves.*

Nudibranchia, enormous Bivalvia such as the giant thee foot long tridacna, whose psychedelic colors are the result of symbiosis with particular algae; 190 species of fish including shrimp goby, globe-fish, and scorpion fish.

The area has been part of the World Heritage since 1976 and is protected as an integral natural reserve, which extends as far as 1640 feet from the outermost barrier reef. The road to salvation has been difficult; the naturalistic observations of the great oceanologist Jacques Cousteau, who visited Aldabra on his ship Calypso in 1954, did not prevent the British government, who was its owner at that time, from setting up a project to transform the entire atoll into a military base, complete with a port, airport, dikes, roads and logistical infrastructures. The life-scientists of the Royal Society who had begun fundamental research of Aldabra's flora and fauna opposed the plan, but without result. Salvation arrived unexpectedly when the British pound was devalued and military expenditures were cut, so the project was abandoned. In the last century matters were no better; the delicate ecosystems of many of the Indian Ocean islands were irreparably damaged by hunting, guano extraction, the introduction of dogs, cats and goats. The enchanting primordial nature of Assunzione (a three-hour ferry ride from Aldabra), Astove and Cosmoledos has survived only in the underwater habitats. According to Cousteau, these fissured coral islands have the clearest water in the world, but the land sadly shows the weighty signs of intense over-exploitation. Aldabra is barely accessible and not particularly welcoming because of its isolated position, monsoon climate, dangerous landing conditions, and scarcity of drinking water. Yet the bounty of giant turtle meat pushed many to challenge this locale, to the point that in 1820 the species had nearly disappeared, except in Aldabra where there was a drastic decrease in the number of turtles.

In 1874, the great Charles Darwin pleaded for the protection of the species and its habitat. Other voices joined his plea; famous names of natural history such as Thomas Huxley, Joseph Hooker and Richard Owen, the latter a fervent anti-evolutionist and therefore Darwin's implacable adversary in the debates of the time. (A.S.I.)

A GARDEN IN THE OCEAN

136 center The gorgoniae are typical of these depths; here is a fine example in forest formation.

136-137 A giant grouper (Epinephlus Tukula) swims tranquilly in the depths of the underwater park.

137 bottom A longnose hawkfish (Oxycirrhites Typus) immortalized amidst the branches of coral.

ASIA
INTRODUCTION

Let's play at turning the globe and as our finger stops casually on an emerging point of land we will notice at least every third time we touch Asia. The largest continent, in fact, covers 18 million square miles, populated by three billion, six hundred million people who belong to a variety of races. Recent estimates reveal that population density is about 207 inhabitants per square mile, but this is a classic example of statistics that are not always accurate.

In Asia, a multi-faceted territory with an infinite variety of landscapes, human distribution is quite irregular. A square mile of Mongolia has an average population of two, while in Singapore the same space has 5,500. Humans colonized Asia in very ancient times, when their ancestor *Homo erectus* started to feel cramped in its native Africa. At least a million years ago there were ape-men who had reached Java and the extreme southwest island offshoots.

These ancient peoples lived by hunting and gathering, but they did not take long to develop stable settlements and flourishing civilizations. Archeologists say that the world's oldest city is to be found on this continent: Jericho, founded near an oasis in Palestine about ten thousand years ago. Asia's settlers progressively developed according to the availability of food, especially the cultivation of rice, a cereal that is the basis of survival for over half of the world's population. So a number of very fertile zones that are situated in strategic positions for commerce have reached a situation of unthinkable overcrowding, yet in other areas it is possible to travel for days without seeing a living soul. From such dissimilar situations it is obvious that there is little sense in formulating affirmations of a general nature regarding conservation of nature in Asia.

Each race, each country, each region of this immense continent is having to face specific problems and is attempting to resolve them with an approach that varies on the basis of the territory and of cultural tradition. Perhaps there is a constant in that the nature in Asia is of a magnificence that is rarely encountered elsewhere. It is not by chance that Asia was the cradle of all the religions that have influenced the history of humankind. How can we not recognize divine presence in the absolute silence of the "home of snows," the Himalayas, or in the thousand colors that drape Fujiyama, indifferent to humanity that bustles frenetically at its foot? How can we not fear the ire of the sky when the summer monsoons pour their torrential rains on the dried-out earth, or when each day's survival is entrusted to the severity of the desert and its caprice? Oriental

140-141 A tiger chases a young sambar in the Ranthambore National Park in India. The big cat is an excellent swimmer, and the fawn's escape into the water does not dissuade the former from attacking.

140 bottom From the tracks of a tiger that has launched into the chase of a prey, it has been found that its bounds can reach 16 feet in length. The hunting technique, however, depends on the situation and the habits of each individual.

141 top Once it has spotted a potential prey on open terrain, the tiger approaches as near as possible without giving away its presence before giving fast chase at the gallop and with great bounds.

religions, such as Hinduism or Buddhism, are based in large measure on humankind's quest for a perfect harmony with nature and extreme respect for all living creatures. Those of us who are strangers to these cultures find it inconceivable that a pariah can starve to death in a Calcutta street under the placid stare of a holy cow. Yet no one can deny the fascination of many tales (legend? reality?) that tell of the almost supernatural ability of Hindu Brahmins or Tibetan bonzes, who can overcome the limits of the material world by meditation, lifting their minds to total freedom. So let us imagine that we, too, can abandon our bodies and travel as invisible birds flying over this immense continent.

Let us fly at sunset over the red deserts of Arabia, skim the magical tufa peaks of Cappadocia and head bravely ever north, over mountains and plains as far as the great expanses

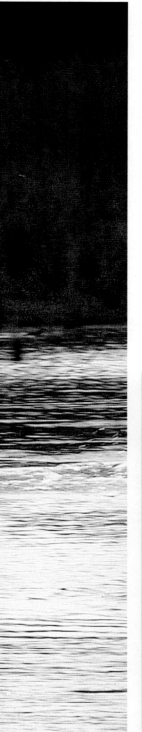

of the Siberian taiga. Let us watch the tiger's ambush in silence; just this once let's cheer on the "bad guy" and hope this rare majestic feline will procure a handsome meal for its cubs. Let us brave the icy tundra and the ticklish flowering cotton-grass as far as the far north of this continent, to Komsomolec, an island beyond the Arctic Circle. Then our yearning for some climatic and human warmth drives us south to equatorial Asia, where hospitable people, sumptuous architecture, crystal clear oceans, and forests brimming with all life forms greet our passing.

Immense China offers a panorama of its teeming yet highly organized cities, fields diligently farmed and surrounded by hills of an incredible sugar-loaf shape, misty woods and a millenary history. Mysterious India seduces with her contradictions and charm.

We would like to linger, but we have to get to the Roof of the World. But here the excessive amounts of trash left by an influx of excursionists are a painful reminder that even such

141 bottom Despite the size of the creature, the tiger's movements are as agile and elegant as those of a cat. It walks with apparent nimbleness, and can cover considerable distances when it is giving chase.

142-143 The largest continent is home to the highest mountain chain in the world, the Himalayas. Everest, as seen from Nepal, looks like a squat rocky pyramid, surpassed in beauty by the pointed white tip of Nuptse.

an incredibly grand and magnificent place desperately needs protection. So, now it is time to get our feet back on the ground; a trip to Asia's most precious places awaits, where wise policies have safeguarded a landscape for us to appreciate and leave us with the satisfaction of knowing that our usually ruinous species can find the right way to do things, every now and again. (A.S.I.)

INTRODUCTION

144 bottom left An encounter with the desert fox, which mainly operates at night, can easily occur in the first light of dawn. Approached with caution, it shows no fear of man.

144 bottom right Besides the coral reef, the Park offers spectacular landscapes consisting of small coves and rocks of fossil coral in succession along the coast.

144-145 Ras Mohammed is the southernmost point of Sinai, where the waters of the Gulf of Suez meet with those of the narrower Gulf of Aqaba.

RAS MOHAMMED
NATIONAL PARK

T he point where Africa and Asia meet is the place where an underwater world unfolds; the Red Sea is in fact the result of the slow tectonic movements of earth's crust, beginning over 20 million years ago, that caused a deep split dividing the two continents. The initial divide was the cradle of the current sea basin, which extends for over 1,365 miles, while the maximum width is just 186 miles.

To the north, the sea is divided in two by the dominating presence of the Sinai promontory, forming a smaller branch to the east composed of the Gulf of Aqaba, and a slightly large one to the west, the Suez. The landscape is characterized by the usual desert tones: rust-colored sandy beaches and bronze reefs that reflect the rays of the broiling sun. Every which way, the environment seems to be lifeless, an uninhabited land; but a surprise is in store for anyone who plunges into these inviting crystal-clear waters, which never drop below 76°F even in the middle of winter. In fact, under water an extremely interesting ecosystem has developed in relation to a highly developed coral reef. The multiple forms of life come from the evolution of marine species that colonized these waters in far-off times, penetrating through the narrow passage connecting this sea with the Indian Ocean.

Adapting to unique environmental conditions, they have undergone a slow indigenous evolution. To safeguard this marine life that is unrivaled the world over, a sea park was established in 1983, Ras Mohammed National Park, which today safeguards an area of 80 square miles in the southern

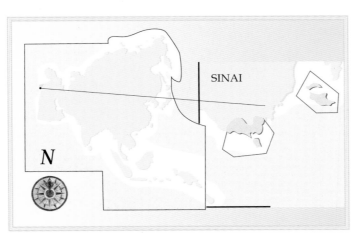

145 top Towards the end of summer hundreds and hundreds of storks interrupt their migration to East Africa and stop for a while in the Park.

145 bottom This promontory, characterized by its pointed shape, consists of a series of fossil coral platforms, which have emerged in the course of millions of years.

146 top left Various environmental
and behavioral adjustments allow
many organisms to co-exist in the
same area interweaving complex food
networks.

146 top right The corals contribute
to the growth of the reef, forming its
framework. They also provide
thousands of organisms with food
and shelter.

146 bottom left The corals can easily
be distinguished into hard and soft.
The former have a rigid support
produced by the colonies of polyps
that live there.

part of the Sinai peninsula, a few miles from the famous
tourist resort of Sharm el Sheikh. The park was named after
the present promontory, a block of ancient rocks connected
to land by a thin strip of earth just a few miles wide. It was
given this name in honor of the prophet Mohammed, a very
important figure in the Islamic religion of the local
populations. However, we must remember that during the
Roman era it was called Poseidon, because the sheer beauty
of the place justified the choice made by the sea god to make
this place his mythical home.

The regulations that must be observed in this park are
very strict and include a ban on touching the coral, taking
material and feeding the fish. In order to monitor any
undisciplined tourists, numerous rangers patrol around the
clock in boats and jeeps to ensure proper respect for nature.
For scuba divers, this place is a dream come true! The
clearness of the water permits excellent visibility even at
greater depths; everything looks clear and spectacular.
Multi-shaped coral covers every rock surface, often
exploding in brilliant colors, first of all the red of the sea
fans, which are so ubiquitous in this basin that they are the
reason it is called the Red Sea.

The inhabitants of this underwater world seem to show a
certain amount of curiosity about us, although considering
the mass tourism of recent years, we probably just look like
the "usual terrestrial intruders." Silvery jacks and whimsical
triggerfish, with their prominent mouths and geometric
bodies, are happy to welcome us. There are numerous
anthias, typically orange in color, that swim in schools,
ready to seek safe refuge amidst the corals at the least hint of
danger. They live in a harem led by a dominant male and
when it dies, the largest female takes its place, changing
gender.

It is not unusual to run into a group of barracudas that,
placidly immobile in the current, observe everything with
apparent nonchalance. These fish, which can grow to up to 7
feet in length, have mouths armed with extremely sharp

146-147 *Famous for the colors that characterize them, the soft corals have a delicate structure that recalls the chiseled work of a patient craftsman.*

147 bottom *Diving in the waters of the park may be the realization of a dream for a scuba diver. Few places can boast such marvels.*

AN UNDERWATER GARDEN

148-149 *The barrier reef is revealed in all its magnificence of shapes and colors, a breathtaking sight for anyone seeing it for the first time.*

148 bottom left *Queens among corals, the gorgoniae form intricate fans of delicate appearance, which can grow to measure as much as ten feet in diameter.*

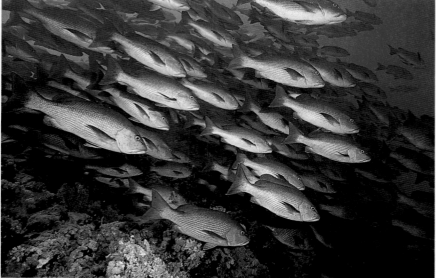

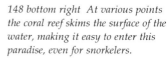

148 bottom right At various points the coral reef skims the surface of the water, making it easy to enter this paradise, even for snorkelers.

149 top The dentex assemble in spring and summer in shoals consisting of thousands of specimens, which form living columns that are almost impenetrable.

149 center Smaller than the other groupers, the coral grouper is easily recognizable on account of the red color of its body on which countless blue dots are distributed.

teeth. They attack their prey suddenly and then disappear into the depths. But you are truly lucky if you can enjoy the pleasant company of the Napoleon fish during your dive.

This gigantic puffy-looking and good-natured labride can grow to nearly 10 feet in length, weighing over 220 lbs. Its good-natured appearance comes from the natural hump on the top of its head, which makes it look like a clown wearing a hat. Its entire head is decorated with a Greek-fret design reminiscent of the tattoos of the Maori tribes, while the color of the green scales that cover its body has subtle yellowish-blue reflections. It is the lord of this sea, a benevolent monarch that greets his guests with a sign of welcome, delicately allowing visitors to stroke its back.

The groupers are just as shy, but quite diffident in that they habitually seek refuge in a safe den, from which they will poke out only their heads, like an inquisitive wife looking out the window. Another fish typical of the coral reef is the small and unmistakable polka-dot grouper (or coral grouper), which is bright orange with an infinite sprinkling of dark-blue dots. There is also another presence that is "sensed" almost instinctively; a sudden and unnatural calm arrives suddenly where before you could see fish playfully chasing after each other. The sharks, the feared

150 top left With a disturbing appearance that recalls the mammals from which they have borrowed their name, the bat fish roam ethereally amidst the reflections of the waters.

150 bottom left The barracudas are voracious predators that love to remain immobile in the current,

while maintaining the group. Their appearance leads to them mistakenly to being considered dangerous.

150 top right With fins similar to wings, which literally make it "fly" through the saves, the manta is one of the largest creatures encountered here.

predators of every sea, are here.

Even if everyone knows that only a few species are dangerous for man and that none of them live so close to the coral reef, no one can deny that a shiver runs down their back as soon as the unmistakable blue shape of a shark is detected. The white-fin shark is typical of the reef environment and they are named after the light spot at the tip of their dorsal fin. It is electrifying (to say the least) to watch them swim slowly in circles above us and then alongside us, apparently uninterested, as they wander slowly, lazily swishing their tails every so often. Suddenly, tired of the novelty, they go off as silently as they arrived.

Hidden in the crevices and ravines of the rocks most of the time, morays wait patiently for the right moment to lay a trap and close in on their meal. The moray's appearance, by no means reassuring, results from a mouth filled with small but sharp teeth. The shape of its eyes, giving it an evil look, have contributed to creating a long series of popular legends on this animal's danger to man. In reality, the rare attack can be attributed to an error on the moray's part, confusing a person's hand for an octopus, its usual prey. A moray bite is very painful because it causes deep wounds. As opposed to the Mediterranean species, tropical morays reach substantial dimensions (they can grow to up to 22 lbs), but it is rare to see a full-sized specimen — unless it decides to "change house" in your presence — swimming with sinuous snake-like movements to seek a better refuge. (C.B.)

150-151 Few encounters can be as thrilling as those with the most playful and lovable creatures in the sea, the dolphins.

151 bottom left The shark always awakens ancestral fears, which are completely unfounded since the barrier reef species, such as the White Fin, do not attack humans.

151 bottom right The silvery livery of the carangids lights up the depths of the sea. These predators often swim in close, compact shoals.

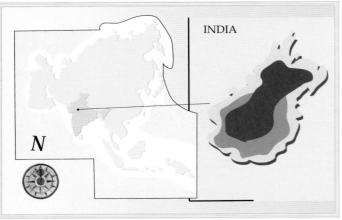

INDIA

N

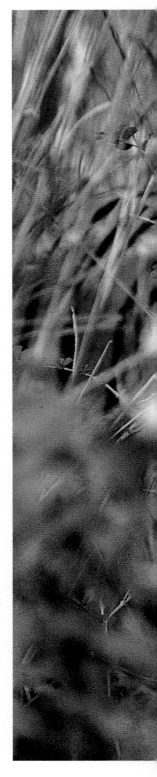

RANTHAMBORE
NATIONAL PARK

To the north of the Indian subcontinent, in the region of Rajasthan—the ancient land of maharajas (kings) and ranas (princes), extraordinarily rich in palaces, temples and old fortresses—Ranthambore National Park extends over 150 square miles. This natural reserve has its own story to tell, one that is closely tied to the region in which it is located. In fact, for a long time this area was a private hunting reserve belonging to none other than the maharaja of Jaipur, who brought his most

illustrious guests here to experience the daring tiger hunts or simply to strengthen political alliances with representatives of foreign countries. It was precisely the will to safeguard this majestic feline that, in 1973, allowed this small reserve to become one of India's most important national park. This event was known as the "Tiger Project," an ambitious undertaking set up by WWF and promoted personally by Indira Gandhi, established to rehabilitate the tiger populations and protect them from extinction. With it, nine natural parks were established (which later grew to twenty-three), inside of which several smaller "cushion areas" were identified, with natural vegetation in which limited anthropic activities were permitted.

There were also other zones in the center of the parks that were strictly off-limits to men and cattle, and inside them certain areas were created exclusively for the tigers to use, as indicated in the statute: "*reproduction nucleuses from which the extra animals can emigrate toward the outlying forests.*" This is a step that was as urgent as it was necessary, considering that just thirty years ago the number of specimens had drastically and dangerously dropped to less than a tenth of its initial value. Today, Ranthambore National Park is backed by a non-government organization, the Ranthambore Foundation, which functions as a link between the need to preserve the area's natural wealth and the growing economic needs of the inhabitants of the surrounding villages. This natural oasis is located in Rajasthan and is divided by the desertic zone that lies north by the Aravalli mountain range. The region is characterized by monsoon climate with heavy seasonal rainfall that makes it fertile and fosters the lush growth of vegetation. This is one of the few places where you can still see tigers in their natural habitat, either at the first light of dawn or sunset as they lay ambush, follow their prey or take a nap in the shade of the undergrowth. You may even be lucky enough to spy some tigresses in the dense scrub as they lovingly take care of their young.

Although tigers have made this park famous there are also many other animal species that the visitor may encounter while traveling the trails in the areas accessible to jeeps. The variety of landscapes heading to the interior will never cease to amaze anyone who enters the reserve for the first time. It is not unusual to stumble over the ruins of tombs, shelters and walls,

152-153 The existence of
Rathambore Park is closely tied to the
presence of the tiger. The number of
specimens of the largest feline in the
world was reduced by more than
ninety percent in the last century.

153 bottom left The tiger is a
solitary animal. Each specimen
defines its own space within which it

does not tolerate outsiders, unless
they are members of the other sex
during mating season.

153 bottom right A tiger in the
Rathambore Park, one of the most
important protected areas of those
included in the Tiger Project. The
program for safeguarding this species
began in the early 1970s.

152 center The saving of the few
thousands of Indian tigers left is
connected to the preservation of a
land in which poverty dominates.
Here, man too has to fight to survive,
and even today the tiger may still be
seen as a danger.

152 bottom Unlike other felines, the
tiger is at ease in water. It stays there
to refresh itself, and in case of
necessity proves to be an excellent
swimmer. But on the other hand it is
not good at climbing, due to its large
size.

154 top When environmental conditions permit, the sambar lives in populations of high density. Generally, however, it does not form very stable herds, as is the case with other species of deer.

154-155 Completely immersed in water, these sambars eat the floating leaves of water lilies. It appears they can also feed off poisonous plants, which are inedible for other animals.

which act as silent witnesses to a rich and pompous past, and now the royal residence of colorful peacocks that court the females by proudly displaying their marvelous tails.

The entire area, almost completely enclosed and at one with the natural countryside, is dominated by the hilltop fortress of Ranthambore, which dates back to the tenth century. The privileged position of this landmark allows visitors to enjoy a spectacular view from the southwestern end of the park, characterized by marshy areas and typical grassy stretches.

The main marshes section is Padam Talao, near the Jogi Mahal, the maharaja's hunting palace and the last sign of its ancient function as a reserve. Its distinctive blue lakes, surrounded by enormous *Ficus bengalensis* trees whose branches are densely interwoven with a labyrinth of typical aerial roots ,

represent another suggestive feature of Ranthambore. Numerous families of lively langurs, ever watchful for predators, dominate the territory.

During the late afternoon or evening you can often see many groups of sambar deer on the lake shore, mixed with dappled deer and noisy Indian boars which are characterized by a mane of bristly hair at the napes of their necks. This may also be the right time to witness the exciting hunt of a tiger as it searches for food. And with a bit of luck, you may even run into the very rare fisher-cat, a feline that, unlike its domesticated "cousins," is not only unafraid of water but specializes in catching fish as its main source of food from ponds and lakes. And if you should happen to see a threatening shadow fly over your head, there is no need be alarmed, for it could be an Indian flying fox, a large but

LAND OF TIGERS AND MAHARAJAHS

innocuous bat with diurnal habits and a frugivorous diet, as it seeks a quieter perch to continue its upside-down nap.

The inhospitable swamps, nearly suffocated by stretches of aquatic plants, are the reign of crocodiles and gavials. The latter can easily be distinguished from crocodiles because of their typical but unmistakable long and narrow snouts.

A good dose of insect repellent is essential due to the abundant presence of ravenous mosquitoes. You might also see the little-known dorcas gazelles or desert gazelles and blue antelopes, in a carefree race across these open spaces in search for grass and plants. The park also offers shelter to the small

thick-lipped bear, also known as the juggler bear because of its evident aptitude for skillful balancing acts. It has now become increasingly rare to see it at sundown, as it is intent on leaving its refuge on a tree branch to move quickly into the forest in search of food. Its favorite foods include ants, which it catches by sucking with its outstretched lips after destroying their nest and (like all bears) the tasty honey made by wild bees.

Also worthy of note is the local bird life; a great variety of birds lives in the park, starting with the little flycatcher of paradise, proverbially famous for its faithfulness to its mate. It is not always easy to sight, however, because it is so shy, hiding at the slightest noise. Nevertheless, it still deserves a long and silent wait in order to admire the incredible nuptial plumage that the male flaunts during the mating season; its long tail with ribbon-like feathers can measure up to a foot in length!

On the banks of the pools, which are almost entirely covered by palustrine plants, it is quite easy to distinguish the typical white heads of countless water pheasants possessed of long "fingers" that have very well-developed nails that perform the "miracle" of walking on water (in reality, they rest their

lightweight bodies on the plants, assisted by the special shape of their feet). The white wagtail is a rather common bird that can often be seen flying in search of insects, its sole source of nourishment in open areas, mainly near lakes or ponds. Predatory birds include the crested serpent eagle, which loves to catch snakes and helps keep the number of these reptiles in check.

If you decide to spend the night at one of the lodges on the reserve, you can experience the thrill of the unusual and evocative appearance of the park at night, when the other animal species that are present but as yet unseen come out—including the leopard, which howls softly in the dense undergrowth, ready to pounce on some unsuspecting animal. A feeling of danger can come from knowing that you're in the land of tigers, the world's largest predator; nevertheless, the pleasure of experiencing your surroundings and hearing something as the deep dark cry of the rare royal owl as it leaves its daytime hiding place in the cavity of a tree makes the adventure of the Rathambore National Park well worth it. (C.B.)

155 left The axis, or dappled deer, lives in Nepal, India and Sri Lanka. It can be found both on the plain and in the hills, at the foot of the Himalayas and at the mouth of the river Ganges, usually in environments rich in water.

155 right The sambar is the largest cervid in south Asia, and males can weigh more than 770 lbs. Its horns, however, are not particularly large.

CORBETT
NATIONAL PARK

Corbett National Park is quite famous and is included in almost all tourist itineraries recommended to nature-lovers. The park has a surface area of about 200 square miles and is an important protection oasis Indian flora and fauna. It belongs to the state of Uttar Pradesh, or North State as is also known, which stretches from the Himalayan chain to the fertile Ganges lowlands, and is one of the most important territories of northern India. Founded in 1936, thanks to the iron will of Major Jim Corbett, a hunter and passionate environmentalist, it has the honor of being the first Indian national park.

During its history it has been renamed several times. It was initially called Hailey National Park, in honor of Sir Malcolm Hailey, governor of Uttar Pradesh at that time. After the British withdrew from India in 1947, the park became Ramganga National Park for about ten years, named for the river that crosses the territory. It was then given the name it retains today, in memory of the person who had so strongly desired its creation. Together with other Indian parks, its

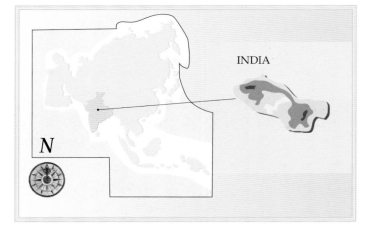

INDIA

N

territory was involved in Project Tiger in 1973, sustained by the government to exorcise the risk of the tiger's extinction in India.

Corbett National Park territory is closed to the north by the Kanda mountains that rise from 1,300 to 4,000 feet in altitude. The hill zone is mainly covered by dense forest, constituted by sal-trees and the more famous teak, which can reach 200 feet in height and is most famous in the West for production of furniture and parquets. *Ficus religiosa*, known locally as peepul tree, is also abundant and is called "religious" because an ancient Indian legend relates that Buddha received the revelation of Truth under one of these trees. For this reason it is common to find the peepul tree planted near or within temples. As we ascend to greater heights, the vegetation progressively changes, and your attention will be caught mainly by the elegant pyramid foliage of the Cedar Deodara, whose wood is so resistant that it is known as the "tree of the gods."

Almost at the heart of the park flows an arm of the Ganges, the River Ramganga. Over thousands of years its many tributaries have created the park's most important valley, as well as a series of small but especially lovely canyons. To the south of the park, near the town of Kalagarh, a dike has been built to block the course of the river and form a vast artificial basin, with a marshy area of almost 15 square miles, an ideal place to do some birdwatching.

Carefully concealed amongst the shore vegetation it is possible to observe herons and cormorants as they make their

156 center The sun is about to rise over the river Ramganga. The "changing of the guard" is starting in Corbett National Park and before long the diurnal animals will gradually take the place of those that have been active during the night.

156 bottom left A splendid specimen of Semnopithecus Entellus hides with her baby in the Corbett forest.

157 Two timid dappled deer find refuge in the dense undergrowth of the park. The luxuriant vegetation offers a hiding place for prey and predators.

characteristic dives, disappearing into the lake waters and re-emerge, gripping their prey in their beaks. If the purpose of your visit to the park is to find yourself in an exciting encounter with great mammals, it is worth moving towards Dhikala, the reserve's most important tourist center. Here, there is an ample, grassy plain that resembles African savanna in many aspects. There are raised observation stations here, specially installed to allow better views of the habitat.

This is the right type of habitat for a meeting with deer,

antelopes and Indian elephants. If there is a herd it will almost certainly be a group of females with their young, led by a wise, experienced older female. The young males form smaller groups and the solitary individuals you may see are adult males or maimed animals. Elephants are accustomed to spending the warmest hours of the day under shady trees or soaking in water, while the mornings and evenings are dedicated to procuring food, using their long trunks as if they were the fingers of a hand to pick up leaves or pieces of hard bark, that are then chewed at length. Local populations

THE ELEPHANTS' KINGDOM

have elected these pachyderms as a symbol of strength and •long life because of their majesty, their unbelievable power and extraordinarily massive structure, as well as their longevity (many live over eighty years).

The Indians also have reserved a great honor for this animal; according to Indian mythology, Indra, one of the most important masculine divinities, chose an elephant as his mount. Those who enjoy panoramas will want to climb Mount Kanda, towards the northern park border, which dominates the Dhikala plain and the artificial Ramganga basin. Here the distant snow-capped peaks of the Nanda Devi chain can be glimpsed as they tower over 25,580 feet. Closer are Paterpani's lower, gentler hills. If close contact with its massive body is not a problem, it is also possible to take a short excursion on a tame elephant, whose back is actually one of the best observation points for total immersion in nature, and an easier way to approach park animals. What is more, this is the safest means of transport for negotiating forest paths, accompanied by the experienced drivers called mahaut.

In the Jangal, or jungle, whose luxuriant growth is attributable to the monsoon climate that characterizes the whole region, (there may be as much as 7 feet of rain a year), there lurks an almost invisible specter, the king of all predators, the tiger. The great tangle of trees and brushwood is its almost impregnable kingdom. Yet here, as elsewhere, this superb animal has risked extinction, because of illegal hunting that supplied bones and other body parts for traditional Oriental medicine, above all Chinese, which is firmly convinced of the therapeutic powers of the tiger. It is difficult to sight, but its spine-tingling presence may be perceived if the mahaut is clever enough to identify an old track in the dried mud underfoot.

Another intriguing inhabitant of these forests is the

rhinoceros hornbill, a strange medium-sized bird whose trademark is its enormous beak, and which can be heard as it flies noisily from tree to tree. It also behaves curiously towards its mate; in order to protect the female when she is brooding, the male encloses her in a hollow trunk, leaving only a tiny opening through which food is passed. This continues until the young are totally weaned.

The most likely place to sight large numbers of animals however, is near expanses of water where they gather for the evening watering rite. The sighting of Indian vultures may indicate that the cadaver of one of the reserve's inhabitants lies waiting to be eaten. The vultures, and with them hyenas and jackals, offer an important though hardly noble service to the entire reserve community; they eliminate the remains of animal carcasses.

In the reserve, as throughout the rest of India, there are extremely dangerous reptiles such as the king cobra, infamous for the number of human victims they reap, though it is unlikely that you will perceive their presence. The largest of the cobra family, this reptile reaches truly exceptional dimensions. Generally the adults are approximately nine feet in length but in some cases they can reach 12 or even 15 feet. They lurk in the vegetation and lay in waiting for their victims—often other snakes—striking with poisonous fangs almost an inch long and injecting a venom that is almost immediately fatal. They become even more dangerous for humans during the mating period, because they are much more aggressive and will suddenly attack anything that moves near. If you happen to see a cobra while you are with a local, you will immediately distinguish the relationship between the Indian population and the snake, which is characterized by a mixture of fear and respect. Yet, even though they are very dangerous, cobras are never hunted for they are the chief predators of the mouse, a tremendous scourge of barns and food reserves. (C.B.)

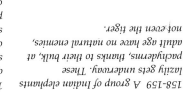

158-159 A group of Indian elephants lazily gets underway. These pachyderms, thanks to their bulk, at adult age face no natural enemies, not even the tiger.

159 top left and right On the banks of the River Ramganga the gavials share space and food with the crocodiles. The extended narrow snout of the gavials and their long projecting teeth are specialized for catching fish.

ROYAL CHITAWAN NATIONAL PARK

I n central southern Nepal, on the Indian border, visitors can set off from the town of Bharatpur and head for Royal Chitawan National Park, perhaps the most famous of the Nepalese parks and the home of the now-rare Indian rhinoceros. This oasis has 400 specimens, well protected by severe Nepalese legislation that even contemplated capital punishment for those who kill the rhinoceros. The park stretches for almost 370 square miles, with the massive silhouette of the Himalayas as its spellbinding backdrop. It was created in 1959 by the King at that time, Mahendra (father of recent monarch, Birendra), who declared the eastern part of the current territory a protected area and gave it his name. The local population immediately voiced its disapproval and the eastern part was occupied for planting crops. After 1963, the government offered the King strong support and the inhabitants of villages falling within the park were forced to evacuate. This zone, with another 180 square miles, was then definitively declared a "Protected Oasis for the Indian rhinoceros." It was not until 1973 that the park was officially and legally recognized, and it is now a leading tourist destination, contributing support to a nation with a sadly weak economy. Geologically, two thirds of its territory is occupied by the luxuriant Siwalick Hills that stretch across the Southern Himalayas, originating from a progressive accumulation of detritus. These highlands are split by a series of valleys that generally open lengthwise and are a specific characteristic of the area. The remaining part is lowland of alluvial origin, formed by progressive accumulation of fluvial detritus from the erosion of high mountains in the north. It forms the eastern part of the vast Ganges Plain.

The park's boundaries are mainly constituted by two great rivers: the north-flowing Rapti, which is a favorite place for exciting two-day rafting excursions, and the Reu, which flows south. The point where the two watercourses divide is rich in swamps and an ideal place to linger for a glimpse of the pachyderm that gives the park its name: the great Indian rhinoceros. This plain is the rhino's ideal habitat and it is not rare to see them bathe in the water, seeking some relief from voracious parasites, or intently pasturing for their abundant ration of daily grass.

These armor-plated giants, who measure 5.5 feet at the withers, are in serious danger of extinction. For countless years, they have been protagonists of legends and superstitions, and have been hunted for centuries by those who sought their unique horn to grind to powder and use as a panacea for all evil.

Today the Indian rhinoceros' distribution area is slowly extending and the naturalists of Royal Bandia National Park have used specimens from Royal Chitawan National Park to populate their reserve and put into effect a project established in 1986, which envisaged the re-introduction of this species to Eastern Nepal. Each year the rains and floods of the monsoon season bring enormous quantities of water during summer months, conditioning the life of all park animals.

High temperatures and strong humidity here create the ideal environment for the growth of tropical plants, such as the Dalbergia, an extremely tall leguminous with thick branches throughout, offering a perfect hiding place for animals like deer and boar. Just as abundant is the Bauhinia, with its curious bilobate leaves, which blooms throughout the summer, and the acacia with its thorny branches. Many grasslands where great herbivores pasture are positively affected by the local population who still undertake an age-old practice of burning terrain to encourage a faster growth

160-161 An example of an Indian rhinoceros seeks refreshment in a pool at the dawn of a new day.

161 bottom From the bank of the Rapti it is possible to admire the splendid snow-covered mountains of the Himalayan range, soaring in the background and providing the landscape with an unrivaled backdrop.

160 center The park is home to a large number of dappled deer. Their fawn-colored coat has white patches on it, giving the animal an elegant appearance.

160 bottom Two Indian rhinoceros taken by surprise in the thick of the undergrowth. Almost driven to extinction, this protected species now survives only in parks and reserves.

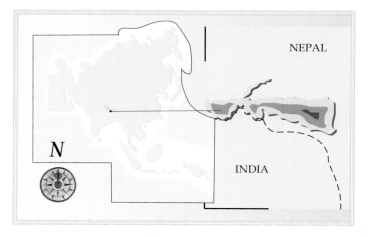

THE LAST KINGDOM OF THE INDIAN RHINOCEROS

162-163 The rhinoceroses love spending the hottest hours of the day in the water. The horn that this specimen shows, unique in the Asiatic species, has a corneous starting point similar to that of hair.

162 bottom Generally mild-tempered, rhinoceroses can suddenly charge if frightened or bothered. In spite of their bulk, they can run at great speed, sweeping away everything in their path.

of new tender shoots that the herbivores seek out and enjoy with gusto. The fire also slows down the growth of advancing forest and ensures that open meadows survive, as an important and fundamental feeding point for rhinos and elephants.

To enter the forest, it is necessary to reach higher altitudes where park guides are quite happy to accompany tourists along the paths that penetrate the jungle, but only on foot. The small amount of exertion required is definitely rewarded by the extraordinary spectacle that unfolds before the visitor; the dense foliage appears to form an overhead cupola—a cathedral of indescribable loveliness.

The tall trees are at one with the air plants that have found a home on their trunks and with the ramblers that gently encircle them in a dangerous embrace; these include easily recognizable orchids, whose delicate blossoms are quite famous in the western world. A large number of

163 left As it is possible to see from the photo, the Indian rhinoceros has a very hard thick skin. The presence of numerous folds make the animal look as though it is protected by a veritable suit of armor.

163 right A rhinoceros is procuring food for itself. These pachyderms feed off grass and leaves, which they are able to tear off thanks to their upper lip with its pensile fingerlike appendage.

animals use the dense woods as a shelter, although they are difficult to spot on the ground — perhaps just a trace remains of their passing.

There are small muntjacs, shy deer with curious tiny curved horns that rarely leave the denser areas of the undergrowth. In the branches, noisy and thus easy to spot, are lively langur monkeys, who are almost objects of worship in this area of Asia. They are dark in color, unlike the lighter species that inhabit the southern part of the Indian subcontinent. Their loud, playful screaming is a safety alarm for all the inhabitants of the forest, for it means that no predators are lurking.

The langur's greatest enemy is the leopard, especially the melanic or increasingly rare black panther, who can, hunting by night, conceal itself totally in the dark, as it competes with the park's other great predator, the tiger. A sudden loud noise betrays the presence of a rhinoceros hornbill in flight. These extremely large birds, with their characteristic hooked beak, have a consolidated bond between couples whereby that the male protectively walls his mate and offspring behind mud and twigs in a hollow tree trunk, and sets off on a ceaseless search for food for himself and his family.

To see as many animals as possible and often all together, the best place to go is along the river. Here you will see thirsty mammals such as hog-deer, dappled deer, samburs, Indian wild boar and Indian bison (also called a jungle ox because of its gigantic size). These animals are six feet at the withers and their unmistakable black silhouette looms against the horizon, with ornate horns that can reach 3 feet. Usually the herds are led by an adult male and try to keep near the densest vegetation. The merest hint of danger thrusts them back into the vegetation where they disappear without trace. They communicate by frequent warning hisses that can become loud bellowing if the danger materializes.

The riverbanks abound with ducks and other aquatic birdlife, including migratory species that land here in winter, ready to set off again for the north when the fine weather arrives. It is not unusual to see a brown-backed bird of prey with a white head and wings that suddenly takes flight from some point on the riverbank. This is surely the osprey that rises in flight with such graceful and harmonious movements that watchers may experience a moment of silent admiration. When the osprey reaches about 100 feet from the ground it suddenly plunges downwards and hits the surface of the water, then rises again with a prey gripped in its claws. This falcon's ability means it rarely misses a target.

Far stiller are the swamp crocodiles and Ganges gavials that snooze away the hot hours. Lurking amongst the lacustrian plants they cope with their long elaborate digestion in quite ungainly positions. Until a few years ago another inhabitant of these river waters was the Ganges platanist, a slim, streamlined dolphin measuring eight feet long that could swim upstream for many miles, moving in small shoals. (C.B.)

SAGARMATHA
NATIONAL PARK

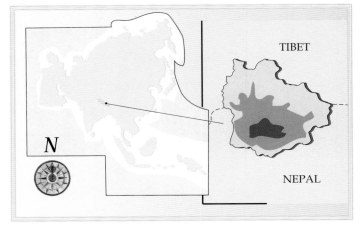

Y ou're short of breath, your heart is in your mouth, your head aches, you have nausea, your lips burn, it's cold, you're fatigued, you can't swallow food, you can't sleep and you could easily die. So why go all the way up there? Why climb the world's tallest mountain? Sir Edmund Hillary, who is thought to have been the first—but in any event was not the only one—had an answer: "because it's there."

Sagarmatha for the people of Nepal, Chomolungma for the Tibetans, Everest for the most recent arrivals, is a single rush skyward, the tallest thing there is, above which there is nothing else, not even air. Some have done it: about a thousand people, practically nothing compared to the rest of mankind that, while living here, has always venerated the tallest peaks on earth from below (from below in a manner of speaking, because around here, a valley floor can be higher than any peak in the Alps).

The highest national park in the world could not be located anywhere but here, and it could bear no other name but Sagarmatha, the goddess of the heavens. Established in 1976 and covering 470 square miles, it includes the upper basin of the Dudh Khosi River. Climbing up the valley, you come to the entrance at the park near Jorsale, at an altitude of nearly 9,184 feet. There are 19,680 more feet to go to get to the top of the world, and this difference in height follows different climatic zones and vegetations.

At the lower altitudes, the environment is characterized by forests, composed of conifers, birches, junipers and rhododendrons. The latter are full-fledged trees that during the month of June, after the first monsoons, display countless colorful blossoms. The altitude, the climate and the ensuing short vegetative period mean that only a few short and twisted trees can survive at altitudes of more than 14,750 feet, where the plant covering is transformed into an expanse of shrubs that become more stunted as you go up. This is followed by a zone of increasingly spare grassy vegetation composed of species that can endure the harshes conditions imposed by the environment. Lastly, at about 18,696 feet, you cross the snow line and enter the kingdom of ice, rocks and glaciers. Only mountain-climbers

venture any further, attracted by the summits of Lhotse (27,932 ft), Cho Oyu (126,899 ft), Nuptse, Ama Dablam and dozens of others, including, of course, Mount Everest (29,021 ft).

A classic route for hikers crosses the forest to Tengboche, at 12,677 ft. The magnificent monastery here was destroyed by a fire in 1988 and was subsequently rebuilt. A little past this, Pangboche is the site of the oldest monastery in the region of Khumbu. Khumbu is also the name of one of the most important glaciers in the national park and its moraines rise rapidly toward Kala Pattar (18,450 ft). From here—clouds permitting—you can admire the world's tallest mountain. Although it is not a difficult route to climb, it nevertheless requires prudence because of the altitude, and the various legs must be faced slowly to allow the body to become somewhat acclimated. Otherwise, the effects of mountain sickness will force hikers to descend to a lower altitude.

Only the Sherpa seem unaffected by the problems of high altitude. Originally from eastern Tibet, they came here between the late 1400s and early 1500s, and about 3,500 of them live in the different villages inside the national park. Their economy, traditionally an agricultural one, has become more and more dependent on tourism. Even the local culture, with its Buddhist monasteries, now represents one of the leading attractions for visitors. The character of these people is surprising in that it contrasts sharply with the harshness of a territory that tests the limits of man's ability to survive.

Cut by deep ravines with impetuous torrents, shaped by the movement of the glaciers, Sagarmatha National Park also hosts very interesting fauna. One of the inhabitants of the forests is the musk deer (*Moschus moschiferus*), an odd little deer without antlers but armed with extraordinary upper canine teeth: real tusks that are about three feet long. At higher altitudes you'll find the Himalayan tahr (*Hemitragus jemlahicus*), a mountain goat distinguished by the bristly mane that covers is neck and shoulders. Carnivores include the Asian black bear (*Selenarctos thibetanus*) and the small panda (*Ailurus fulgens*), the smaller fawn-colored cousin of the better-known Chinese giant panda. Over a

hundred bird species have been recorded in the park, and they spread their wings amidst the forests but also soar to the highest peaks of the Himalayas. However, sighting animals—particularly mammals—is no easy task.

The main attraction of Sagarmatha is the grandeur of its scenery. Alongside the mountains, the Nangpa, Ngozumba, Khumbu and Imja glaciers the largest in the national park are a truly magnificent sight. Due to the climate, however, the park cannot be visited year-long. During the summer, from June to September, monsoons make any movement difficult and prevent visits to the higher altitudes. On the other hand, the winter is very cold and, as a result, only the intermediate seasons are suitable for tourism, particularly the springtime, with its milder temperatures. (G.G.B.)

SKYWARD

164 bottom A Himalayan valley as it appears at the lowest levels of the Sagarmatha National Park. The slopes are covered with dense forests consisting for the most part of conifers, such as the Himalayan fir tree (Abies spectabilis).

164-165 In 1862, after much measuring, the topographer Radhanath Sikdar announced to his superior; "Sir, we have found the highest mountain in the world." Despite the local toponymy, the summit was dedicated to the English topographer Sir George Everest, first director of the Survey of India.

165 bottom left The light of sunset highlights every detail of Ama Dablam, a summit coveted by mountaineers.

165 bottom right The magnificent and rare snow leopard weighs up to 88 lbs, and has a thick downy coat.

166-167 The clouds, which usually hide Everest from view, have joined with the wind and the light of sunset to create an exceptional sight, which the photographer has captured from Mount Pumori.

WOLONG
NATIONAL PARK

Steep mountains wrapped in a blanket of fog, ice crystals that elegantly swing from the branches of bamboo, a carpet of snow destined to stay on the ground at least until March; this is how the Wolong Reserve, in the mountainous Chinese region of Sichuan, looks in the winter.

With the arrival of spring, the silent and still forest comes to life; buds poke through the snow, the river at the bottom of the valley — at an altitude of 3,280 feet above sea level — swells as the cold waters of the thaw flow into it and the fauna reawakens from its winter languor. For people as well, it becomes easier to travel the sole and often impassable trail that leads to the research center of the reserve.

But why such interest? Elsewhere, the "Land of the Clouds" (this is what Sichuan means) offers locations that are safer to reach and far easier to access. What has driven eminent scholars to spend decades of their lives at Wolong and convinced a country like China, which is expanding at a dizzying rate, to preserve this place as a park, taking it away from essential agricultural use? All of this can be explained simply by the presence in Wolong of the *Ailuropoda melanoleuca*: the giant panda. Adored by children all over the world because of its playfulness and tender glance, highly respected also among adults, who have made this animal the symbol of environmental protection, in China the panda has officially been named a "national treasure." It has been known in its native land since antiquity, as shown by an embalmed specimen found in the museum of an empress who lived in 200 BC, while for the rest of the world it is a far more recent discovery.

The missionary Armand David was the one who introduced the friendly bear to the West in 1871. The panda's fame certainly did not bring good luck, which for decades found its forests — already infested with bandits — teaming with hunters after its pelt. This was an ugly period, during which the panda population dropped dramatically. This phase was followed by a period in which the animals were captured alive for export. Owning a panda became a must for zoos all over the world and during the 1930s, anyone who wanted easy notoriety simply had his picture taken holding one in his arm; newspapers very appropriately referred to this as "pandamonium." Thirty years later, when only two of all the poor pandas abroad were left in China and the Maoist revolution had captured the public attention, more pressing problem such as growing rice to feed the population were considered far more urgent than preserving

168-169 *This is the treasure of Wolong: the giant panda. It is a bearlike creature with a massive body, which can reach as much as 350 lbs in weight. Its projecting cheekbones enlarge its head, and its black and white coloring make it unmistakable.*

169 bottom left *With elfish ears and a shrewd expression, the lesser panda is a carnivore with nocturnal habits that lives in the mountainous woods east of the Himalayas. Its elongated body is covered with impressive reddish fur.*

168 top *Even a fragile fractured trunk can become an unusual seat. This lesser panda (Ailurus fulgens) uses it to make a great show of its climbing skill.*

168 bottom *The peaks of the Qionglai mountains emerge from the clouds as protecting divinities. The chain surmounts the woods of the Sichuan region, where Wolong is situated.*

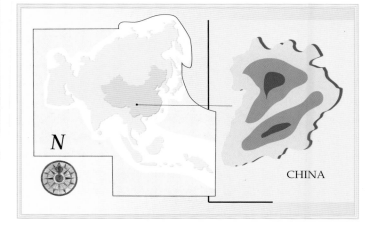

N

CHINA

bamboo or chasing poachers.

In its natural habitat, the panda eats only bamboo, even though it seems to recall its forefathers when it occasionally catches small rodents. The particular life cycle of bamboo, which after a long period of vegetative life suddenly blooms and dies over vast areas, is now the main danger. Research for the protection of the panda has thus spread to predicting the blossoming cycle of the various species of bamboo and to studying the possibility of feeding other plants to the wild pandas.

In Wolong, a team of Chinese and American scientists (the first example of this type of collaboration) studied the pandas in the wild with the help of remote-control collars, discovering the animal's timid and reserved nature not only toward man but also toward its companions. The female is fertile only one or two days a year: the probability of encountering a partner and bearing its young is thus quite low, and even in captivity the births are exceptional events. In addition, the fragmentation of

the territory into many poorly connected reserves (Wolong is the largest) has impoverished its genetic heritage, putting the survival of the species at an even greater risk. However, the world commitment to save the panda is such that it will certainly succeed in saving the black-and-white bear.

Its unmistakable coat has a legendary origin; many years ago, when their fur was still completely white, the pandas took in a little girl abandoned in the mountains and raised her as their own. When she grew up, however, the young woman died in an attempt to save one of the pups in her adopted family from a leopard. Out of respect for her courage, all the pandas went to her funeral with black arms and legs, but were so moved that when they disconsolately hung their heads between their paws, they also turned their eyes and ears black — the color of mourning. There are far too many legends surrounding the panda to recount them all, but it is interesting to note that there are no malicious stories about pandas. (A.S.I.)

171 top right The panda is able to climb, but usually moves around at ground level, in an habitual area that does not exceed 3 sq. miles. It has scent glands, which it uses to mark the places it frequents, and it is solitary, even though it does not delimit its precise territory.

171 bottom The panda has twilight habits. In the panda's day at least ten hours are dedicated to eating. Bamboo is not very nutritious, which is why an adult has to eat around 35 lbs of it a day.

ELEGANCE IN BLACK AND WHITE

170-171 In the course of evolution, the panda has adopted an almost exclusively vegetarian diet, based on bamboo. Its front paws are modified to this end, in that they have an opposable "sixth finger" that facilitates grasping this foodstuff.

171 top left In the breeding season, between March and May, the males go in search of a companion, leaving signs of their presence. It is the panda's only social period; there may be fights between competing males and, naturally, mating takes place. Births are rare since the female is fertile for a very short period of time.

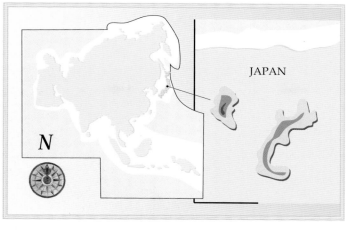

JAPAN

N

JOSHINETSU-KOGEN
NATIONAL PARK

172 *What might look like an irregular furry snowball is in reality a macaque busy quenching its thirst with a handful of fresh snow.*

173 top *When a baby gets a bug in his ear (not just a proverbial one), his big sister helps with the cleaning, with a tenderness that is somewhat surprising.*

173 center *The eyes of the macaque have met those of the photographer, but holding the gaze of a dominant specimen is considered by the latter to be a very serious affront, sometimes punishable with a violent attack.*

173 bottom *Its thick fur protects the macaque from the rigors of winter, and camouflages it in its woodland environment. Its red nose is characteristic of the species; it can signal the state of health and mood of its owner.*

According to Japanese mythology, the mountains are places best left undisturbed, especially during the icy winter. Otherwise, there is a risk of meeting supernatural beings who are not always benign, such as the *Yuki Onna* (ladies of the snows), who, after having enchanted the unlucky wayfarer with their ethereal beauty, carry him off by means of a snowstorm; or the spiteful and cruel Kappa, the water goblins, or the awful *Tengu* demons with their forbidding faces and evil nature. Whether they exist or not, these secret entities have still played a role of remarkable importance in terms of safeguarding the natural landscape, by discouraging plunderers and thus allowing several strips of forest to be preserved intact up to the present day.

In a densely populated country where for centuries wood has been the main, if not the only, building material and where frequent earthquakes, typhoons, landslides and other disasters make almost incessant building activity necessary, this is nothing short of a miracle. In 1949 the government supplanted the ancient legends, transforming into a national park a stretch of 470,000 acres, which includes the most outstanding peaks of the chain of the Japanese Alps, including Mount Kurohime. The central part of the park, the Shiga Plateau, has been declared a biosphere reserve by UNESCO. The Joshinetsu Kogen area is home to the highest and most beautiful mountains in the Land of the Rising Sun. Yet, despite the park's remote proximity, threats prevail. We are in the prefecture of Nagano, the resort where the Winter Olympics were held in 1998, and it is not hard to imagine the level of impact on the environment an event of such as this may have caused. The environmentalists are noting with great concern how the engulfing presence of human settlements is becoming increasingly threatening; a megalopolis, with its accompanying sprawling infrastructures, has an enormous influence on the territory, and the park lies only 124 miles from Tokyo. Rather, Joshinetsu Kogen deserves to be

protected with great determination, and not only on account of
the majesty of its mountains—among which Tanigawa stands
out as the most beautiful of all its seventy small lakes, the
primitive power of its two active volcanoes, Asama and Shirane;
or the pleasantness of the countless hot springs of thermal water.

The main reason for interest in this albeit charming resort
lies in its most typical inhabitants: a dense population of
macaques of Japan (*Macaca fuscata*). It is amazing to find
monkeys on the snow-covered slopes of the Japanese Alps; we
are used to identifying these animals with regions with a milder
climate. Instead, the macaques have also adapted to this rigid
climate, in which the temperature in winter can even fall as low
as 14°F. With the exception of man, the macaques are the
primates with the largest area of distribution. Protected by a
thicker skin than that of their tropical cousins, and equipped
with a robust build and a life cycle that concentrates births in
the tepid spring, these monkeys represent a constant source of
surprise not only for zoologists, but also for behavioral
psychologists.

They began to be noticed in 1953, when it was discovered
that specimens of this species were capable of learning from the
experience of others (a capacity considered to be the exclusive
privilege of *Homo sapiens*). On the island of Koshima, a female
named Moja began washing sweet potatoes in salted water, to
clean them and flavor them, and this clever behavior was

rapidly adopted by the whole community. At Jigokudani, a
thermal resort not far from the Shiga Plateau, a dense colony of
macaques lives in absolute freedom under the discreet gaze of
scholars. They show the typical behavior of primates, such as
grooming (when individuals of the same clan delicately pick
fleas off one another, more to strengthen family ties than for
actual hygienic necessity), the habit of moving in packs that
recall a military detachment on the march, and the
hierarchization of roles within the community. Then quite
unexpectedly they surprised the scientists by exhibiting
characteristics that we would not hesitate to define as more than
human; in fact how else could the case of Moja be explained?

This female from the Jigokudani pack was born without
hands and feet; natural selection would give rise to the rapid
death of a specimen with such limitations. However, the
solidarity of the pack allowed Moja (who was not even capable
of climbing up trees) to survive and even to reproduce. Scholars
see a primitive form of morality in this behavior, which
evidently is not the exclusive prerogative of our species. Other
behavior also recalls that of human beings in less noble aspects.
For example, the macaques have learned to assemble enormous
balls of snow, on which they sit to show their high level in the
hierarchy of the pack; the greater the height of the "throne," the
greater the prestige of the specimen. They also resemble us in
the search for well-being, idling about and playing in the hot
water of the volcanic springs. Observation of the macaques
attracts enthusiasts from all over the world; the monkeys
tolerate the presence of man as long as he does not dare to look
them directly in the eyes: such effrontery would be repaid with
a demonstration of their long canines in action. Evidently,
patience does not feature among the semi-human gifts of our
macaques. (A.S.I.)

LORDS OF THE SNOW

174-175 Water and snow do not put a brake on the exuberance of these young macaques, intent on a battle that simulates in every respect the clashes that, as adults, will permit them to acquire their legitimate position in the hierarchy of the troop.

175 bottom The macaques of Joshinetsu Kogen love water, partly because the volcanic morphology of the terrain makes it rich in thermal spring. The tepid waters provide a real relief from the freezing cold as well as offering an opportunity for relaxation and social interaction.

KOMODO
NATIONAL PARK

East of the island of Sumbawa and west of the island of Flores, in the center of southern Indonesia, there is a small archipelago where time seems to have stopped in the Mesozoic Age. Not content with having granted these islands the gift of a constantly mild and not-excessively rainy climate, nature has provided them with transparent waters and fantastic beaches, an unparalleled luxuriance of underwater life, a people who have made welcoming visitors a constant tradition, and a creature so unique that, it alone, would fully justify a trip here just to be able to see it. This special paradise is the Komodo Island National Park.

The uniqueness of this landscape, and the need to safeguard it for future generations, was realized a long time ago; in fact, this area has been protected since 1938, while the foundation of the National Park dates back to 1980. Since then the Park Authority, in collaboration with the Commission for Nature Conservation and the Indonesian government, has been doing its utmost to plan for the management and development of the territory in a way that is ecologically compatible, but also respectful of the customs and needs of the local people. The entire international community has also recognized the enormous importance of the Komodo National Park by declaring it a Mankind and Biosphere Reserve and a World Heritage Site.

The park covers around 160 square miles of land, consisting of the three main islands of Komodo, Rinca and Padar and many other smaller islands. The park also includes an additional 500 square miles of sea water; these marine ecosystems are in fact the most fragile, the most threatened by the impact of human activity, and the most in need of protectionist intervention.

The archipelago has volcanic origins; the slopes of the hills normally look dark and relatively bare, dotted with slender lotar palms and tamarinds, but then become a lush green with the arrival of the violent rains brought by the monsoons. On the island of Komodo there is just one village where nearly 450 people live. There are two more villages on the island of Rinca, so that, overall, the human population residing within the confines of the park numbers some 2,000 inhabitants. The population of Komodo consists of a mosaic of different ethnic groups, which form a perfect mix even from the point of view of their professional specializations. The Lombok and the Bima are traditionally merchants, while most of those who work in the public sector, such as teachers, are of Manggarai origin. However, most of the inhabitants, belonging to the Bajo and Komodo ethnic groups, are involved in the fishing industry, which is the area's most important economic resource and, as a consequence, poses the greatest risk for the delicate ecological equilibrium of the park.

The ancient methods of fishing, handed down from generation to generation (nets are used for squid, bamboo traps for rock fish, free diving or homemade snorkels are used to gather mother of pearl), have co-existed for thousands of years with the coral reefs, allowing for their natural regeneration; these are, however, much less profitable than methods that are unfortunately extremely destructive, such as those requiring the use of dynamite. More than half of the coral reefs within the park or immediately bordering it have been shattered by underwater explosions.

Other portions of the seabed seem to be dominated by populations of soft corals, those with no calcareous skeleton and no capability of constructing reefs. These species prosper precisely where the barrier has been damaged, and are home to a much smaller number of species than the original coral barriers. The revival of the building species is thus hampered by these presence of the opportunistic soft corals. The massive growth of underwater tourism (the Komodo National park has more than 30,000 visitors a year), can be a very precious resource, but if it is not carefully controlled and regulated, it causes disturbance and damage to the coastal habitats. Moreover, tourism brings with it an increase in sea traffic and a flourishing of holiday resorts, with

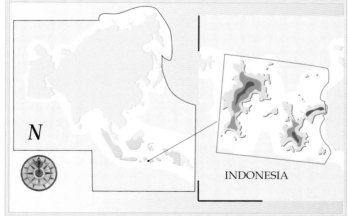

176-177 Two bagans, typical fishing boats, prepare to land on a crescent-shaped beach on the Island of Padar. The currents are very treacherous; the link between islands can require a voyage of several days.

177 bottom left Seeking refreshment, a monitor has found a small stretch of water, at Poreng.

Despite its size, it is a good swimmer; it propels itself by waving its robust tail.

177 bottom right There are around ten resurgences on Komodo, where it is possible to get fresh water. However, it is not wise to trust what at first sight might look like a floating trunk!

INDONESIA

N

178-179 The long shadows of the early morning stretch onto the beach, where a solitary monitor enjoys the salt deposit with his long forked tongue. Before long the high temperature will force him to take shade in the forest.

178 bottom The transparency and iridescence of the sea of Komodo allows us to guess what marvels await divers in search of the coral reefs that surround the main island of the archipelago, and many of the smaller ones too, which are splendid uninhabited paradises.

179 top left The silhouette of this bat cannot help but conjure in our minds terrifying scenes from horror films. However, this is completely unjustified; the flying foxes feed only off fruit and are very useful to plants because they help with the dispersion of seeds.

consequent pollution problems that were totally unknown until just a few decades ago. When you land on these islands, defying the currents that here, at the confluence of the Pacific and Indian Oceans, are particularly violent and unforeseen, you will be welcomed by shouting groups of ever happy children, and if you are lucky enough to meet the head of the village, you may be disconcertingly surprised to learn that he is more than a hundred years old! But living in Komodo is not easy; most of the population, unfortunately, do not even reach the age of forty. Often the inhabitants have to reckon with a hostile environment: highly venomous snakes on the land and in the sea, sharks, thousands of species of insects that are still

not completely classified and, naturally, the giant monitor.

Whilst the rest of the world rightly thinks it has to defend Komodo from the actions of man, the local people struggle daily to save their children from Komodo's rigors. The Park Authority works very closely with the inhabitants, maintaining that local support is essential. It operates primarily by suggesting to the local people productive activities that are compatible and not destructive, such as eco-tourism, deep-sea fishing and mariculture. In addition, it promotes educational programs for the correct use of the environment and forcefully intervenes against those who infringe upon protection regulations.

Thanks to this multi-faceted project for training and monitoring, dynamite fishing has decreased by 80% in the last five years, and the local community is able to welcome tourists (and all the advantages they bring) with only a moderate

179 top right The tropical fauna is very rich in invertebrates, and among these are numerous spiders. Sometimes they are of a considerable size, like this female Nephelis. The male, however, is much smaller.

179 center It looks like a scene from Jurassic Park; however, the huge creatures moving away from the fresh water well are not digitalized images, but alive and kicking monitors of Komodo.

impact on the environment. The Park Authority is also carrying out research to explore the incredible biodiversity of this ecosystem. From an extensive study conducted in 1995, around 1,000 species of fish were found to be present in the seas of the park. This makes the Komodo National Park one of the richest habitats of fish fauna in the world. In addition, there are more than 250 species of builder corals, among which the organ pipe coral is particularly abundant (*Tubipora musica*). This species has an unmistakable shape and is responsible for the highly distinctive pink color of the archipelago's coral beaches. Around 70 species of sponge also abound on the coral reef. The encrusting varieties prevail, since the reefs are battered by

strong sea currents. These currents are incredibly rich in nutrients and plankton, thus contributing to a high level of biodiversity in this habitat.

In the waters of the archipelago swim shoals of friendly dolphins, and occasionally you can spot whales, since their migration routes run very close to Komodo Island. Large sea turtles such as the green sea turtle (*Chelonia mydas*) and the Hawksbill turtle (*Eretmochelys imbricata*) can be found in plenty in the waters of the park. Threatened by intensive hunting of their tasty meat and beautifull shells, they find a precious place of tranquility in the Komodo National Park. Here, the Hawksbill turtle reproduces on the sandy beaches, and at the

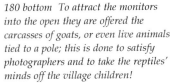

180 bottom To attract the monitors into the open they are offered the carcasses of goats, or even live animals tied to a pole; this is done to satisfy photographers and to take the reptiles' minds off the village children!

181 The monitor's meal is a grisly sight: the males close their jaws on the prey, which is torn apart with abrupt jerks backwards and swallowed in large pieces. Its gastric juices can digest even the hardest bones.

180 top left The indigenous name of the monitor is "buaya darat," land crocodile. Its stocky robust limbs allow it to reach a considerable speed. In order to control its territory better, or to impose its dominance, it is capable of rising up on its hind legs.

180 top right The west learned of the existence of this antediluvian being only in 1910, when the Dutch hunter Aldegon sent to the Museum of Buitenzorg, in Java, a skin he had bought from the natives. With the

typical sensationalism of the age, the newspapers were to speak of "monsters 40 feet long": in reality, however, the monitor is not even as much as 14.

180 center The smell of food normally attracts a large number of monitors, and the meal is shared. Naturally there is a hierarchy based on size; a young monitor that refuses to give way would in all probability pass to the role of prey.

WHERE DRAGONS
ROAM FREE

moment when the eggs hatch hundreds of minuscule specimens will totter awkwardly to reach the open sea and safety. But who is the chief enemy of the little turtles, and of the fat wild pigs in the hinterland? Who is the largest predator, which, heir to the great dinosaurs, makes the Komodo Park an absolutely unique place for the tourist who wishes to be immersed in a scene that seems to take us back millions of years? It is the largest member of the family of monitor lizards, the so-called dragon of Komodo (*Varanus komodoensis*), whot is the master here. Just think that in the territory of the park the number of monitor lizards is equal to that of men: around two thousand specimens, of which a thousand are on the island of Komodo and the same number on Rinca.

Although the monitor lizard is protected everywhere in Indonesia, the largest population is actually the one in the National Park. Almost 13 feet long and more than 286 lbs in weight, with a formidable appetite that leads it to prey on practically any animal smaller than itself, this huge lizard, which can live as many as a hundred years, certainly deserves the name of dragon. It does not breathe fire, but it constantly darts its thin forked tongue between its lips. This is the special mechanism with which the monitor lizard detects the scents of its territory. The odorous particles deposited on its tongue are then analyzed by a special organ located inside its mouth, and provide information on the presence of prey, potential companions or tourists curious to admire it. The local foresters will often attract the monitor lizards to the lookout points by offering them goats' and pigs' carcasses. Although it is a skillful hunter, the monitor lizard does not turn its nose up at a free meal, thus giving all the spectators the opportunity to imagine what mealtimes must have been like in the dinosaur age. And after a sight like that, we might need to relax in the balmy safety of a rose-colored beach; the Komodo National Park is just the right place, and is in need of aware and respectful tourists, prepared to be enchanted by this splendid little paradise. (A.S.I.)

DANUM VALLEY
FIELD CENTER

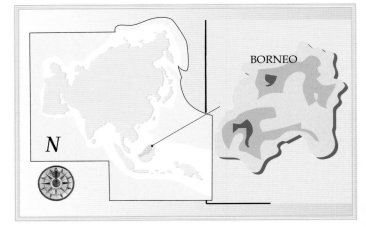

Borneo, a large island, third in the world for surface area, is completely covered by dense, stratified rain forest that is extremely difficult to explore; we must admit that Borneo is an ideal subject for writers of adventure stories! Reams of fascinating pages have created in our childish minds a world of fierce head-cutting Dayaks, man-eating tigers, explorers armed with machetes seeking gold, and proud native populations battling against western dominators who are incapable of understanding the profound equilibrium that

must exist between the environment and all the creatures that populate it, including humans.

Today this island is divided into three states: Indonesia, the rich Sultanate of Brunei and the Malaysian Federation that also comprises the two Sultanates of Sarawak and Sabah. In the latter, which occupies the northernmost part of the island, we find Danum Valley, located about fifty miles from the coastal town of Lahad Datu. There are truly a multitude of reasons for visiting this special but almost totally unknown place. The main reason is, without doubt, the possibility of seeing and enjoying a taste of how the world must have been before humanity set foot (and chain saw) here. The protected area of Danum has a surface extension of 170 square miles of a 60-million-year-old rain forest. Scientists have quite rightly defined it as "the greatest expression of life on Earth." Here, we perceive that all that surrounds us is alive and breathing in a frenzy of activity, and in perfect harmony.

If one of the aspects that most characterizes our race is its desire for knowledge, especially in regard to the mysteries of Nature, this park offers the challenge; we are still a long way from having a scientific classification of all the creatures of the jungle. The pace at which we acquire knowledge is in any case far slower than the one which evolution spawns new species. So those who become famous in history should carefully observe the insects, great and small, that can be encountered around the Field Center (the area's only infrastructure), able to host a dozen researchers. If they are lucky, they may even find an insect not yet described and definitively baptize it with their name.

Thousands of plant species host, nourish and conceal a multitude of animals, even some that are larger in size. Some species have their final refuge here; we are well aware of how vulnerable the tropical forest is and how elsewhere fires, deforestation, subsoil exploitation, and the increasing pressure of an increasingly intrusive human population have

182 center The orangutan, the "man of the woods" of Borneo, is an anthropomorphic monkey, which is now very rare, as a result of hunting and destruction of its habitat. It moves among the branches with agility, but on the ground it is rather clumsy.

182 bottom The delicious flower of a wild banana tree provides a snack for this charming little bird, known as the "bespectacled" spider-hunter, on account of the gaudy yellow border around its eyes.

182-183 The rainforest that covers the lowlands of the Danum Valley emerges from the morning mists; the dipterocarps, about 40 feet high, are the first to enjoy the sun's rays.

183 top left The blossoms of the Rafflesia, the largest flower in the world, certainly do not go unobserved. Less pleasant is their smell; the main pollinators are saprophagous flies, and to attract them the Rafflesia emits a stench of rotten meat.

183 top right Along the Segama River stretches a particularly lush tropical rainforest, which can also be observed from the suspension bridge built near the Research Center.

184-185 *In the arms of its mother, who for now is its whole world, this three-month-old orangutan is the very picture of fragility. It will grow to a height of more than 51 inches and will weigh 198 lbs, and has an average life expectancy of thirty-five years.*

184 bottom *Discovering the marvels of the forest, a small orangutan puts itself to the test in climbing. Not being natural predators, orangutans live a peaceful life; the young ones play, while the adults spend a lot of time searching for food: fruit, leaves, bark, as well as earth rich in minerals, eggs and small invertebrates.*

LAND OF THE ORANGUTANS

cut its area down to a few continually impoverished acres. Danum Valley, final rampart of a truly uncontaminated nature, hosts the rare Sumatra rhinoceros, famous for its single horn of pressed, hardened hairs, and a medium-sized population of elephants; among the carnivores, there is the clouded leopard. Stratified plants that can reach hundreds of feet in height constitute an ideal habitat for flying squirrels and several species of monkey.

The sound track to our visit will certainly include the

185 top Orangutans are weaned at about three years of age, but a young one remains with its mother until it is six or seven, and only separates from her for good when it reaches the age of sexual maturity, at around ten years of age.

185 bottom Seen from ground level in their original habitat, these giant Ficus certainly do not look like the plants, which, in fact, belong to the same genus that is so popular in homes worldwide.

howls of the gibbons, who make their presence known both to their family and to their neighbors. They swing through the branches and swiftly cross the curtain of trees, moving with long, strong arms and an agility that makes them seem like cotton puffs blown by the wind. The rare proboscis monkey, with its disproportionate nose, leads us to suspect that perhaps nature does indeed have a sense of humor. A reddish shadow, the flash of an almost human face amongst the leaves, is all we may be able to discern of the orangutan, an extremely elusive and quite rightly diffident animal. (According to local legend, however, the orangutan is not a monkey but in reality a man—orangutan means "man of the woods"—who astutely pretends not to be able to speak to avoid being forced to work!)

Poachers kill the adults to sell the skull as a souvenir and kidnap the young to feed a black market of exotic wildlife. Fortunately, there are many who dedicate their lives to make up for the damage, creating rehabilitation clinics for wounded

or orphaned orangutans, so that they may be re-introduced to their jungle habitat.

We could continue to list the entire 110 species of mammals present, but we would disappoint the birdwatchers. Danum Valley is a must for these wildlife aficionados. The reserve symbol is the giant pitta (*Pitta caerulea*), accompanied by other different kinds of pitta, colorful Bulwar's pheasant, and Storm's stork. About 275 species, some endemic, others more common but no less beautiful or interesting, can be heard and encountered along the network of paths that surround the Field Center, which also includes the suspended bridge over the Segama River and observation stations set 130 feet above ground. The infrastructures for visitors are certainly not suitable for mass tourism, but they are sufficiently comfortable and safe to allow those truly determined to plunge into this fascinating Jungle (with a capital J) with the means to do so. (A.S.I.)

OCEANIA
INTRODUCTION

Virtually the entire austral hemisphere—isolated in relation to other land surfaces and to other major routes of communication and trade—this was the last continent to be discovered by Westerners and was why it was called "new." This mosaic of earth and water is Oceania, and as its very name suggests, its physical and geographical features make it different from all the other continents. Its surface, composed of thousands of islands scattered throughout the Pacific Ocean, represents only 6% of all land surfaces. To its inhabitants, however, the water separating the archipelagos, atolls and large and small islands are like an extension of terra firma, vital for cultural and trade exchanges. What dominates over all this is the massive shape of Australia, covering 2.9 million square miles (all of Oceania isonly 3.5 million square miles). The other major islands, New Zealand, Tasmania and half of the territory of New Guinea, together with Australia, comprise 99% of Oceania's land surface. The rest of the continent, composed of a myriad of smaller islands, is divided into three major geographical groupings: immediately northeast of Australia is Melanesia, or the "Black Islands"—including the famed Fiji Islands and the New Hebrides. To the north is Micronesia, or the "Little Islands," an appropriate name given that the largest one covers just 222 square miles; these include the Marshall Islands and the Mariannas. Lastly, in the middle of the Pacific is Polynesia—"Many Islands"—including Samoa and Tahiti, with the easternmost landmasses that stretch across the Equator.

Many of these smaller islands are of volcanic origin but, particularly in Polynesia and Melanesia, they are also coral islands. Typical ones include the atolls, composed of the calcareous skeletal material of coral; these are typically shaped like large rings of land with a lagoon in the middle. In the collective imagination of Westerners, many of these islands symbolize clean beaches and clear blue seas, and they are a sought-after destination for tourists from all over the world. However, in these tropical paradises the management of tourism has not always coincided with respect for the environment. Fortunately, people today are also becoming aware of the fact that the deterioration is irreversible and, above all, counter-productive. The different countries to which these archipelagos belong, particularly the US, New Zealand, Chile, France and England, are taking steps so that future generations can also enjoy the "marvels of the South Seas." If we leave aside the above archipelagos and smaller islands, Oceania can be considered an extremely old continent, from a physical standpoint, despite the adjective "new" used to describe it. Only in New Guinea and New Zealand are the geological formations fairly recent. In the southern island of New Zealand, the mountains are clearly marked: with Mount Cook in the Southern Alps reach an altitude of 12460 feet. To the west, they drop off rapidly toward the sea and the power of the river water erodes the coast, forming a series of suggestive fjords.

On the northern island—in the national park that goes by the same name—is the snowy peak of Mount Egmont, one of the tallest volcanoes in New Zealand. Instead, Australia is a flat continent composed of ancient rock, where the wind and other erosive elements have worn down nearly every rugged feature over the ages. The only true mountains are the Australian Alps, which snake along the southeastern coast. However, their summits do not exceed 7,200 feet. Although it is completely surrounded by water, Australia is not considered an island: because of its size, the interior is not affected by the sea. The central-western areas are covered almost entirely by deserts.

186 left On account of the quantity of marvels that live there, like this soft coral with a curious broccoli-like shape, the coral reef is considered by many to be a true paradise. It is also where, however, the fragile equilibrium that governs all the inhabitants may be irremediably destroyed as a result of human negligence or indifference.

186-187 The Great Barrier Reef of Australia, formed by an enormous quantity of rocks and small atolls, is 1240 miles long and is the largest natural habitat in the world.

187 bottom left Erskine Island: one of the three hundred small sandbanks or cays dotted all over the Australian Great Barrier Reef, and one of the few covered in vegetation.

187 bottom right On Big Island, Hawaii, the goddess of fire Pele constantly reveals her anger: the gigantic caldera of the volcano Kilauea, which belches out a red river of lava, is her home.

Because of the lack of glaciers and the high level of tropical evaporation, there are no rivers worthy of this name. Instead, the west coast offers what remains of a lush tropical-forest environment. Programs have been carried out for several decades to preserve the marvelous scenery and unique flora and fauna of Australia and New Zealand. In fact, they are the countries in the South Seas that have looked furthest ahead in terms of environmental protection, to the great benefit of the thriving tourist industry.

Since 1987, there has been a Conversation Department in New Zealand. It handles the management not only of the numerous National Parks, but also the State Forests and Marine Parks. Australia, with over five hundred national parks distributed throughout the territory—rainforests, broad stretches of savannahs and deserts, monsoon forests, coast dunes, vast wetlands and, last but not least, the Great Barrier Reef National Park—beat every record of environment protection. All these areas are, infact, administered by the federal government, which ensures respect for the regulations that protect it. Many Australian parks that have both cultural and naturalistic importance have demonstrated their right to become part of the list of places that are part of the World Heritage, drawn up an authoritative institution like UNESCO. (C.P.)

188 bottom In the setting of the Bungle Bungle chain, Western Australia, towers another termites' nest, the silent refuge of a highly active city of insects.

189 The extraordinary rock formations of Purnululu National Park, Western Australia, are reminiscent of enormous striped beehives almost 1,968 feet high.

190-191 Detail of Uluru, or Ayers Rock, in the national park of the same name. The strange signs of erosion on the monolith have acquired important symbolic meanings in Aboriginal cultural history.

188 center left In a world of marsupials, there is one Australian mammal that is not: the dingo (Canis familiaris dingo) a wild dog found throughout Australia.

188 center right In south Queensland, on the seashore, a young oriental gray kangaroo (Macropus giganteus), a heavyweight among marsupials, scans the horizon.

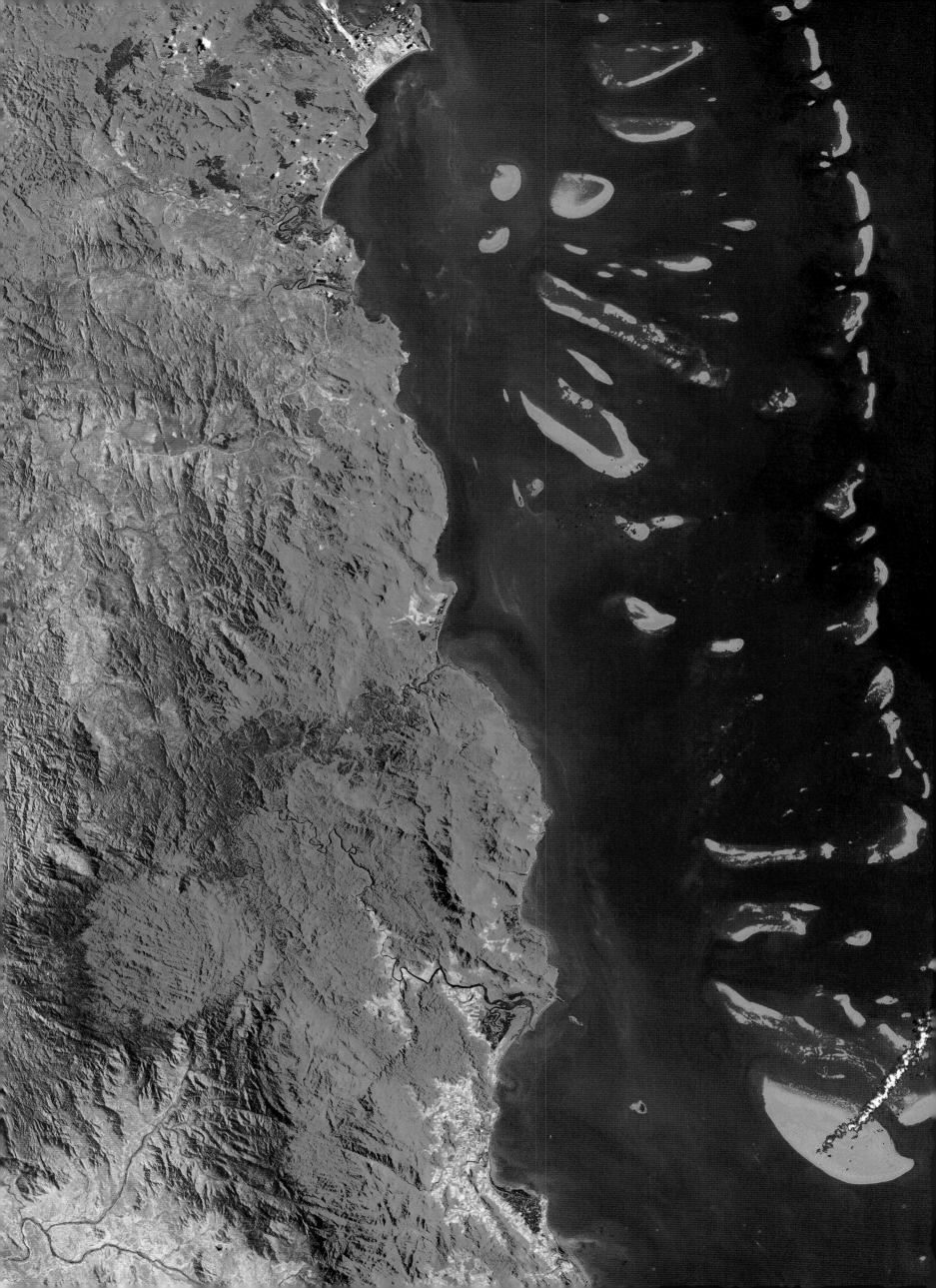

192 The coral reef seen from a satellite. This is the largest construction made by living beings visible from space.

193 top left A teeming school of bluestripe snappers moves in unison with perfect synchrony, thus creating a curious chromatic effect.

feet of living space is shared by various species of coral, sponges and a giant clam with open valves.

GREAT BARRIER REEF
MARINE PARK

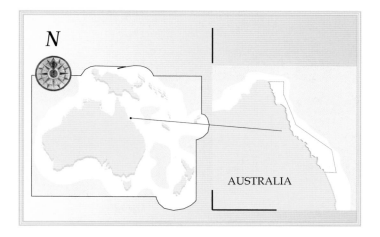

AUSTRALIA

Few places on Earth manage to arouse in man such intense emotions as the underwater world that gravitates around a coral reef; and if this reef happens to be the Great Barrier Reef, we are faced with a veritable universe of awe-inspiring shapes and colors. In order to fully appreciate the magical beauty of this place, diving with oxygen bottles is a must; in fact it is only in this way that we can delude ourselves (albeit temporarily) that we, too, are part of this paradise.

The Great Barrier Reef is the largest construction built by living beings (including man) in the world; it is more than 1,240 miles long and extends in a half-moon shape off the northeast coast of the Australian continent. It consists of thousands of separate reefs, some above sea level, while others are completely or occasionally submerged by the tides; these reefs can be circular or half-moon shaped, or they can be proper breakwaters. To protect this area, which is unique in terms of its variety of living species, the Australian government founded in 1975 a marine park that safeguards both the land above sea level and the surrounding waters. It remains one of the largest marine parks in the world.

Nowadays the aims of the park include checking on commercial activity, regulating the exploitation of natural resources, limiting tourism in the area and at the same time carrying out important research to preserve the habitat and the species present. One glance at this world is enough to be amazed by the incredible variety of underwater life and to realize how fragile and precarious the balance is that regulates existence in these depths.

Dive into the crystal-clear water and you will be enveloped in a whirl of blue while witnessing a fairytale garden opening beneath you. This garden is not enchanted though; it is a multicolored expanse, embellished here and there with shells and nudibranches and almost entirely covered with thousands of sponges and corals of the most fantastic shapes: some like fans, funnels and globes and some similar to human brains, while others are indented like tender young broccoli. Scientifically, their names are madrepore, gorgonia, turbinaria and alcyonaria. Silent and motionless, they lead their life as creatures, preying on microscopic particles of food with the small stinging tentacles of their polyps. The rest of these organisms, with the help of very extensive colonies of green and red calcareous seaweed, will contribute, in future years, to the construction of another barrier, just as the past generations have done for millions of years in these parts. They will create the habitat of an infinite quantity of animals, including many fish whose variety of shape, color and size is impressive, to say the least.

It may seem incredible, but it is thought that there are 1,500 tropical marine species living here, and that many more still have to be classified. Some are of indescribable beauty, such as the butterfly fish, which appears in the form of a disc with a thin pointed little nose growing at one end, with which they delicately tear the polyps off the corals. Equally splendid in terms of shape and color are the angel fish, which allow us to experience the sensation of being immersed in a gigantic aquarium. It is fairly common to observe between the tentacles of the sea anemones small orange fish with black and white stripes: these are clown fish. These fish find shelter amidst the stinging tentacles of the sea anemone no less, which are harmless to them thanks to their protective covering of scales. But the surprises seem to be endless. One creature that seems to have come straight out of a child's imagination is the cow fish (*Lactoria cornuta*), with the unimaginable shape of a box. The pair of horns that stick out above its eyes are the feature that justifies its name; in constant search of small algae, it swims slowly with short strokes of its fins. It is possible to find

playmates here too: first and foremost are the giant groupers, which reach 330 lbs in weight and seem to have a good-natured attitude towards scuba drivers, as evidenced out by their peaceful and playful behavior.

And can a meeting with a green turtle be defined as any less thrilling? Because of man's merciless hunting, the number of representatives of this species has fallen dramatically in the course of recent years. Even if the Great Barrier Reef is home to the largest population in the world, it is still thought to be a great stroke of luck to come face to face with one of these creatures. Moving its fins in a graceful way it almost seems to be flying in the water, as though it was not weighed down by its voluminous carapace. Named after the color of their flesh, the female green turtle make a nest every two/four years, digging deep holes on sandy beaches, inside which they deposit more than a hundred eggs. The young that are born, abandoned to their own devices, head for the sea, the vulnerable prey of seagulls and crabs. They will return to their birthplace after 20 – 30 years to give life to a new generation of the species.

Of course, there are two sides to everything; this world, where everything seems to belong to paradise, is also home to creatures that can spell danger for any imprudent person who ventures too close. Among these is undoubtedly the stone-fish, or *Synanceia horrida*, from the family of the Scorpaenidae. Up to a foot long, it has a vertical mouth and eyes positioned on the top of its head, which justify its scientific name. These characteristics are not immediately noticeable, or rather, they mingle with the rocks and corals when it is in its natural environment, half-buried by the sand and perfectly camouflaged with the sea bed, lying in wait for a prey to pass. Big trouble is in store for the unlucky person who should inadvertently tread on it! In fact, through the thirteen spines on its dorsal fin, the fish injects a powerful venom that quickly leads to muscle paralysis and cardiac arrest.

On the theme of danger, remember to approach another inhabitant of the Great Barrier Reef with great caution: the blue-ringed octopus, which grows up to 4 inches long. It can be found in the low waters of the natural pools that are formed among the rocks when the tide is low. It is precisely its color that attracts tourists; in fact when the creature is excited, iridescent blue rings appear on its body, which are so beautiful that they cannot be passed by unnoticed, especially by children. Its bite is not painful, but the venom in its saliva is highly toxic and often lethal.

Other dangers appear at sundown when large predators such as barracudas and sharks appear and, protected by the dark, capture their prey, completing the perfect circle of life and death in this splendid sea. (C.B.)

194 top A large barracuda shows its perfect teeth. These predators of proverbial voracity form groups consisting of hundreds of specimens.

194 center A giant grouper can exceed 330 lbs in weight. In order to approach these rather mistrustful colossuses, it can be useful to have a few morsels of fish on hand.

194 bottom These hammer-headed sharks, with their characteristic and unmistakable head, can reach 13 feet in length.

195 More than 65 feet deep, the gorgoniae develop their branches until they reach a giant size.

196-197 These soft corals, called alcyonaria, can reach a remarkable size. Their shape suggests personal and bizarre interpretations to each of us. The vast chromatic variety helps us give free rein to our imagination.

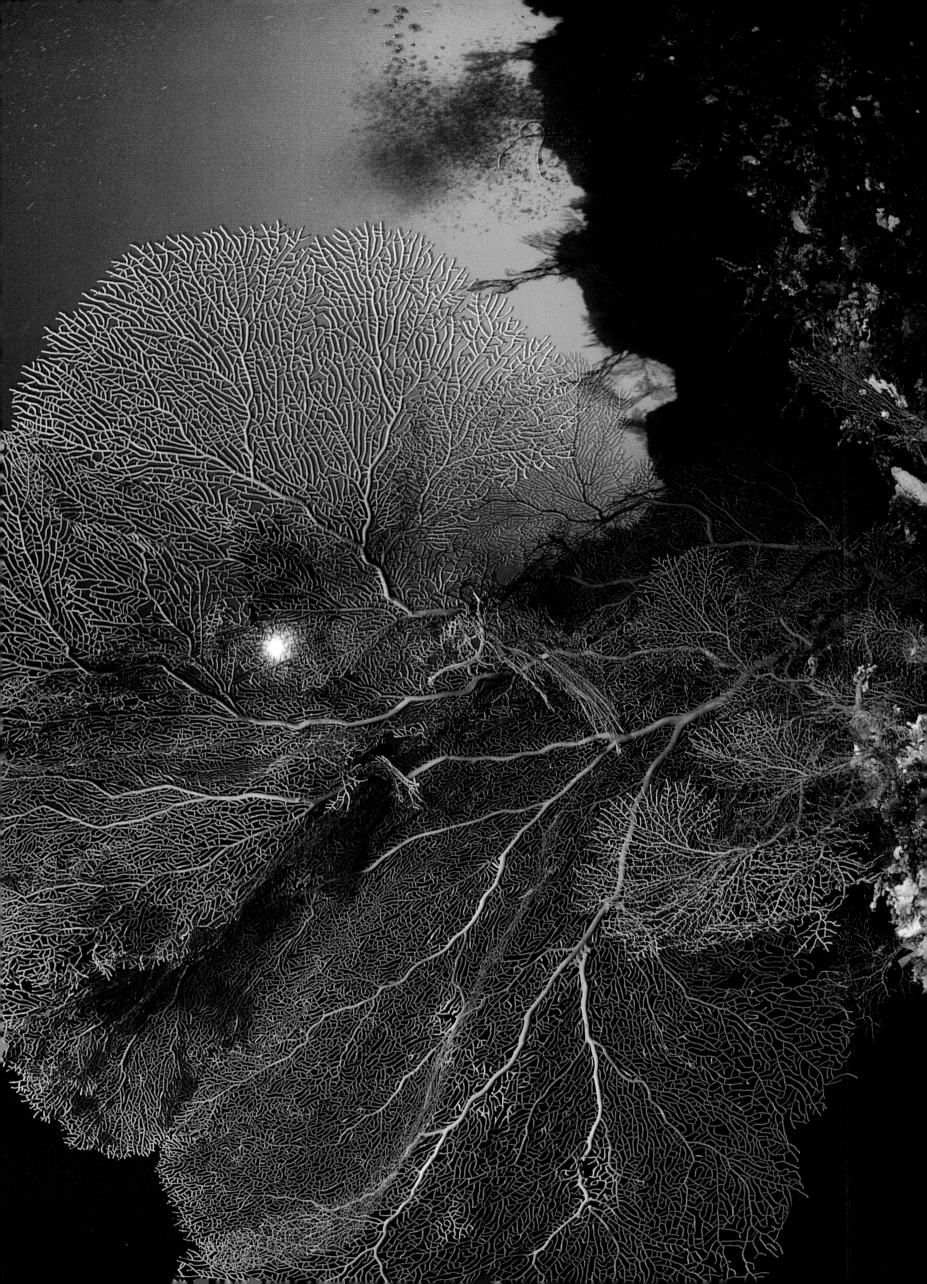

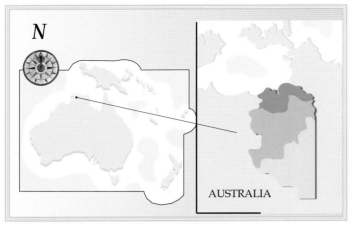

AUSTRALIA

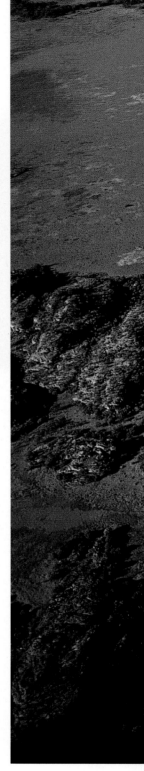

KAKADU
NATIONAL PARK

A visit to Kadadu National Park will disappoint neither the naturalist nor the anthropologist; the relaxing beauty of the landscape is, in fact, accompanied by numerous expressions of one of the oldest aboriginal cultures in Australia. It is no mere chance that in 1991 Kakadu was included in the list of places considered by UNESCO to be the "World Heritage," and it is one of the few examples in which the reasons for choosing it were both naturalistic and cultural.

As in the whole of the Australian territory, in Kakadu the history of the Aborigines is inextricably tied to the environment. Everywhere in the park the presence of this cultural heritage is palpable; today the aborigines of Kakadu, owners of the national park to a great extent, are willing to share their deep knowledge of this land with visitors, and express the hope that the latter will learn to appreciate its natural and spiritual values.

The name Kakadu is a degeneration of "Gagadju," the most spoken language here at the beginning of the twentieth century. After the 1960s, the Australian zoologist J. Calaby sensed that the area had the potential to become a world-class park. His vision became a reality on April 5, 1979, with the proclamation of the Kakadu National Park. Situated in the Top End, the region at the apex of the Northern Territory, about 124 miles from the city of Darwin, Kakadu extends for 7,750 square miles, including the entire drainage basin of the South Alligator River and parts of other rivers: the Wildman, the West Alligator, the East Alligator and the Yellow River.

Around 140 million years ago, Kakadu was submerged by a shallow sea, whose shores today is represented by the majestic escarpment of Arnhem Land, which marks the eastern border of the park, and beyond which stretches a territory wholly owned by the Aborigines, which can only be visited with special permits. This spectacular sandstone wall, which can be admired from various lookout points, is between 330 and 660 feet high and winds its way for about 310 miles, forming the natural border of a harsh plateau. The numerous watercourses that furrow the plateau plummet from the escarpment in the form of thunderous waterfalls, which then submerge the vast flood plains, in the months from October to May, the period better known as "the wet." It is almost incredible that, only several months later, some of these tracts, previously impassable on account of water as

198-199 Ubirr, Canon Hill: a view of the sandstone formations that emerge from the brilliant green of the flood plain.

199 bottom left The wide-open jaws of the sea crocodile (Crocodylus porosus) – the most aggressive and dangerous reptile in Australia, if not in the world – are truly impressive.

199 bottom right A large specimen of a sea crocodile (Crocodylus porosus) in its most congenial surroundings: the calm waters of an estuary.

198 top Aerial view of the Twin Falls, situated in the central-southern region of the park. In the dry season the flow of water diminishes, but never disappears altogether.

198 bottom A splendid example of Kakadu rock art, at the foot of the steep Nourlangie Rock, sacred to the Aborigines, with stylized human figures representing the Dreamtime.

much as ten feet high, are perfectly dry and can be crossed in a jeep. This happens because the whole of northern Australia is part of the monsoon band, with a succession of such diverse seasons that the appearance of the landscape is radically altered (because the climate is tropical, however, the temperatures never drop below 68°F).

In the summer season known by Australians as "the dry," not all the watercourses withdraw completely; in some areas, permanent pools known as *billabongs* persist. Often their surface is carpeted with water lilies, whose roots are sought by Aborigines, who dig in the mud to find them and eat, sometimes raw. Large numbers of *melaleucas*, trees with a typical papery bark that comes off in thin sheets, border all the flood areas, streams and billabongs; during the wet their base is submerged by usually shallow water, while in the dry they serve as a reference point to indicate the level of the winter flood.

For lovers of birdwatching, the billabongs are a true paradise; a cruise at dawn on the Yellow River is an excellent opportunity to spot herons, little egrets, cormorants and pelicans, but also more characteristic are species such as the *jabiru*, the Australian stork with a saddle-shaped beak, red feet and iridescent plumage, which has become something of a symbol for Kakadu.

Along the coast and the estuaries, dense forests of mangroves encourage the accumulation of great quantities of debris dragged from the rivers every season, visibly increasing the surface area of the park. The mangroves are a natural breeding ground for dozens of species of fish, including the famous *barramundi*, or *Namarngo* (in the language of the Aborigines), with the most delicious meat. However, the

inhabitant of the rivers and estuaries with which a close encounter is most feared or most hoped for, depending on your point of view, is the crocodile. In fact, the Australian Top End has the greatest concentration of the largest reptile now existing in the world, the sea crocodile, with a length of 23 – 24 feet. It is affectionately referred to as *saltie*, from *saltwater*, since, unlike other crocodiles, it is fond of living in brackish water and even in the sea. The *saltie* is known for its aggressiveness; there are danger signs everywhere warning visitors not to carelessly approach the river banks or attempt to swim in the inviting waters at the foot of a waterfall.

The sea crocodile, which lives in salt and fresh waters in the whole of southeast Asia, must not be confused with another species of exclusively Australian crocodile that lives in Kakadu with which it shares its fresh water habitat; this time its nickname is *freshie*, from *freshwater*. The *freshie* is smaller than the *saltie*, has a narrower snout and seems harmless, although it is not advisable to try to find out whether this is true. Kakadu is the home of another 120 species of reptile; during the wet

you may have the opportunity to see a frilled lizard running on two legs, with its comical little frill erected, or you may even witness the rustling of a python fleeing from your approach.

Kakadu is not only an immense wet area, however; about half of its surface, the southern part, is in reality dry lowland, with woods and grassland. The predominant tree type here is undoubtedly the eucalyptus, and the best known is the *Darwin woollybutt*, a medium-sized tree, whose trunk is used to make the *didgeridoo*, an ancient musical instrument used by the Aborigines. Its bark is very thick and thus provides it with good protection against the fires that regularly burn down the grassland. Fires are important for the life cycle of the woodland; for thousands of years the Aborigines have used it as a regenerating process.

The woodland habitat is home to the greatest number of species in the whole of the park. The black red-tailed cockatoos, together with various other species of parrot, enliven the highest branches of the trees, while in the sky, the white-breasted sea eagle and the black falcon circle in full view. The mammals are more difficult to spot: various types of small

about the creation of the world and the birth of the Aboriginal law. For the natives of this region, the paintings are a highly-valued source of knowledge about their traditions, a sort of historical archive, given that they have no writings.

Among all these marvels, however, a threat hangs over Kakadu. Since the 1950s, small deposits of uranium within the park have been found and tapped immediately. In 1973, the largest superior-quality uranium mine in the world was discovered in Jabiluka. For some years it was forbidden to tap it, but since 1998 work there has been authorized. The Aborigines look on in puzzlement and undoubtedly realize the danger of contaminating their territory. It is everyone's hope, however, that contamination will not effect this corner of Australian nature in order to preserve the Aborigines' culture in the future. (C.P.)

kangaroo, such as the black *wallaroo* and the short-eared rock *wallaby*, can be seen jumping amidst the rocks only at sunset or in the early hours of the morning. The other marsupials, the *possums* and the smaller *bandicoots*, are mainly nocturnal creatures. At the bottom of the escarpment, scattered patches of monsoon forest are home to gullies and shady declivities; this is a type of rainforest adapted to a severe climate, which passes from extreme humidity to extreme drought. Small birds and fruit bats, or flying foxes, are essential in maintaining a link between the isolated pockets of the forest, encouraging both pollination and dissemination.

In addition to the great variety of habitats, Kakadu is also rich from an artistic point of view. The rock art in this place is a heritage of universal importance, one of the oldest and best preserved in the world. Although the park contains several thousands of sites of archeological importance, most of these are not accessible to the public, especially the most ancient, which date back as much as 20,000 years and generally depict legends

200-201 The noisy take-off of a flock of galah (Cacatua roseicapilla), *the commonly found pink and gray Australian parrots, is a very frequent sight in each part of the Park.*

200 bottom A broad bend in the East Alligator River; the extraordinary abundance of wildlife in the park depends on its rivers.

201 top A jabiru, or black-beaked stork (Ephippiorhyncus asiaticus) *takes flight. Highly skillful at capturing fish in low water, it uses its pointed beak as a spear.*

201 bottom Ubirr, in the north of the park. The rocks here are veritable art galleries of rock paintings, which give us important information about the history of the Aborigines.

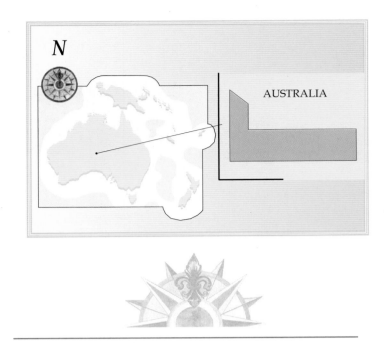

ULURU-KATA TJUTA
NATIONAL PARK

Uluru, Ayers Rock, or more simply "The Rock," has virtually become a must for anyone visiting Australia. Its unmistakable red outline is present on all tourist brochures and the agencies compete to offer the most advantageous tour packages. To withstand the enormous onslaught of visitors in the middle of the desert (over 400,000 a year), the town of Yulara, located outside the park about 12 miles from Uluru, has expanded and set up facilities, becoming an excellent base for excursions. Despite this modernization, however, there is still a sacred atmosphere within the park itself.

The visitors' center is an Aborigine cultural center where people are virtually led by the hand to learn about the rich cultural tradition of the *Anangu*. According to the *Tjukurpa* (the Aboriginal law laid down during creation), the ancestral beings that modeled the entire landscape of Uluru-Kata Tjuta still live in their descendents, the Anangu, the last guardians of this ancient land. As legend would have it, Uluru was built by

children who were playing in the mud after a thunderstorm, right in the middle of the intricate network of *song paths* that cross every inch of Australia's territory. In 1985, the sacredness of the place forced the Australian government to recognize the Anangu as the legitimate owners, who in turn began "renting" the place to the National Park Administration for ninety-nine years in exchange for a fixed annual income and 25% of the revenue brought in by the growing tourism trade.

Until 1993, this national park was called *Ayers Rock-Mount Olga*, a name given to it by the first explorers, Ernest Giles and William Gosse, who at the end of the nineteenth century discovered these unique formations. Sir Henry Ayers was then president of South Australia and Olga was the queen of Wurttemburg.

Uluru and Kata Tjuta are located at the southern edge of an ancient area that once held a shallow sea, referred to by geologists as the Amadeus Basin. This depression in the earth's crust was formed about 900 million years ago and was then filled with layers of sediment for another 600 million years. The moment the process stopped, erosion then began to sculpt it: wind, rain and sand are what shaped one of the world's largest natural attractions. Uluru-Kata Tjuta National Park, together with ten other Australian sites, is included on the list of places considered by UNESCO to be part of the "World Heritage."

Uluru boasts of one record in particular: it is the largest monolith in the world, and in some ways it has become the symbol of Australia. It rises to a maximum of 1,140 feet from the immense sandy red plains, and its base, roughly elliptical in shape, has a perimeter of 5.8 miles, for a length of 2.23 and a width of 1.5 miles. At certain points, the slopes have a gradient of 80°, but the summit is flat.

The rocky formation, which appears perfectly solid from a distance, is furrowed by deep vertical and parallel fissures. It has countless ravines, niches, little valleys and even an enchanting hidden lake. Uluru is composed entirely of coarse sandstone, rich in feldspar that settled after the erosion of granitic mountains that have now disappeared. It is likely that two-thirds of the monolith actually lies beneath the surface of

203 bottom left When threatened, this lizard of the Agamidae family (Amphibolurus barbatus) *extends the fold of skin bristling with spines on its throat; this is why it has earned the name of "bearded dragon lizard."*

203 bottom right The bearded dragon lizard, a typical agamid of the arid forests of Australia, is able to change color according to its mood. If disturbed, its skin gradually changes from dark gray to yellow-orange.

202 left A bearded dragon lizard (Amphibolurus barbatus) *caught while eating its meal. Its favorite foods are insects and other invertebrates but, when these are not available, it will make do with a vegetarian diet.*

202-203 Ayers Rock, the mountain sacred to the Aborigines, for whom it is Uluru, rises solitary in all its grandeur in the boundless desert expanse of central Australia. In the background are the Olgas Mountains, or Kata Tjuta.

THE MONOLITH

the sand. The cleavage of the surface of Uluru is the result of the oxidation of ferrous minerals present in the sandstone; the characteristics rusty color of the chips is rust (as sandstone is actually gray). The red color of Uluru, which shows off all its possible hues at sunset, attracts hordes of tourists all year, even during the austral summer, between June and October, when the night temperature drops to about 32°F; hundreds of people swarm to an enormous parking area set up at a distance in order to enjoy the show. But the rock can also be observed up close. It takes about three to four hours to walk the entire perimeter, but it's worth the effort; this is the only way to admire the caverns and rock paintings.

Along the way, there are many places that are sacred to the Aborigines which cannot be photographed. Many visitors come to Uluru simply to climb it. Along the western side of the rock is the departure point of the only route leading to the top. The climb covers one mile and the first part, which is extremely steep, even requires a chain for people to pull themselves up. The violent gusts of wind and the extremely high temperatures in the period from December to March make the task even more arduous. An increasing number of people have nevertheless

chosen not to climb the mountain sacred to the Anangu, in order to respect their wishes. Capitalizing on such "altruism," however, there is an enormous profit in the sale of T-shirts and gadgets of all types with a picture of Uluru and the words "I didn't climb it."

Located about thirty miles west of Uluru are the Olgas, or Kata Tjuta, a group of monolithic rocks that are smaller and rounder than Uluru. The tallest monolith reaches a height of 1,790 feet. The aboriginal name Kata Tjuta means "many heads" and is associated with a series of Tjukurpa stories that are revealed only to the men of the tribe, since they are linked with male initiation ceremonies. From a petrographic standpoint, the sedimentary rock of the Olgas is a conglomerate of gravel, composed of small and medium-sized pebbles and larger stones that have been cemented together by sand and mud. Many of the stones are granite or basalt and from up close, they give the conglomerate a variegated appearance. Following the path that runs along the gorges between one rock and another, you can reach the lookout points to enjoy a view of all the "heads," often

in complete solitude because Kata Tjuta has far fewer visitors than Uluru.

Although the park is located in the middle of the desert of central Australia, many plants have managed to adapt to the sandy red soil and to the long dry spells. Nearly all of them are quiescent for a good part of the year, but then they revive and blossom, following the heavy rains that generally arrive between December and March, when the north of Australia is prone to daily thunderstorms and tempests.

The tree that is probably most typical of the park and of all the dry areas in Australia is the *mulga*, a type of acacia. The Anangu use every part of this tree to produce boomerangs, digging sticks or parts of lances, shelters and firewood. While frequent fires can destroy the tree, in order to germinate its seeds it actually needs high temperatures, thus furnishing the ideal solution for the survival of this species. In the more sheltered areas between the tall dunes or near the rock faces, we can find small copses of *desert oaks*, a tree with a resinous bark that is most widespread in this area. But the park would have a completely different appearance if the sandy soil were not carpeted with an endless series of *spinifex* cushions. This is a herbaceous plant and, as anyone who has walked over it with sandals knows, is also painfully spiky. It has an immense root system which keeps the sand compact, preventing it from blowing away.

The fact that the stories of the Tiukurpa always have animals as their leading characters is proof that this territory is not really as inhospitable as it might seem. There are about twenty types of marsupial mammals that live on plains and in the ravines of the rocks of Uluru-Kata Tjuta. They range from the large red kangaroo that jumps heedlessly over the spinifex to the small and much more reserved marsupial mole. These are prevalently nocturnal animals that are thus more difficult to observe. If you are lucky, you might see a dingo, a wild Australian dog, circling about in the dunes. But the birds are what will give you the most satisfaction; their presence is felt everywhere, their cries resound amidst the gorges and over the plain, and the trees offer them plenty of food and shelter. There are the ubiquitous parrots, the pink cockatoo with its white crest, finches, magpies and doves. Not to mention the giant of Australian birds, the emu, which can't fly but dashes quickly across the desert.

Rocks, wind, sand and living creatures: all of this constitutes the sacred world of the Anangu who have a profound knowledge of the ecosystem in which they live, from the characteristics of the flora to the habits of the animals. This is the reason that the park administration consults them for surveying work and in developing conservation programs. The goal is to learn more about this unique environment and preserve it in the natural conditions in which the Anangu have maintained it since time immemorial. (C.P.)

204 top A sand monitor (Varanus gouldii) as it explores the environment with its long forked tongue. In Australia the monitor is called "goanna," a word most likely derived from a degeneration of the term "iguana."

204 center Even the desert of Central Australia can blossom; among the pads of spinifex some brightly colored flowers appear.

204-205 With a threatening hiss, wide open mouth and large extended chlamys, a frilled lizard (Chlamydosaurus kingii) seeks to frighten an aggressor.

205 bottom The first lights of the dawn light up the great sandstone monolith in the National Park.

206-207 Less famous than Uluru, the rock complex of the Olgas Mountains has an extra appeal, since it is possible to penetrate and explore it. The name that the Aborigines give it, Kata Tjuta, means "Many Heads."

208-209 The proliferation of these
"rainbow" mushrooms, as they are
known, on the dead trunks of the
rainforest creates a strong contrast
with the bright green of the ferns.

208 bottom A November view of the
mountains in Lamington National
Park; in the late southern spring the
high humidity and temperatures
often give rise to mists.

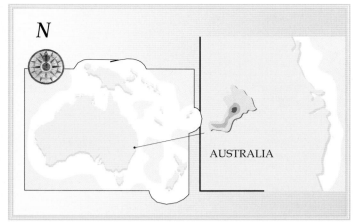

AUSTRALIA

LAMINGTON
NATIONAL PARK

About sixty-two miles south of the capital of Queensland, Brisbane, in the wild McPherson Mountain chain, lies an area of uncommon beauty, with unique flora and fauna. Its name is Lamington, after Lord Lamington, governor of Queensland in 1915, when the entire area was declared a National Park. This decision was largely influenced by Robert Collins, an Australian traveler who had visited Yellowstone, the world's first national park, in 1878. Inspired by this original concept of protecting nature, Collins spared no efforts in the following years to ensure that the McPherson Mountain chain, might meet with a similar fortune. Since one of the purposes of national parks is that they should also be enjoyed by people, Collins succeeded after a few years in getting a trail opened, running along the whole plateau, up to a lookout point, so that the first visitors could enjoy the matchless view. Today in Lamington there are more than 100 miles of paths, catering to all levels, including trails for the blind, and rope suspension bridges to admire the canopy of the forest from above.

Lamington's present-day landscape is the result of two large, ancient volcanoes which have now vanished, the Focal Peak Volcano and the Tweed Shield Volcano. 6,560 feet high around 24 million years ago, they erupted hundreds of cubic feet of lava that covered up the pre-existing lower hills of sedimentary rock, giving rise to the mountainous ranges that characterize the park today. Within its borders, the mountains reach an altitude of 3,608 feet, but a large part is occupied by a vast plateau interrupted by deep wooded valleys, gullies and caverns, and freshened by waterfalls and small lakes. In just 80 square miles, Lamington is home to an astonishing seven different types of rain, subtropical and temperate forest, with hundreds of different vegetable species.

209 top The canopy of the hot subtropical forest of Lamington National Park is so dense and rich in epiphytes that the lower strata always remain in the shade.

209 bottom A small kangaroo, known as the red-necked pademelon (Thylogale thetis), is captured by the photographer's flash while it roams the forest at night in search of food.

THE LAND
OF THE
SEVEN FORESTS

On the western side of the mountain chain, looking towards the coast, humidity is very high: precipitation here reaches 8.2 feet a year. The forest is often wrapped in fog, which, together with ferns, lianas, orchids and the carpet of moss that covers everything, gives the landscape a fairytale appearance. Several trees, such as the strangler fig and the *booyong*, a sort of Australian oak, even grow as high as 131 feet.

Between 1,640 and 4,920 feet in altitude, where there are frequent snowfalls, grows a tree common throughout eastern Queensland, the small Antarctic beech. Never reaching more than thirty-three feet and found in small dense woods, it turns a beautiful shade of red during the southern spring, the period in which the leaves begin to change color. The western side of the McPherson chain, on the other hand, is in rain-shadow and it is primarily eucalyptuses that grow there, trees that need a lot of light and could not survive in the foggy forest.

Other dwellers of the misty forests of Lamington are the delightful *pademelons*, smaller relatives of the large red kangaroo and, in lesser numbers, gray kangaroos, which make their appearance at the hour of sunset. The Yugambeh, the Aboriginal tribe that has lived in Lamington for thousands of years, traditionally used to tame dingoes, wild Australian dogs, to help them hunt these sought-after marsupials.

Unlike the mammals, which are for the most part nocturnal and therefore difficult to see, the birds play the lord and master during the day. In Lamington, in the thick of the forest, you may be able to watch the industrious male *satin bower bird*, relative of the birds of paradise, as he constantly embellishes his small bower with flowers, feathers and stones—preferably blue in color—all gifts that will be offered to the female, who will be attracted by the most beautiful little bower.

In the Green Mountains district you may be pleasantly assailed by hordes of parrots, large and small, landing on your head and on your shoulders. Among these, is the amazing *rainbow lorikeet*, one of the most colorful birds imaginable; its head is violet, its neck yellow and its back green, while its chest is orange and abdomen blue. Its eating habits are also unusual; it is fond of feeding off nectar, which it sucks from the corollas of flowers with the tip of its tongue, thus acting as a pollinating agent as well.

It is also in the Green Mountains that the historic O'Reilly Guesthouse is located, named after the first brave pioneers of those mountains, who in 1912 built the first primitive lodging. In those days the only way of reaching the small settlement was by a rough track 9.3 miless long, which was only passable on foot. It was in 1914 that the O'Reillys began to receive their first visits from friends and mountain enthusiasts, and their hospitality soon became legendary. In 1920 the first proper inn was completed. Today, the celebrated O'Reilly Guesthouse is the most sought-after place to stay for anyone wishing to spend a few days in this splendid park. (C.P.)

210-211 *A flutter of wings and one of the most common parrots in the park appears; in the plumage of the crimson rosella (Platycerus elegans) the crimson is teamed with an incredible cobalt blue.*

211 bottom *A splendid close-up of a male king parrot (Alisterus scapularis). This species shows a high sexual dimorphism; the female has such different colors she seems to be another type of bird.*

212-213 *Among the bushes of spinifex, a solitary eucalyptus* (Eucalyptus leucophloia) *emerges from the red earth of the plateau; in the background are the soft contours of the Hamersley chain, at the back of which is the Karijini National Park.*

212 bottom *An extraordinary display of violet-colored mulla mulla flowers* (Ptilotus exaltatus), *at the beginning of the southern spring, cheers the landscape of the park, which is normally more severe.*

213 top *A specimen of* Macropus agilis, *or agile kangaroo, covering an open space with its rapid bounding gait, a characteristic of many Australian marsupials with proportionally longer back feet.*

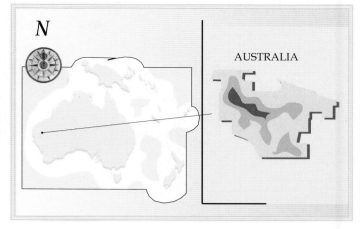

213 bottom A female agile kangaroo
(Macropus agilis) with her joey,
which has come out of the pouch to
stretch its legs. This species is easily
recognizable on account of the white
stripes on its cheeks.

KARIJINI
NATIONAL PARK

A wild world of gorges and canyons, crevasses and ledges, waterfalls and lakes, the rugged Hamersley Mountain chain is one of the biggest attractions in Pilbara, the region of western Australia formed by rocks of the venerable age of two and a half billion years. These fossil-bearing rocks, rich in iron and silicon, now form mountainous spurs and a vast plateau which is about 3,280 feet high, but were once a seabed. The rivers dug the very deep crevices that now constitute the extraordinary gorges, red because of their wealth of iron oxides and characteristic of the present-day landscape of the area. The highest mountains in the Hamersley chain are Mount Meharry, the highest peak in western Australia, which stands out on the plateau at an altitude of 4,100 feet; and Mount Bruce, just a little lower. The destination of excursions allow visitors to enjoy a fine view of the whole plateau.

Discovered by western explorers in 1861, the area is today a national park extending over 2,500 square miles. Its name is *Karijini*, the name given to it by the *Banyjima* Aborigines, who have lived there for more than 20,000 years. They have learned to co-exist with the extreme natural environment and with long periods of drought, since rainfall is very low and concentrated in the southern summer, when temperatures often reach 104°F. At the beginning of spring the park, even in the rocky precipices, is covered with a mantle of yellow, blue and crimson wild flowers, which add new color to the variegated shades of the layers of rock; this is the best period to visit it.

In the southeastern corner of the reserve a modern visitors' center, run entirely by Aborigines, provides a warm welcome and excellent information on how best to spend one's time within the park. One reason Karijini is one of the most popular parks is that its spectacular scenery is accessible to everyone; you can park your car just a few steps away from a lookout point, to admire the entire length of a canyon, with waterfalls that form pools of emerald green water at their foot. It is believed that Oxers Lookout is a place where you can enjoy one of the most beautiful views in Australia. This is also the meeting point of the four gorges of Karijini: Weano Gorge, Red Gorge, Hancock Gorge and Joffre Gorge.

The Joffre Gorge has a formidable curved wall that looks like an immense amphitheatre, easily visible from the Joffre Lookout, and it is particularly spectacular after heavy rain, when a great waterfall makes 328 foot drop. However, the truly unforgettable experiences in Karijini are linked to the

exploration of the depths of its famous gorges. Some of these excursions can be very dangerous and it is therefore necessary to be in good physical shape and avail oneself of the help of expert guides. By taking a very steep path it is possible to reach quickly the bottom of the picturesque Weano Gorge, in which an inviting lake appears, surrounded by eucalyptus trees. The narrow and craggy Hancock Gorge is the most amazing; descending into it seems almost like a journey to the center of the Earth. After a stretch that is equipt with a metal stairway, the descent continues and becomes increasingly daring when, in order to proceed, it is necessary to cling tightly onto the cornices of rock that jut from the wall with mother of pearl reflections. At the bottom of the ravine comes the reward: a crystal-clear pool of water reflecting the whole precipice. But the gorges are not the only marvel in the park. The surface of the plateau also offers many interesting opportunities for nature enthusiasts. All around, the sinuous outlines of eucalyptus trees, the symbol of the park, emerge from the low scrub, which consists of acacias and cassia plants. After rainstorms the dozens of different species of *mulla mulla*, graminaceous bushes typical of the Pilbara region, put out multicolored flowers. Another essential feature of the landscape are the giant termites' nests, silent monuments to the engineering skills of these archaic social insects.

Great curiosity is aroused by the mounds of small round pebbles that rise between the prickly round pads of grassland spinifex; these indicate the presence of the very rare *western pebble mound mouse*. This minuscule marsupial lives only in the Pilbara and its behavior is quite extraordinary. With an average weight of around 35 ounces, it tirelessly transports dozens of

214 A pair of budgerigars (Melopsittacus undulates) flirting on a branch; these delightful little parrots, known throughout the world as household pets, are very common all over Australia.

215 top right The confluence of two of the deepest gorges in the region of Pilbara, the Hancock Gorge and the Red Gorge, offers a view that should not be missed during a visit to the park.

215 center left A steep wall of Mount Bruce, where the eucalyptuses are the only trees in a world of small bushes and spinifex. The rocky stratification is evident in the places where the vegetation has not taken root.

215 bottom right A spectacular view of the Dales Gorge, where the erosive action of the river, flowing on the gorge bed, can easily be seen. Even in the craggiest places the walls are covered with vegetation.

pebbles that weigh half as much as it does, and places them on the pile with its front paws until it has built a lair, intersected by tunnels. Many generations can contribute to building one of these piles; their circular base can even measure as much as two and a half feet.

Aside from the natural beauties, however, Karijini brings with it evidence of a tragic experience as well. At the northernmost tip of the park is the ghost town of Wittenoom, inhabited in the 1950s by nearly two thousand people who worked in the asbestos mines, located in the thickness of the rocks of the Wittenoom Gorge. Contact with this deadly mineral decimated the residents and other workers in the course of just a few years. Today the Australian government has reclaimed the entire area and there is nothing to be feared from visiting this historic part of Karijini, which is still one of the most interesting national parks in Western Australia. (C.P.)

MOUNT COOK
NATIONAL PARK

New Zealand is famous for its national parks. The most spectacular is Mount Cook, located in the heart of South Island. This formidable peak, part of the Southern Alps chain, towers far above the others. The formation of these mountains is an adventure that began about two million years ago, when a trial of strength started between two powerful rivals, the Pacific and Indo-Australian plates. The result was a rapid generation of one of the world's most sensational alpine chains, which characterize New Zealand's South Island.

The Maori have another version of this story, however. In their language Mount Cook is called Aoraki, which means "one who breaks through the clouds." The legend tells of the canoe Araiteuru that was wrecked on the eastern shores of South Island, in a place called Matakea, where today the remains can still be seen of the Moeraki rocks. A group of survivors ventured onto the island; Aoraki was a child, carried on the shoulders of the chief, his grandfather. The first light of dawn turned the castaways to stone and Aoraki, who was the tallest of them, became Mount Cook.

The name Cook was given by Captain Stokes, of the scout ship Acheron, in about 1850, in honor of the explorer James

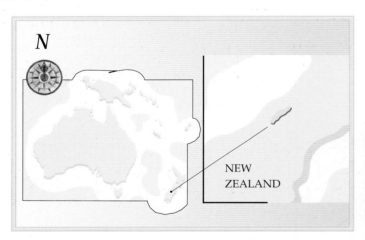

Cook. In 1885-87, the nucleus of the park became a reserve, but it was not until 1953 that the national park was founded, and in 1987, together with Westland Park National, it became part of World Nature Heritage.

New Zealand has twenty-seven mountains that are over 10,000 feet in height, and twenty-two are to be found in this park. Mount Cook is the tallest at 12,345 feet, not just in New Zealand, but in all Oceania. This height was defined in 1881 by G.J. Roberts and remained such until December 1991, when a gigantic avalanche of 32,800,000 cubic feet of snow detached from the eastern summit, reducing it to its current 12,313 feet.

In the history of mountaineering, Mount Cook plays a prominent role; the first attempt to scale the peak was undertaken by the Irishman, Reverend W. S. Green, who set off with two Swiss guides. They got just 656 feet from the top but did not complete the ascent. The record must therefore be credited to three New Zealanders: Tom Fyfe, Jack Clarke and

George Graham, who got to the top on Christmas Day, 1894. Many other famous mountaineers, including Sir Edmund Hillary, his son Peter and Graeme Dingle have used this unique towering mountain as a training ground. It is always a difficult and dangerous enterprise; more than 140 climbers have died on these slopes.

Mount Cook is this national park's major attraction but certainly not the only one. There are 270 square miles, a third of which is covered by perennial snow and glaciers. Twenty-two peaks over 10,000 feet spiral skywards in this park, including Mount Tasman, which is second in height at 11,470 feet. There are fantastic views of Mount Cook and the other mountains in the park to be enjoyed from the legendary Hotel Hermitage, New Zealand's most famous hotel and certainly that with the best panorama. The building that stands today is the third, built after the fire that destroyed its predecessor in 1957, which in turn replaced the first construction, dated 1884, which was swept away by a flood in 1913; at that time the hotel could be reached only by several day's walk from Christchurch.

In the context of the park all the glaciers play an important role, but there are five that are worthy of note and certainly the most extraordinary is Tasman. Two miles wide by seventeen in length it is one of the widest glaciers in the world that is not found in polar regions. If in the higher area, Tasman glacier is a splendid, impressive, white expanse, whereas from below it can be frighteningly dour. The glaciers of New Zealand, as in the rest of the world, are in a withdrawal phase, but the

217 bottom left *On a splendid winter's day the peak of Mount Cook, "the mountain that pierces the clouds," belies its name, soaring against a clear sky.*

217 bottom right *The wide valley dug out by the Tasman glacier in the Mount Cook National Park is crossed in its final part by the Tasman River, whose meandering course is easily visible in this aerial photo.*

216 bottom *Throughout the Southern Alps there are very sizeable populations of thars (Hemitragus jemlhaicus), bovids originating from the Himalayan regions and introduced some time ago to New Zealand, where they have adapted splendidly.*

216-217 *The grandeur of the glaciers of the Southern Alps in New Zealand can only be fully appreciated by flying over them. In the background the peak of Mount Cook is recognizable, while in the foreground there are other glaciers of the Westland National Park.*

Tasman is unique—its final miles are almost flat so that recently it has contracted vertically rather than horizontally.

During the melting process, boulders, stones and pebbles stop on the slopes and on the bottom of the excavated valley and are not pushed forward as the ice around them melts. Thus in the ablation zone the glacier is filled with detritus that slows down the melting of the ice and renders the environment gloomy and desolate. The never-ending noise of loosened stones that rattle downhill contributes to the landscape's overall sense of uncertainty. Despite the thawing that is currently in progress, in some points the ice is still over 1,968 feet thick.

Given its mid-high altitude, Mount Cook National Park has particularly severe winters, but offers visitors a milder climate in the spring, although this may often be late in arriving. During austral summer, between December and January, temperatures at lower altitudes can reach 86°F. Although humidity is less intense than on the western slope of the continental watershed, it is still high. Precipitation is extensive—rain at lower levels and almost exclusively snow on the peaks.

In this remote and apparently hostile habitat, some life forms of flora and fauna do flourish. When spring arrives the escarpments, precipices and mountain slopes are covered by tufts of grass, scattered with thousands of flowers, mainly daisies and buttercups. Of these latter, one endemic specimen is worthy of note—the candid Mount Cook Lily (*Ranunculus lyallii*), which is the world's biggest buttercup and flourishes throughout this region. The expanses of grass are scattered with bushes and small forests of southern silver beech, a dwarf tree that prospers in this regional climate. Carpets of moss and lichen that cover every surface are unequivocal proof of the humidity here. The park is the home to no less than forty different kinds of birds, which have adapted to life here. The only permanent high quota resident, however, is the tiny rock wren, which manages to survive severe winters in the higher rocky basins.

Hawks and black-backed gulls streak through the air at great heights. Next to the park, black storks are returning to nest on the tormented Tasman River bed. This territory's most typical and interesting bird is, however, a member of the parrot family, called the *kea*. Usually these birds are associated with tropical areas, but here we there is an exception; the kea is a parrot that loves high mountains, hence cold, wind, and ice. The kea has a playful nature and is extremely sociable— even a snowstorm can be a moment of fun and games. This parrot does not have the highly-colored plumage of its forest

cousins, but is more of a grayish-green color, so it is well camouflaged by the stony slopes. The wing interior is reddish, however, and makes it easy to recognize during its flight. It has a very powerful flight and can hover in the sky against the strong icy mountain winds, its hoarse cry echoing "ke-to," hence its name. This call is so characteristic that New Zealand's Southern Alps would not be the same if it were not heard to float regularly through the valleys. Unfortunately, in the past the kea enjoyed a poor reputation—blamed with killing sheep for many years, it was hunted and poisoned. In reality, it would seem more likely that the kea approached animals that were already dead and tore shreds of meat from the carcasses with its sharp beak, probably to integrate with protein its almost exclusively vegetarian diet. It is a curious and confident bird, and many researchers have paid the price for encountering flocks of these parrots by having their equipment, tents and sleeping bags systematically and minutely demolished.

Another animal, present in great numbers in the park and therefore easy to spot, is the mountain goat or *thar*, of Himalayan origin, which was introduced to this area some time ago and has adapted very well. The thar is a talented rock-climber and manages impressively on this soft and crumbly terrain. Its park companions are the red deer, which prefers lower altitudes, and a type of chamois that shares the steeper slopes with the thar. On South Island and all over New Zealand (before the arrival of humans), there were no indigenous mammals except several species of bats, so the mammals we now encounter in the park are not natives, unlike the birds and invertebrates.

One way to appreciate the national park's geological beauty is from the air—in a plane or a helicopter. It is a breathtaking experience that will not, however, offer any direct contact with the inhabitants. For this, the visitor must opt for one of the many guided excursions—on horseback or at higher altitudes by cross-country skiing—perhaps the best ways to enjoy the fascinating nature of these antipodean Alps. (C.P.)

THE MOUNTAIN THAT HOLES THE CLOUDS

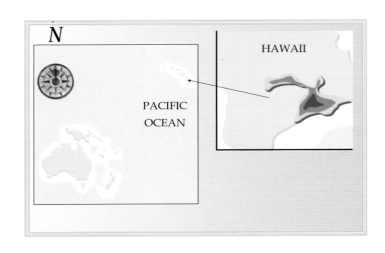

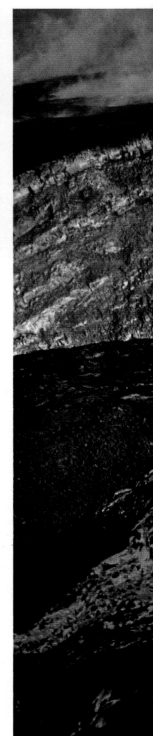

HAWAII VOLCANOES NATIONAL PARK

Aloha! Welcome to the Hawaii Volcanoes National Park. According to legend of *Pele*, the fascinating Hawaiian goddess of fire lives here, characterized by her very long hair, black as lava. Pele's first home was *Niihau*, one of the smaller islands in the western area of the archipelago; she was driven away from there by her sister, the goddess of the sea, who then followed her from island to island destroying her every refuge. Finally, Pele landed on Big Island, the largest and youngest island in the archipelago, and went to settle in the crater of the volcano Kilauea, of which she is still the mistress.

The Volcanoes National Park was set up in 1916, thus becoming the twelfth national park in the United States. It was basically created to enhance the unique volcanic phenomena present in this region, but also its flora, its fauna and the fashinating history of the ancient Hawaiian people.

When you visit the park, you will notice the extreme variety of the scenery; in fact it sweeps from the tropical beaches of the coast up to the summit of Mauna Loa. With a subarctic climate; it is home to entire areas of rainforest, rich in arboreal ferns and slashed with great black scars, the residue of lava flows, on which a new pioneering flora timidly grows. The fascination of this place is, however, linked to the presence of its volcanoes.

Wherever you look you can see cones of ash, hills of pumice, smoking rocks, solidified rivers of lava of the *ha-ha* type, with a very uneven surface or *pahoehoe*, of the stringed kind. It is possible to walk on the bottom of the crater of the Kilauea volcano and down long paths with dramatic names such as *Devastation Trail*, where the gray skeletons of *ohia*, the island's most typical tree, are silhouetted against the black backdrop. It is also possible to admire, at the hour of sundown, the unforgettable effect of the meeting of a white-hot torrent and the cold waters of the Pacific.

All of these are highly atmospheric experiences, which seem to take us back in time, when nature was the absolute ruler of the world. The volcanoes themselves are a celebration of the origins of the Earth, the proof that its primordial forces are still at work. Indeed, what makes this park special is the concrete possibility of

witnessing a volcanic eruption, some more spectacular than others but thrilling nevertheless. The Hawaii Volcanoes National Park is one of the very few places in the world where one can observe this extraordinary natural phenomenon up close and with minimal risk. In fact, unlike the continental volcanoes of explosive type, the more fluid and less gassy eruptions of the Hawaii volcanoes, which are typically "shield-like," are almost never violent. They produce incredible fountains, up to 1,640 feet high, and rapid rivers of lava, which end by fixing new strata to the already existing black rock, thus conferring on the landscape a strange alien aspect.

The volcanoes are prodigious "constructors"; the whole Hawaiian archipelago, a true chain of summits of undersea volcanoes, 1,488 miles long, is proof of this. Yet, while the western islands have shown no volcanic activity for some time and are undergoing erosion, Big Island, or *Hawaii*, the

easternmost and youngest of the islands, is continuing to enlarge and its countryside is in constant evolution. Roads have been permanently blocked, entire villages have vanished under thousands of feet of cubed lava and the outline of the coast is eternally changing.

Kilauea and Mauna Loa, the giants of Big Island and two of the most active volcanoes in the world, are situated right inside the national park. Kilauea is about 100,000 years old and geologically it is almost a baby; Mauna Loa, the other big shield-like volcano that rises west of Kilauea, is much older, maybe millions of years old. Mauna Loa is the highest mountain in the world, if measured from the base, which lies on the bottom of the

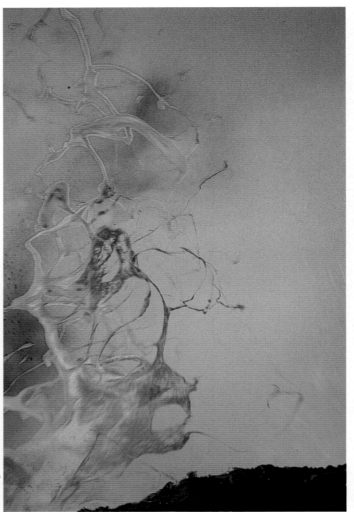

ocean, from which it rises for almost 29,520 feet before emerging more than 16,400 feet from the surface. Yet, comfortably seated in your car, you can reach the top of one of these giants, and it is hard to believe that you are on a volcano.

Instead of the classic summit with a pointed cone, the summit of these volcanoes is a plateau, which slopes down at the sides — giving the whole mountain the appearance of a warrior's shield — and surrounds an enormous depression with steep walls called the *caldera*. The Kilauea caldera, which has a diameter of around 2.5 miles, with many paths that can be traveled on by foot, is the product of a series of sudden depressions in the summit of the mountain, followed by centuries of new refilling. Each time that a submarine eruption takes place, it removes an enormous volume of rock fused to the underneath of the summit of Kilauea, which tends to collapse under its own weight.

In 1790, the last explosive eruption occurred, which killed a group of unlucky Hawaiian soldiers who were supposed to be fighting the native chief Kamehameha. For the inhabitants of the island this was a clear demonstration that the goddess Pele had taken sides with Kamehameha the Great, who became the absolute chief of Big Island and, in the years following, managed to reunite all the other islands as well. The soldiers were suffocated by a rare cloud of poisonous gas; the shower of ashes and boiling mud solidified around them, leaving a permanent cast of their imprints, which can still be seen today. However, the volcanoes are not the only attraction in this park.

The Hawaiian islands, situated right in the middle of the Pacific Ocean, are by far the most isolated place on the planet.

222 left A thick cloud of smoke and a deafening roar accompany the spectacular burst of flame produced at the moment the lava reaches the ocean.

222 right Fragments of molten rock are projected to a considerable height following the "clash" between water and fire, the Pacific Ocean and the Kilauea volcano.

222-223 Cascades of lava come out of the numerous apertures along the sides of Kilauea, thus providing an outlet for the volcano's eruptive fury.

223 bottom Towards the end of its course, the river of cooling lava becomes so thick that it slows down and begins to solidify in the shape of pahoehoe, or "corded lava."

Located about 3,100 miles from the continental masses, this has posed a real challenge for the settlement of forms of life. In the millions of years that have seen the gradual emergence of the bare volcanic summits from the ocean surface, hundreds of species of plants and animals, fortuitously crossing the Pacific Ocean, have somehow reached them. Only some, however, have been able to colonize and their descendents have given rise to almost 9,000 animal and vegetable species, with characteristics that are unique in that they represent a real reservoir of biodiversity and a laboratory for evolution experts.

Unfortunately Hawaii, once celebrated as the "evolution islands" no less risks becoming renowned as the "extinction islands." In fact, more than 25% of all endangered species in the United States are Hawaiian and, of the 2,400 native species that remain, half are at risk.

The introduction of extraneous species by man has forever changed the conditions that had permitted the original biodiversity. Hawaii Volcanoes National Park is, however, now a refuge for native plants and animals, or rather for what remains of the immense variety that has been lost forever, and exists as an important area for the reintroduction of several species that are seriously threatened. Within the park, for example, the population of wild boars and mongooses, some of the most

224 left With a black sky as background, a great bubble of lava explodes on contact with the cold water, giving rise to a sort of fireworks display.

224 right As though in an enormous and noisy smithy, masses of white-hot lapilli are flung to a considerable height by the power of the volcano.

224-225 Only an aerial view can give an idea of the grandeur of this peaceful eruption of the Kilauea volcano, made even more suggestive by the nighttime hour, when the colors of the lava are particularly vivid.

225 bottom A fountain of lava at least 1,640 feet high, originating from the untiring Kilauea, lights up the Hawaiian night with its warm colors.

harmful mammals introduced by westerners, is kept under strict control, to prevent the forests of *hapu'u*, the Hawaiian arboreal fern, from being damaged, and with it the habitat of a vast number of birds and invertebrates.

The bird that is the emblem of the state of Hawaii, the Hawaiian goose or *nene*, has also escaped extinction as a consequence of the specific protection programs set up here, although it remains on the list of species in danger. In certain areas it is nature itself that has provided an insurmountable barrier for extraneous species: *Kipuka Puaulu* is a sanctuary for Hawaiian plants and animals, an oasis of around 247 acres of native forest, supposedly saved by Pele 400 years ago and surrounded by a sea of lava rock.

The tallest tree in this wood is the *koa*, on whose humid trunk grow ferns and amidst whose branches nest three species of small birds with a curved beak, whose names in the Hawaiian language sound like: *amakihi*, *apapane* and *iiwi*. It is the hope of nature-lovers that they will be able to continue to see these creatures and to use such musical words to define them: it would mean that the will to conserve one of the last tropical paradises is still alive, enclosed within the confines of none other than Volcanoes National Park. (C.P.)

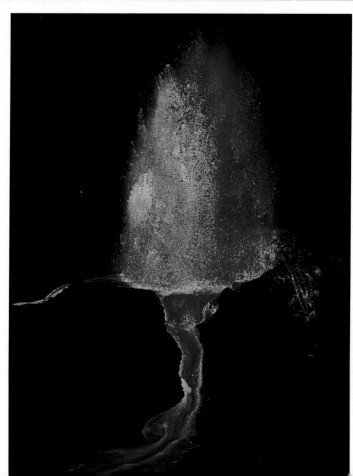

NORTH AMERICA
INTRODUCTION

Two oceans, the Atlantic and Pacific, separate this territory from the rest of the world, and only a thin strip of land unites it with South America: North America, which includes Canada, the United States and Mexico, is truly a world within itself.

An incredible diversity of climates and natural environments make this continent extremely varied both biologically and culturally. At its northern limits, above the 70° parallel, a labyrinth of inhospitable frozen islands surrounds the Great North. Tundra dominates, populated by caribou and musk bulls and is the typical landscape of Northern Alaska and the Canadian territories, which stretch from Baffin Bay to Hudson Bay and the Beaufort Sea. Here, the sun remains below the horizon for five months a year. Further to the south, immense northern pine forests, a source of precious timber, can be found: this is the undisputed kingdom of bears, wolves, elks, deer and beavers.

In lower latitudes, forests of broad-leaved trees dominate the landscape, with maple and oak in abundance. East of the first spurs of the Rocky Mountains, lie the endless prairies, home to bisons. The southeastern regions of the United States are bathed with the tropical influence of warm and humid winds that

226 left At the Olympic National Park, near Seattle, there is an immaculate blanket of enormous glaciers, a further example of the variety of the landscapes in North America.

226-227 Banff National Park, in Canada, has a wealth of water sources: from thermal ones to icy ones originating from glaciers, to tumultuous torrents and waterfalls and placid lakes such as Moraine.

227 top left This male elk is in the midst of the mating season and the enormous antlers he flaunts will make him irresistible to females.

227 top right An aerial view of the Glacier National Park communicates the main impression that the visitor to North America receives:

everything here is large and majestic and our gaze sweeps over immense horizons, giving us the true measure of our humanity.

227 bottom On the high mountains of the north it is the glacier that shapes the terrain, as in this photo of the Glacier National Park.

ascend from the Gulf of Mexico. On the Pacific coast, California is an oasis with its Mediterranean like climate but if you go a little further to the east, out of reach of the humidifying ocean winds, the subtropical region becomes desert, dotted with bizarre shaped cactus: this desert continues southwards into the heart of Mexico.

The internal waterways of the North American continent are of notable importance: more than 250,000 small and large lakes have been counted in Canada alone. On the border between Canada and the United States lies the Great Lakes system, the largest in the world. Five enormous basins (Superior, Michigan, Huron, Erie and Ontario) are connected to each other by the St. Lawrence River and a multitude of partly man-made canals. In the United States, in the foothills of the Rocky Mountains, on a plateau situated at a

228 bottom right An aerial view of Death Valley National Park in California. Despite its lugubrious name and torrid climate, this park attracts hundreds of thousands of tourists each year.

229 The puma (Felis concolor), also known as the "cougar" or "mountain lion," has the largest geographical distribution of any American feline. Highly adaptable, it can live in deserts, high in the mountains or in marshy regions.

230-231 In Alaska, a grizzly bear (Ursus arctos) seizes a salmon that is swimming back up the waters of the river. To exploit this abundance, the bears often come a long way.

228-229 In the Sonora desert lies the Saguaro National Park, with the largest concentration of giant cacti (up to 60 ft. in height), known in fact as "saguaro" (Carnegiea gigantea), which from above look like an army of men.

228 bottom left Scattered specimens of Organ Pipe Cactus (Stenocereus thurberi). In the foreground is a group of Teddy Bear Cholla (Opuntia bigelovii), another particularly thorny type of cactus.

height of 4,215 feet, can be found the Great Salt Lake, which has 10% salinity. Across the central plains, several large rivers form an extensive navigable system of waterways. The Mississippi is, after the Nile, the longest river in the world. It has its source on the eastern side of the Rocky Mountains and becomes navigable when it joins the Missouri River, before finally flowing into the Gulf of Mexico through a delta system that is still considered to be in pristine condition and an important wetland nature reserve. Meanwhile, in the west, rivers run their courses through dry ground and have assumed the role of 'canyon builders,' modelling the landscape in an unmistakeable fashion.

The North American continent has on average, a relatively low population and its mosaic of uncontaminated, natural

Services to "conserve the landscape, natural and historic elements, the present day flora and fauna and to maintain them all for the enjoyment of future generations."

Today, the United States National Park System is an extremely efficient organization—probably the best in the world—and handles with ease the ever increasing demands of national and international tourism. It is not only an excellent protective organization, they also go to great pains in the visitors center of each park to explain to the public how best to enjoy the parks without spoiling the often delicate environment, and offer guidance for each kind of visitor, from lazy to adventurous. UNESCO has declared many National Parks in North America "World Heritage Sites." One example is the International Peace

environments is made even more precious by the immense amount of land that it covers in comparison with inhabited areas. This great wealth of varied and sometimes unique landscapes, such as the Grand Canyon or the Sequoie National Park, the mountains of Alaska or the volcanoes of Hawaii, have for a long time made the North American authorities especially sensitive to the need for environmental protection, and it has become one of their oldest traditions: the first National Park to be established in the world was at Yellowstone, in the State of Wyoming in 1872. In 1916, the United States Congress officially declared the fundamental aims of establishing protected areas within their own territory and gave a full mandate to the National Parks

Park, Waterton Glacier. It was the first protected area in the world that spanned national borders, when in 1932, the Waterton National Park in Alberta (Canada) was united to the National Glacier Park in Montana. Some National Parks have, in addition to their environmental value, historical and cultural importance as well. A perfect example of this is La Mesa Verde, which in Spanish means the green table, a plateau covered with dense forest, found at the borders of Colorado and New Mexico. It is a canyon that conceals within its ravines the ancient homes of the Anasazi tribe divides it, and provides some of the most important evidence of human presence on this continent, which was one of the last to be populated by man. (C.P.)

INTRODUCTION

DENALI
NATIONAL PARK

Denali National Park is home to the impressive Mount McKinley, whose 20,316 feet make it the highest peak in North America. It reigns in silent isolation on a territory of extreme contrasts, more than half-covered by a blanket of perennial ice about 35 feet thick. Not many places in the world make the visitor feel so small and fragile, faced with nature's majesty and the precariousness of survival in this hostile habitat.

At the same time, however, the measure of infinity can sing in a crystalline sky that covers vast and boundless plains, with cloud-capped peaks that make it easy to imagine a divine presence. This is the heart of Alaska, in a mountainous territory that originated 65 million years ago from the collision of two

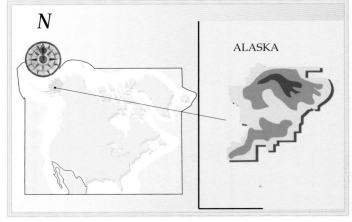

tectonic plates corresponding to the Denali Fault, which is North America's most impressive crust fracture. It extends for over 1,240 miles, from the Yukon border westwards on to the Aleutian peninsula. From a geological standpoint the zone is still very lively: active volcanoes exist, earthquakes of moderate intensity are frequent in the Park, and the Alaskan Mountain Range, of which McKinley is a part, continues slowly to grow in height.

The park also owes its contrasting beauty to the Denali Fault: multicolored peaks and steep granite spires, vast lowlands and

impressive highlands (there are many besides Mount McKinley that exceed 13,000 feet), forced to face the continuous erosion caused by immense, eternal glaciers that descend the slopes of the Alaskan Mountain Range and severe temperatures that prevent melting. Numerous rivers that flow in the valley bottom are born from these glaciers, where the climate is milder and the tundra typical of higher slopes gives way to evergreen boreal forest— called by its Russian name of *taiga*—composed of many firs but also larches, birches, alders and poplars.

In reality, the rivers are so young and rich in suspended deposits (called rock flour) that they flow in their ample valleys, tracing courses that change from day to day and renewing a landscape that would otherwise seem unchanging. Strong contrasts also characterize the park's inhabitants; it is ironic to notice how some of the planet's biggest animals, such as the stately moose, can survive in this region thanks to extremely small plants. Tundra flora, in fact, comprises mainly miniscule dwarf plants, able to withstand harsh winter cold as no others can. During the frequent storms, winds can reach speeds of 150 miles/hours, with tundra terrain permanently frozen through and summer thaw affecting just a few inches of the surface.

This limited resource still permits the growth of small but tenacious plants, true pioneers in this wild territory. It is not by chance that Alaska has chosen as its state symbol the shy forget-me-not, that brings about the park's most striking transformation from endless winter snow to the kaleidoscope of colors offered by the brief Arctic summer, when the night lasts no more than four or five hours.

Visitors are often is astounded by the simple beauty of the tufts of white cotton-grass, blades of sharpest sedge and cushions of bright tiny flowers that attract the few insects that live in this hostile climate; but this should not distract us from consideration of their immense ecological importance. The line-up of mosses, lichens, mushrooms, trailing and flowering plants capable of completing their life cycle in just a few months, supports a food

232-233 *The massif of Mount McKinley in a rare picture. Usually the mountain is hidden by a thick blanket of clouds.*

233 bottom left *An immense glacier, from which only the highest peaks manage to emerge, reminds us of the world in the far-*off ice age, and makes us realize how precarious life is in this hostile environment.*

233 bottom right *A large flock of Dall sheep is ready to face the rigors of winter, when just a few lichens and mosses will provide them with their main source of food.*

232 top left *A male caribou in the prime of life prepares for the mating season, in which it will engage in combat for the conquest of a harem of females. The antlers which it is so proud of will fall off before the winter.*

232 bottom left *Shy and elusive, a beaver is taken by surprise by the camera while busy munching on a willow branch. The dams built by these skillful engineers create valuable microhabitats for many other species.*

chain that culminates with the great tundra and taiga mammals such as Dall's sheep, caribou, moose, grizzly bears and wolves.

The park is home to thirty-seven mammal species (among the "small" there is the charming, versatile lemming) and 156 species of birds, both permanent and migratory, all perfectly adapted to survival in such a selective habitat. The decision to found the park, however, is attributable to the large species. In fact, a natural reserve instituted in such a remote region was

determined mainly by the desire to protect the subartic populations of great mammals from the threat posed by intensive hunting and progressive degradation brought by human colonization.

The "father" of Denali National Park was Charles Sheldon: hunter, naturalist and conservationist, who explored the Mount McKinley area extensively between 1906 and 1907 in order to define the boundaries for an area to be protected and repopulated with big game. When Sheldon returned east in 1908, he launched a campaign to found a national park. It wasn't until 1917, however, that his efforts were rewarded by the official opening of Mount McKinley National Park. Its first superintendent was Harry Karstens, an experienced mountain climber who had been the first to scale McKinley and was also Sheldon's guide during his explorations. Mount McKinley National Park was a great deal smaller than today's Denali park, and in fact it did not even contain the entire McKinley massif.

Sheldon had originally proposed calling the park Denali, as it means "the tall one" in the Aleutian language and was what generations of Athabaska natives had always called McKinley, long before white men discovered and explored the region. His suggestion was finally accepted in 1980 when the state of Alaska formulated important legislation for the protection of local nature and re-christened the park as Denali, extending the territory to over 11,780 square miles. Denali was declared a Biosphere Reserve in 1976, and on December 2, 1980, President Jimmy Carter signed an official decree declaring it a national park. Now Denali is administered as three separate units: the Denali Wilderness, which corresponds to the original McKinley National Park, a zone dedicated entirely to the protection of fauna and flora; Denali National Park additions, which allows traditional subsistence uses by local rural residents; and Denali National Reserve, which allows subsistence uses as well as sporting, trapping and fishing.

The area of Denali National Park remains as the Aleutians knew it thousands of years ago and is one of the last true frontier zones. In the areas annexed to the park in 1980, the local rural populations are actually allowed to undertake traditional survival activities (hunting, trapping, fishing, gathering). This is out of respect for native Athabaskan customs, a tribe that has challenged the hostile climate and impervious territory since time immemorial. They were nomadic by necessity; from spring to autumn they hunted caribou, sheep and moose on the hills of Denali's northern border, picked berries to preserve for winter and fished with nets. With the first snowfall they migrated downhill, nearer to the rivers, to an area that gave greater guarantees of survival against harsh winters.

Within the park there are also two hunting reserves, where both traditional and sport hunting and fishing areas are allowed, controlled by Alaska State laws. The presence of careful, competent Park Rangers, who also accompany tourists along the fascinating trails, ensures that the park and the animals that populate it are truly safeguarded. As with flora, fauna also have to make the most of the fine weather from late spring to autumn, and give up any activity in winter that requires high energy investments. Many permanent animals, such as the grizzly bear, devote the winter to complete rest. Reputed to be North America's most dangerous animal, the grizzly is omnivorous; in fine weather its primary nourishment is composed of vegetables, but also of insects and the occasional young caribou or moose, nor does it disdain carrion (characteristic behavior for grizzlies in Denali Park, but quite rare elsewhere). In winter, the grizzly takes shelter in its den and falls into a long, deep sleep during which it consumes its fat reserves and may lose over 200 lbs in weight. This is the season when the female gives birth to two (rarely one, three or four) defenseless pups that she nurses for four months and then spends another three to four years with thereafter. Their greatest enemies are the adult males of their own kind; in fact as long as there are cubs around, mothers will not mate again.

Among the park's herbivores we find the caribou—a unique deer (the only one of its kind in the cervid family) in which both sexes have antlers—living in herds that periodically migrate so they can make the best of the harsh climate. They abandon the mating zones south of the Alaskan Mountain Range and spend the winter on the northern plains, feeding chiefly on lichens. The Denali Park herd in particular has suffered great fluctuations in the last thirty years. Today it is easy to sight about twenty specimens that pasture calmly on the roadside, but not long ago there were thousands. These are, for the most part, natural oscillations, but they help us understand how difficult life is in this hostile territory, and therefore the importance of the protection offered by Denali National Park. (A.S.I.)

234-235 *Clearly distinguishable because of its large size and the presence of a considerable "hump" on its back, the grizzly is the undisputed master of the Denali terrain.*

235 bottom left *The Alaska Mountains clearly show the modeling action of ice.*

235 bottom right *In the Denali Park, around the Savage River, which runs in a northerly direction from the Alaskan Range, extends a dense undergrowth of shrubs.*

236-237 *The tepid sun of the extreme north rises over Mount McKinley.*

234 top left *A ptarmigan in its summer plumage while it wanders cautiously among the thin grass. It is considered a delicacy by all the predators in the park: bears, wolves, foxes and birds of prey.*

234 top right *A young male elk lowers its head, perhaps to allow us to admire its antlers, which are now still covered with velvet. By eating around 45 lbs of grass a day it will become an adult; it will then grow to in excess of 1,760 lbs in weight, and its antlers will reach up to seven feet in length.*

JASPER AND BANFF
NATIONAL PARKS

In Canada's Rocky Mountains there are four neighboring national parks: Jasper, Banff, Yoko and Kootenay. There are also three provincial parks: the Mount Robson, the Mount Assiniboine and the Humber. In total they constitute one of the world's greatest protected areas (and certainly one of the best equipped) that UNESCO has included as part of the Natural World Heritage program. Jasper is the biggest, with a surface area of almost 4,247 square miles, and it is the furthest north. Banff is the oldest, founded with only 10 square miles in 1885, with the aim of controlling the excessive exploitation of the precious sulphurous thermal springs and now extends 2,564 square miles. Its name derives from the town of Banff, a tourist

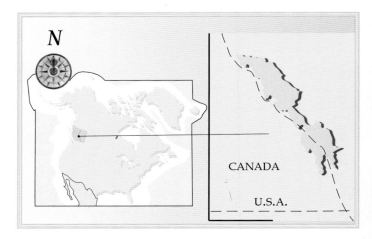

resort that is always packed with visitors. It is easy to explain this popularity; where else in the world would we come face to face with a handsome wapiti stag grazing undisturbed on the flower borders of a town center hotel? In the past, this area was famous for forest bison, smaller than the better-known plains bison, but now made extinct by hunting.

Inside the Banff National Park several specimens of bisons from Wood Buffalo National Park (Northwest territories, Canada) may be observed in a Buffalo Paddock, where they pasture and ignore the flashing cameras. Just outside the paddock a small hill hosts a large ground squirrel community; in the Canadian Rocky Mountains there are numerous species that have tunneled the area with their underground lairs. But Banff is not the park's greatest attraction; one of Canada's most famous sights is Lake Louise, whose waters are 295 feet deep and shimmer a particularly brilliant green because of the minerals brought in by the Victoria Glacier.

A detour that is only possible in the summer is Ten Peaks Valley. At the entrance words cannot describe the spellbinding landscape that greets us: the ten snow-capped Wenkchemna Peaks frame Lake Moraine and are mirrored in its waters. Visitors who walk the lakeside paths will encounter sparkling streams, flowers and multicolored mushrooms. We pause every now and again to close our eyes, breathe in the perfume of musk, ferns, pines, firs, and listen to the sounds of nature.

Banff's greatest lake is Minnewanka and those who enjoy diving should explore Minnewanka Landing, which rests on the lakebed. On the one hand, the visitor is greeted by a sense of peace and tranquillity transmitted by the expanses of water, but the impetuous torrents, rapids and waterfalls transmit the vigor and energy that is typical of the Canadian Rocky Mountains. Johnston Canyon and Mistaya ("very windy" in Stoney language) Canyon are Banff's most startling sights.

Park fauna is varied and abundant, but rather elusive; short walks through the woods betray only the tapping woodpecker

238 left Lake Moraine, one of the jewels of Banff, was created when a large mass of stone appropriately called "the tower of Babel" collapsed, causing the obstruction of the outflow of the surrounding glaciers.

238-239 The Mount Patterson massif, with its slopes covered with a thick northern forest of conifers, is reflected in Peyto Lake, whose shape clearly reveals its glacial origin.

239 bottom left In the bighorn herd the hierarchy of the males is decided by the size of their horns; their fights are totally ritualized and cause no injuries to the contenders; only their pride gets hurt.

239 bottom center The pure white and very thick fur of the snow ridge mountain goat is perfectly adapted to life high up in the mountains. This species is endemic to the Rocky Mountains, on which it shows off its climbing skills.

*239 bottom right This young Dall
sheep seems to be smiling, happy with
the spring flowers that grow beneath
its hooves, but it is always alert; a
predator might be lying in wait.*

and the call of numerous bird species. Some, such as Steller's Jay (symbol of British Columbia, with its blue and black plumage), spend much of its time near picnic areas and will go so far as to eat from a tourist's hands. In such situations the tourist is incapable of obeying the total ban on feeding wild animals. When traveling by car, large mammals may be seen, including mule deer and white-tailed deer, far more timid and fleeting than their cousin the wapiti, elk, coyote, foxes, raccoons.

The European tourist who comes to western Canada is always astounded by how immense the landscape is. Those who are used to roads in the Alps, Apennines or Pyrenees, with their

steep ascents and hairpin bends, will find it extraordinary that it is possible to reach 6,560 feet of altitude on a practically straight road the Icefields Parkway where even a camper the size of a bus can drive safely. As altitude increases, the countryside and the vegetation belts gradually change; the dense pine, common silver and Douglas fir forests give way to subalpine meadows, where vivid splashes of color are left by rhododendrons, mountain anemones, gentians, arnica and the red branches of the cornelian cherry. Past 6560 feet there are dwarf willows, heather, mosses and lichens that reach as far as the perennial glaciers.

The wide road cuts though the forest and is bordered by flourishing bushes, so it easier here than elsewhere to spot a bear (almost always black bears and rarely grizzlies) hunting tasty blueberries, black currants, raspberries or bearberries. It is not easy to predict an encounter with a bear, and tourists may pester

240 left The meanders of the Saskatchewan River cross the Jasper Park. Pioneers have challenged these lands, enchanted by the mirage of gold. Today we have come to realize that its true value lies in these unspoiled landscapes.

240-241 Tiny Spirit Island rises from the waters of Maligne Lake, in Jasper, once known as Great Beaver Lake. It is a destination for many visitors, who on a ninety-minute cruise can make the most of the geology, the history and the natural beauties of the lake.

A BOUNDLESS WORLD OF CRYSTAL-CLEAR WATERS

241 bottom left A bighorn, on the shore of Talbot Lake, looks around before taking a drink. We are at the beginning of winter, and the carnivores are particularly active. The bighorns fear the wolves, the coyotes, the eagles and the pumas, even though only the latter might be dangerous.

241 bottom right Placidly sleeping on a poplar and relying on a balance that to us might seem precarious, a black bear, or baribal, reminds us that this is "Bear Country" in which we are just guests.

the park rangers for advice on how to get a close-up, but Canadian locals buy rattles and bells in the hope of scaring them away with noise. It is vital never to leave food or scraps within paw distance, however, as between 1950 and 1980 over 500 bears were killed in Banff and Jasper parks (and just as many were captured and released elsewhere) since they had learned to eat in the houses nearby and became aggressive towards anyone who approached their sources of food.

Since this time, bear-proof waste containers have been installed and visitors are told that the cute, lazy-looking glutton could run twice as fast a person when angry, and black bears were even known to follow their victims up trees. Observation at a distance was encouraged. Now, with a pair of binoculars, it is even possible to identify candid mountain goats that scamper up bare rock peaks where their predators have trouble hunting them

242-243 *From the shores of Herbert Lake the Canadian Rocky Mountains appear in all their majesty, showing the altitudinal succession of the various bands of vegetation from the forest to the tundra.*

242 bottom *A view of Lake Louise in Banff Park highlights the very special color of the waters, resulting from the presence of mineral salts and its great depth.*

down. The highest part of the route through these parks (halfway between Banff and Jasper) skirts the Columbia Ice Field, an incredible expanse of ice that covers more than 186 miles and is more than 984 feet deep.

Further down the valley the impetuous water that plunges from the glaciers has formed marvelous waterfalls such as Sunwapta Falls and Athabasca Falls. They are not so high, but they seem to express all the vigor of these places: the water that thunders and foams in rainbow effects amidst the quartz-rich rocks permits the few who arrive this far to shut off the rest of the world for a while and draw new energy as the natives did in the past. There are numerous excursions around Jasper, the town founded in 1907 after which the park was named. The more daring can challenge the Mount Edith Cavell Peak, while the lazier can use the modern cableway that ascends to Marmot Basin.

Here the marmots are a special color: the whitish back contrasts with the black paws, and their scientific name *Marmota caligata*, means marmot with boots. Lake Maligne is the ultimate destination for those who visit Jasper; a tiny island of just a few feet, with a group of majestic pines, rises from limpid emerald waters in a lake surrounded by snow-capped peaks.

Maligne is the Canadian Rockies largest lake and the second largest in the world of glacier origin, taking its name from the effluent Maligne River, baptized by a Jesuit missionary who was trying to cross it and lost his horse and provisions, dragged away by the violent current. Those who seek greater excitement can try rafting on the hair-raising rapids, down the sinuous and magnificent Maligne Canyon. All the while, a curious puma may be looking on, well-concealed by the vegetation. (R.M.S.)

243 left *Among the caribou, uniquely among cervids, both sexes have antlers: the male has them in the mating season, while the female is equipped with this precious weapon in winter, when the scarcity of food and pregnancy make her more vulnerable.*

243 right *Lake Moraine in the setting of the Wenkchemna Peaks (the name means "ten" in the Stoney language) is a place filled with magic and peace. Be sure not to deprive yourself the pleasure of walking along its shores.*

244-245 The icy water of Firehole River, in Yellowstone National Park, is mitigated by the numerous hot springs located nearby; two eastern elks (Cervus canadensis) *take advantage of the situation to cross the river at their leisure.*

244 bottom left *An evocative photo of the Morning Glory Pool, a pool of sulfurous water situated in the Upper Basin of the Geysers. In its depths bacteria and algae manage to survive, giving the water a varying color depending on the light.*

244 bottom right *During the harsh winter, the predominant color in Yellowstone Park is white; the hot steam of the thermal springs does in fact mingle with the snowy landscape.*

245 top *The American bison (Bison bison) is the most massive mammal in all of North America, reaching a weight of almost a ton; several* thousands of them live in Yellowstone National Park.

245 bottom *In the Upper Basin of the Geysers it is possible to witness the eruption of Castle Geyser, so called because of the structure at its base, which looks like a medieval castle but is nothing more than a deposit of mineral salts.*

YELLOWSTONE
NATIONAL PARK

Colter's Hell: this is how the area of Yellowstone was defined for nearly fifty years after 1807, when John Colter (1775-1813) an American trapper-explorer, gave his legendary descriptions of the sulfurous springs and steam springs in a vast area of Wyoming, an American state that was semi-inhabited at the time. As opposed to many other places in which the white man had found the native culture well-established, no Indians had ever settled here. In all likelihood, they feared the presence of the "turbulent spirits" that made the land so lively and noisy. The natural beauties of Yellowstone were discovered little by little, and almost by chance.

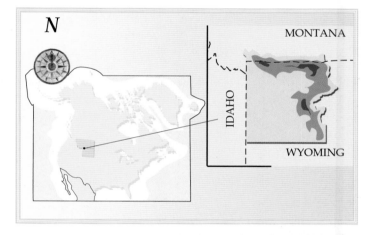

Anyone who dared to venture into those steamy lands full of unexpected dangers did so almost exclusively for two specific reasons: to hunt furs and to search for gold. In 1870, the Washburn Expedition took place, the first official and systematic exploration of the territory of Yellowstone. As they crossed a crest, the members of the expedition were amazed when they found themselves before a fountain of boiling water that, hissing, raised a white jet of steam that was 131 feet high! They waited long enough to see new eruptions and realized that they occurred frequently and at regular intervals.

They did not hesitate to call that oddity "Old Faithful," and even today it is the park's most symbolic geyser. With a wave of enthusiasm over the discovery of something truly unique, government protection was obtained for the entire region and the idea of a national park began to make inroads on a government level. Two years later, the idea became reality; on May 10, 1872, President Grant declared Yellowstone the first national park in the United States. It was also the first national park in the world; but proclaiming the protection of the area only on paper was not equivalent to putting it into effect.

For decades, the park was a land of hunting and vandalism and, in the early 1900s, it was plagued by bandits. The repeated interventions of the army were not enough to ensure the observance of ill-defined regulations. Yellowstone was not placed under the jurisdiction of the new-born National Park Service until 1917, at the same time the rangers were instructed to welcome visitors and tell them the meaning and philosophy behind a national park. The management and behavior parameters developed gradually

originated 600,000 years ago. The intense heat coming from below heats the water that circulates in the intricate subterranean drainage network. In some points, the steam bursts forth violently, like a valve on a giant pressure-cooker, accompanied at times by chains of explosions. These are the geysers—cone or fountain-shaped—the most spectacular natural phenomenon in the park. There are over three hundred in Yellowstone, two-thirds of all those found in the world. The most characteristics ones have been given a name and each of them has a unique feature: Old Faithful, which was the first to be discovered; Riverside, whose angular jet creates a curtain of spray with a

and would become an example for similar areas that were being established.

After discarding the idea of a train to link the geysers and an elevator in the canyon, the next problem faced was protecting an area that had proven to be extremely fragile, despite the violence of its manifestations. During those years, automotive tourism was becoming popular and, with great foresight, infrastructures were created to deal with this, with respect to the ecosystem of the park.

While the number of visitors to the park in 1937 amounted to 500,000, they now average three million a year. The Canyon Village, built in 1950, had to be flanked by numerous welcome areas for tourists. The main attractions at Yellowstone National Park are naturally its hydrothermal phenomena. Within its boundaries is the world's highest concentration of geysers, hot springs and fumaroles.

In no other place is there such a large area that is so close to the inner heat of the Earth. A temperature of 392°F was measured at a depth of 262 feet and it is estimated that molten rock is found just 6,560-9,840 feet below the territory of Yellowstone, which lies on an ancient volcanic caldera that

rainbow of colors on the Firehole River; Castle, with its cone that resembles a medieval castle; Echinus, whose explosive jet goes in all directions like fireworks; Steamboat, the world's largest geyser, which pulses like a massive steam engine during its rare but memorable eruptions with an incredible jet of 390 feet!

The hot springs are another of the hydrothermal phenomena that is very widespread in the park. At Mammoth, in the northern area, the landscape is truly evocative; steaming terraces of fragile white and yellow travertine are the result of the dissolution and redeposit of limestone and chalky minerals. In other areas, the hot springs create pools with amazing colors. The water of the Emerald Pool has a temperature that permits the growth of bacteria and algae; because of this, the middle of the pool is green, while the edges are yellow and orange.

Hot springs, fumaroles, basins of boiling mud and geysers, evoking hellish scenarios, contrast sharply with the surrounding environment: green pine forests and broad grassy stretches populated by an endless number of large herbivores that graze, peacefully unaware of the presence of tourists. This is paradise for bison, moose and deer, as it is for the photographers who want to record them on film. Black bears, grizzlies and coyotes are more

246 top A view of the northern area of Yellowstone National Park, where residual patches of forest are scattered over a vast area of meadows and pastures.

246 bottom A herd of small eastern elks (Cervus canadensis) with their mothers is caught by the photographer in the morning mist of the park; the males are larger and not very gregarious.

246-247 From the top of the Dunraven Pass, within Yellowstone Park, you can admire the dusk falling on the distant Absaroka mountain chain.

247 bottom left The pools of sulfurous water in Yellowstone National Park, superficial expressions of intensive underground thermal activity, are deep and well-defined.

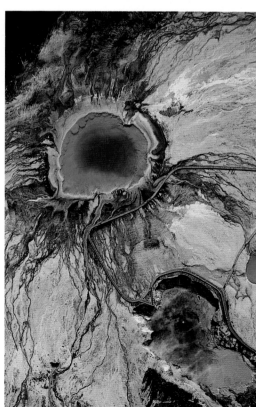

247 bottom right The cold conifer forest in Yellowstone National Park is interrupted by crystal clear water courses, which allow for the survival of diversified creatures in substantial numbers.

248 top A relaxing view of Yellowstone Park: its extraordinary and at times disturbing aspects, such as the thermal springs, the fumaroles and the geysers are in fact concentrated in other areas.

248 bottom A male eastern elk (Cervus canadensis) in a position of alarm: only the males have the typical branched horns and only in a precise period of the year, after which they are lost.

248-249 A herd of American bison (Bison bison) crosses a water course on a spring day; while they are on the move the adults surround their young for greater protection.

249 bottom left The Lower Waterfall of the Yellowstone River is the highest in the Canyon: a drop of around 295 feet, at the end of which the water creates such a cloud of spray that it is difficult to make out the river below.

249 bottom right A picture of the outlet of the Yellowstone River into the vast lake of the same name; we are here in the southeastern sector of the Park, at an altitude of 7544 feet.

difficult to sight and can be seen only early in the morning.

If you go to the southeastern end of the park, you can admire Lake Yellowstone, the largest high-altitude lake in North America. It covers 135 square miles and its water, fed by the Yellowstone River, is a sheet of ice during most of the year. Skirting the river to the north is a segment where the river has etched and continues to cut a deep canyon. The name Yellowstone comes from the color of the walls of the canyon, a dazzling ocher.

The best views of the canyon can be found at the lookouts of Artist Point and Inspiration Point: the river descends impetuously for 656 feet and two main waterfalls can be seen,

the upper and lower falls. The latter, with its deafening noise, drops 295 feet — twice the height of Niagara Falls. Everywhere you go, you encounter the true star of this park — hot and sulfurous water that boils up from the subsoil, constantly changing the appearance of the surface; steam everywhere, making the landscape so peculiar; icy crystal-clear water that runs in the fields and against the backdrop of the canyons; snow that covers the forest and prairie during the endless winters. Water in its various forms has designed the Yellowstone National Park, continuing to touch up the wonderfull portait composed by Nature. (C.P.)

251 center In this photo the snow lets you glimpse the real color of the walls of the canyon of the Yellowstone River, which, as the name suggests, are of a warm ocher yellow.

251 bottom Pelican Valley, in Yellowstone Park, on a splendid winter's day, after a heavy snowfall, which has left the air clear with exceptional visibility allowing us to admire the Shoshone range in the background.

252-253 The extraordinary steaming "steps" made of fragile travertine at the Mammoth Hot Spring is one of the biggest attractions in Yellowstone National Park.

250-251 The recent snowfall cannot conceal the activity of the hot springs, which continue to let off white steam in the Norris Basin in Yellowstone National Park.

251 top Two young mule deer (Odocoileus hemionus) look curiously at the lens; it is easier to catch them in action during the early hours of the morning or towards evening.

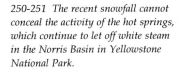

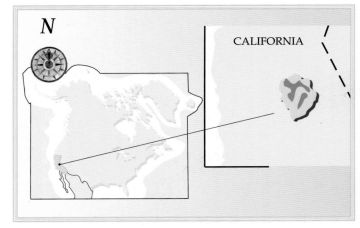

YOSEMITE
NATIONAL PARK

Since the white man discovered the Yosemite Valley in 1833, throngs of writers, artists and photographers have tried to draw a faithful and lively image of this natural wonder. However, no description can recreate the experience of a first-hand visit. And perhaps this is the reason that each year, over three million visitors come to Yosemite National Park, located in central California on the western slopes of the Sierra Nevada. As you approach from the west, a wide bend in the road elicits valley of breathtaking beauty. The desire to preserve this natural gem dates back many years: in fact, it was Yosemite Valley that, originally inspired the concept of a national park, although this role went to Yellowstone Park. Stirred by the ideas of the "environmentalists" of the era, Abraham Lincoln signed a bill of law in 1864, guaranteeing that Yosemite Valley and the forests of giant sequoias located to the south—Mariposa Grove—would be protected by the State of California. Later, the praiseworthy and constant commitment of John Muir, the American naturalist whose famous writings reflected his deep love for the nature of this territory, led to the proclamation of Yosemite as the second national park of the United States in 1890.

The "incomparable valley," as Yosemite Valley was defined, may well be the world's most classic example of a glacier valley, with a perfect "U" shape. The alpine glaciers, carved previously by the Merced River, advanced slowly into the canyon, leaving in their wake steep lateral slopes and a flat valley. This area was once occupied by Lake Yosemite, a typical weir valley formed upstream from the terminal moraine of the glacier that then disappeared after being filled with sediment. Other lakes in Yosemite Valley are following the same destiny.

The granite of the slopes was carved by the action of the ice, which left the hardest sections whole, including monoliths such as Cathedral Rocks and El Capitan. The latter, which has almost a vertical face, measures 3,591 feet from the base to the summit. For years it has been a sought-after destination and true paradise for free-climbers from all over the world; in any season, you can glimpse the outline of a climber hundreds of feet from the ground, in a sixth-degree passage on the granite wall. Along the opposite

256 top The immaculate peaks of the Sierra Nevada, which exceed an average altitude of 9,840 feet, are located in the eastern area of the Park, where a subarctic climate prevails.

256 bottom A stretch of the course of the Merced River, to whose erosive action we owe the initial excavation of the Yosemite Valley, later completed by the glaciers.

slope of the valley is another monolith, which has become a sort of symbol of the park.

It is called Half Dome due to its peculiar profile, similar to a cupola and worn down perfectly in half by the passage of the immense glacier, according to geologists. An Indian legend recounts that Half Dome is a woman from the Payute tribe by the name of Tesaiyac who was transformed into stone by angry spirits. The Indian woman's tears over her unfortunate lot carved furrows down her face, collecting in the basin of Mirror Lake at the foot of the massif. Any climber would be happy to be able to count a climb of the Half Dome among his exploits, as its north face has a gradient of 93%! However, the summit can also be reached by a steep and difficult trail of about 8 miles rising 4,920 feet in height. One of the lookout points visited most frequently in Yosemite National Park is Glacier Point, located on the edge of a vertical drop of about 3,280 feet from which, in a single sweeping glance, you can see the most evocative features of the park; namely, Yosemite Falls. Seen across the valley, with their 2,424 feet, they are the tallest in North America.

The smaller Bridalveil Falls nearby offer a unique sight particularly in autumn, when the water is no longer plentiful. The Ahwahneechee Indians baptized the falls Pohono, or spirit of the wind, because gusts of wind drive the column of water from the rock face to create gleaming spurts. Further ahead, you can see the ring of mountains of the Sierra Alta that act as a backdrop to the scenery. During the spring, the vegetation in the park becomes truly lush, and fields of flowers and forests of conifers and oaks create a unique mosaic. It is worthwhile to head toward the southernmost corner of the park, which features isolated woods of giant redwoods or sequoias (*Sequoiadendron giganteum*), an archaic tree that is now present only on the western slope of California's Sierra Nevada.

The most famous specimen in Yosemite is the Grizzly Giant, with a venerable age of 2,700 years, a height of 213 feet and a base diameter measuring 30 feet. The northern area of the park is the least visited, but it offers opportunities for interesting high-altitude excursions: Tuolumne Meadows is the largest sub-alpine field of the Sierra Nevada and is located at an altitude of 8528 feet. From here, you feel as if you can almost reach out and touch the impressive peaks of the Sierra Alta, which soar to 13,120 feet. Snaking its way over this grassy stretch is part of the famous John Muir Trail, a 198 mile path that links Yosemite Valley with Mount Whitney and pays deserved honor to the explorer who studied and loved this land the most. (C.P.)

257 bottom right Parallel chains of
mountains form veritable buttresses,
which establish the western border of
Yosemite National Park.

258-259 An atmospheric winter
view of Yosemite Valley, made
mysterious and almost disturbing by
the dark sky and the clouds that
conceal the peaks.

256-257 A recent snowfall makes it
impossible to recognize the
appearance of the Yosemite Valley
from one day to the next; the contrast
between the snow-covered rocky
domes and the cloudless winter sky is
even more marked.

257 bottom left A small herd of male
mule deer (Odocoileus hemionus)
is about to wade through a water
course. Their antlers are covered with
velvet, since they have not yet
completed their yearly growth.

NEVADA
UTAH
ARIZONA

260 A classic view of the immense Grand Canyon, in the State of Arizona; not only is the national park important in terms of its landscape, but its formations are also of remarkable geological interest.

261 top right The play of light and shade that is created in the early morning hours among the gullies in the Colorado Grand Canyon, accentuates its majesty.

261 bottom right From the photo taken from the satellite it is clear how erosive forces, over the course of time, have changed the appearance of the Kaibab Plateau, affecting it profoundly through the formation of the Grand Canyon.

GRAND CANYON
NATIONAL PARK

Rising from the slopes of the Rocky Mountains is a water source that has patiently been wearing down the ancient rocks of Arizona for the past million years; this is the Colorado River, flowing 1448 miles from its source to the Gulf of California. The Colorado River has carved out numerous canyons along its course, but its true masterpiece can be seen in the highlands of northern Arizona. This is where its sculpture into the earth's crust has reached its greatest proportions and created a natural wonder that may well be the most famous in the world. We're talking about the Grand Canyon in honor of which, Arizona is named the "Grand Canyon State."

The depth and the width of the canyon vary from one point to the next. The maximum difference in height, measured from the edge of the river below, is 6,000 feet, while its width at certain points reaches over 18 miles. The first westerners to discover the amazing effects created by the erosion worked by the Colorado River were nine pioneers in search of adventure, led by the American geologist John Wesley Powell. In four little wooden boats, they attempted to navigate the river in 1869. Within just a few years, there arose a certain amount of interest in the region because of its wealth of copper and asbestos, but the tourism industry quickly proved to bring out its true potential.

By 1901, the railroad line from the station of Williams, Arizona already reached the southern part of the canyon—the South Rim—and the hotel "El Tovar," which is still in business, was built not far from here. However, the Grand Canyon did not become a national park until 1919, three years after the National Park Service was established under President Woodrow Wilson, and Wilson's successors gradually added a number of acres to the initial territory. Grand Canyon National Park currently covers 1900 square miles and the Colorado River cuts into the boundaries of the park for a length of 276 miles, from Lees Ferry to Grand Wash Cliffs. Further recognition of the park's naturalistic value came on October 26, 1979, the day it was included in the list of sites declared a "World Heritage." A visit to Grand Canyon National Park is a must for anyone touring the United States and as a result, approximately five million visitors come here ever year.

From a geological standpoint, the importance of the Grand

262-263 Grand Canyon National
Park, Arizona, offers five million
tourists each year its splendid views,
extremely interesting excursions and
even the possibility of rafting amidst
the gullies.

263 bottom left and right The first
Europeans to see the Grand Canyon
were the Spanish soldiers in 1540.
The canyon is probably the most
spectacular example of erosion in the
world: the abyss winds for 276 miles
and in some places measures 17 miles
in width.

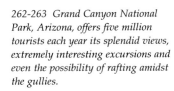

THE MASTERPIECE OF THE COLORADO RIVER

262 left One of the lookout points in
the national park from which there is
a clear view of the main agent of the
slow and inexorable erosive action:
the Colorado River, which has dug
itself, in the course of millions of
years, a more than comfortable bed.

262 right In one of the meanders of
the Grand Canyon, a small waterfall
descends along a furrow dug into the
vertical wall, a demonstration of the
tenacity of the water's erosive action.

Canyon lies in its rich sequence of rocky layers that are well
preserved and can easily be seen along its walls. These layers
document part of the oldest natural history of the continent of North
America. Its vivid colors are attributable to the large quantity of
ferrous minerals in the rocks that have been worn away over time.
The river itself is the main cause of erosion as far as the depth of
the canyon is concerned, but even the erosive action of rain and
snow cannot be underestimated.

Northern Arizona has a semiarid climate with long dry spells.
Nevertheless, the sudden and violent thunderstorms that hit the
area, particularly in late summer, have an enormous erosive power.
The canyon is destined to become wider and wider, stealing land
from the forest that blankets the plateau. The contrast between the
grayish-green surface vegetation, composed mainly of conifers,
and the colors of the canyon walls is another dramatic aspect of the
park. This can best be appreciated by traveling the road along the
South Rim and stopping at sunset at some of the less crowded
lookout points. The spectacle of the vast stretch of tormented rock
rising from the haze evokes a feeling of awe, making man feel
smaller than ever before the unfolding of these natural forces. (C.P.)

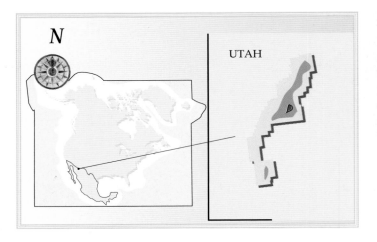

BRYCE CANYON
NATIONAL PARK

"*T*here are deep caves and ravines that look like the ruins of a prison, castles with merlons and fortified walls, churches with their bell towers and their spires, niches and recesses that offer the wildest and most amazing scenery the human eye has ever seen. It is, in fact, one of the wonders of the world.*"

This is the vivid description that the government land surveyor T.C. Bailey wrote in 1877 of the so-called "amphitheater" of Bryce Canyon. These were the years in which the canyon and the area around it aroused great curiosity and various expeditions returned with photographs and maps of the

entire area, which is located in southern Utah. This was the home of the Paiute Indian tribe. According to their legends, the stone pillars inside the amphitheater were actually men who had been condemned by the angry gods to be turned into rock forever.

The arrival of the first Europeans around 1776—mainly Spanish soldiers and missionaries—marked the end of the Paiute civilization's dominance here; the tribe now survives as a small minority on Indian reservations. The Mormon pioneers were the first white men to try to settle stably in the area. Scotsman Ebenezer Bryce, together with his wife Mary, was sent there by his church in an unsuccessful attempt to establish a farm in the Paria Valley and to create an irrigation system to raise crops in the future. The site with the strange rock formations in which the family lived was referred to by everyone as "the Bryce's canyon." When he fled that desolate area for Arizona, Ebenezer Bryce left behind a memorable definition of the canyon: "*an infernal place to lose a cow.*"

The heavy-handed intervention of the white man on this land was destined to alter forever an environment that had been untouched until then: indiscriminate deforestation and uncontrolled pasturing accelerated the disintegration of the rocky formations. It was not until 1920 that a serious conservation program began to be considered. The area was proclaimed a national monument in 1923, and the Union Pacific railroad included it in a tourist circuit that stopped at the leading attractions in the Southwest. On February 25, 1928, the protected area was doubled in size and it was declared a national park.

Today, Bryce Canyon welcomes over 1.5 million visitors from all over the world, and no one is ever disappointed by its spectacular landscape. Let's view the park from one of its

264 top right *The fascination of Bryce Canyon in winter is unparalleled. The peculiar rock formations exhibit their bright ochre color beside the sparkling snow.*

264 bottom *An overall taste of Bryce Canyon National Park, whose characteristics can just be glimpsed between the clouds covering it like balls of cotton.*

264-265 *A few rays of sun manage to penetrate the dense blanket of clouds that obscures the sky, giving emphasis to the warm colors of the walls of the canyon and to the cold whiteness of the snow.*

lookout points: in every direction, the horizon is dominated by the Markagunt, Sevier and Aquarius Plateaus, with an average altitude of 8,200 feet. To the east, this stillness is broken up by the "Amphitheater," an extraordinary example of erosion, created by the Paria River that is still under way even now. To the south we can see the "Grand Staircase," a series of gigantic rocky terraces in different colors that start at the Pink Cliff and descend toward the Gray, White and Vermilion Cliffs.

The geological history of the park is similar to other parks in the American Southwest. The region of Bryce Canyon, originally a sea, was transformed over the ages into a coastline, a coastal plain and a lake floor. Today, its topography is the outcome of the powerful forces of erosion exerted mainly by wind and water. Moving along the natural fault lines of the rock, disintegration and erosion initially led to the formation of long parallel walls that fragmented in certain points into countless pinnacles, some of which are so tall and slender that they look as if they are about to collapse. In the walls, there are natural windows known as "sky holes" and through them, the deep blue of the sky paints a sharp contrast with the red of the rocks. Fragile natural bridges frame immense arches. The rocky pillars in fantastic shapes are called "hoodoos," formations "which cast a spell" on those who observe them, enchanting them with their strange appearance.

RED SPIRES

266-267 *Like the many merlons and turrets of a medieval castle, the walls of Bryce Canyon are silent witnesses to a past characterized by the powerful forces of nature.*

267 left *The semi-desert climate of this region of Utah does not prevent the growth of plant coverage, which can reach all the way to the bottom of the gullies of Bryce Canyon.*

267 right *An aerial view of the Canyon, which shows how the rivers are the principal protagonists of the geological history of the whole south-western region of the United States.*

There's always someone who will be glad to help you pick out well-known silhouettes in some of the hoodoos—relying on your imagination and just the right perspective. They have been given names like *the Pope, Queen Victoria, the Tower Bridge, the Chinese Wall, the Temple of Osiris* and more. And it is the magic of these shapes that makes this canyon so unique, even though it is set in a region characterized by spectacular erosive phenomena.

Tourists flock to admire it mainly in the summer, but the scenery in Bryce Canyon is particularly evocative in the winter, when it is transformed into a dazzling wonderland. The sky is clearer than ever, the pinnacles are capped with snow and the vertical walls appear even redder than ever. Winter is also the time of year the puma comes out. This shy and silent resident of the canyon can be seen more easily since it stands out against the white background. During the winter, other animals in the park such as the mule deer, hares and foxes willingly venture into the depths of the canyon, as the temperature is milder there. The plateaus, dominated by the coniferous and poplar forests, are the home of prairie dogs, squirrels and woodchucks that hibernate in their dens. During this time of year, the canyon can be explored only by cross-country skiers, who can truly get in touch with nature far from the summertime crowds. (C.P.)

268 bottom left An anhinga or water turkey (Anhinga anhinga), very common in the Everglades, spreading its wings in the sun after a dive into the water in search of fish. Its long neck has earned it the name "snake bird."

269 left The environment of the Everglades proves ideal for the American wood ibis (Mycteria americana), a large stork that loves hunting in marshes and wet prairies in search of fish, mollusks, amphibians and insects.

269 bottom right The brown pelican (Pelecanus occidentalis) lives in the area of the coast and estuary of the Everglades. It is able to dive from great heights to catch fish it has spotted on the surface.

268-269 An aerial view of Everglades National Park. The semi-submerged prairies of "sawgrass" stretch as far as the Bay of Florida, where fresh water from Lake Okeechobee mixes with the waters of the Atlantic.

268 bottom left Leaves of water lilies (Nymphaea odorata) carpet the watery areas in the Everglades; water submerges even the base of the sawgrass prairie (Mariscus jamaicensis).

EVERGLADES
NATIONAL PARK

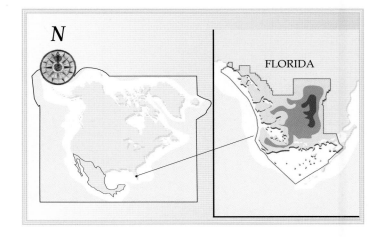

Of all the national parks in the United States of America, the Everglades Park is not the largest nor the most visited, but it is certainly the dampest!

A large part of its territory is under water for most of the year, so that here even the white-tailed deer has adapted to a semi-aquatic life. What seems to be an immense swamp is actually a full-fledged river, though it is difficult to recognize as such due to its width of 50 miles, average depth of 6 inches and the nearly imperceptible slope of its bed. The area around Lake Okeechobee, from which it rises, is just 164 feet above sea level. After a very slow course of about 100 miles, the river flows into to disappear entirely. Today, about half of the original wetlands remain while the flora and fauna have been reduced to about 10%. Understanding the importance of the vast subtropical wetlands of the United States was undoubtedly fundamental for the protection of the entire area. It was President Harry S. Truman who presided over the inauguration ceremony of Everglades National Park on December 6, 1947.

The intricate biological network of the Everglades rests on what was once the bottom of an ancient and warm sea, a porous calcareous floor covered by a thin layer of clay and peat that provide soil for plant life. This is the only place in North America where pines and oaks live side by side with orchids and tropical trees; in the drier part of the park, even conifers prosper,

the Bay of Florida.

As its features are quite different from those of the classic and well-known landscapes of the West, the Everglades, located at the far tip of the Florida peninsula, were not considered areas to protect and valorize. The first colonists long considered them swamps of little value and from the end of the nineteenth century until the 1920s, numerous attempts were made to drain the water to reclaim the land. However, the "grass river" refused

270-271 *Florida puma, a geographical variety of the puma (Felis concolor). This feline has now vanished from all the southeastern United States, but persists in the south of Florida.*

271 left *An example of an American alligator (Alligator mississippiensis), the largest reptile in North America. It frequents the* marshes of the Everglades, together with the rare American crocodile, from which it is distinguished by its wider and more rounded snout.

271 right *The large blue heron (Ardea herodias) is the largest American heron. The Everglades are a real paradise for this lover of both fresh and salt water environments.*

270 bottom left *A storm is announced over the Everglades prairie. During the summer there is almost daily rainfall, which restores the water reserves necessary for the equilibrium of the ecosystem.*

270 bottom right *Pah-hay-okee, in the Everglades National Park, is a marsh densely populated with pond cypresses (Taxodium distichum), deciduous conifers which reach up to 121 feet in high, which prefer terrain so wet they can grow directly in the water.*

272-273 *A beautiful sunset over Lake Pine Glades; the last rays of the sun manage to penetrate the dark* mass of clouds, whilst the silhouettes of the Everglades pines are reflected in the water.

thanks in part to the regenerating action of the fires, now set by the rangers, that contribute continuously to maintaining the composition of the vegetation. Raccoons and opossums find their ideal habitat amidst pine branches, while geckos and lizards sit on their trunks to bask in the sun. These woods are the only corners of the park that can be explored on foot all year long. During the wet season, the rest of the territory is completely flooded and constitutes the true Everglades, or Pa-Hay-Okee (grassy water), as the Seminole Indians called them.

To our eyes, the "glades" look like a single immense prairie, interrupted here and there by tree-covered islands. The rise of just few feet is sufficient to create the deposits allowing small forests of palms and tropical broad-leaved plants to flourish, along with creepers, moss and every type of epiphtye. But the plant that dominates this endless prairie is the kind referred to as "sawgrass," sedge with long, tough saw-edged leaves that will cut deeply into the hands of anyone who tries to rip them up. Sawgrass sets its roots in the layer of clay that covers the riverbed. When it dies, it builds up on the bottom, creating the peat that acts as the ideal soil for willows and magnolias.

The first link in the food chain of this unique ecosystem is the periphyton, together with spongy cylindrical masses of organic matter composed almost entirely of algae—and so plentiful that they cover nearly the entire water surface of the Everglades. Yellowish in color, the periphyton furnishes food for insect larvae, tadpoles, small fish and various other small inhabitants of

shallow water. In turn, they become prey for larger animals, arriving at the top of the food pyramid where the most feared reptile—the American alligator—reigns supreme.

As its home, each alligator chooses one of the deep natural holes in the limestone bed, rightly called "alligator pits." The alligator pits are extremely important balancing elements for the general ecology of the Everglades. Like any good housekeeper, each alligator takes care of cleaning out its pit and always keeps it clear of any decomposing matter. During the dry season, when the surrounding areas dry up, the alligator pits become the sole oasis for the aquatic animals in the park. However, fish, turtles and frogs must risk living alongside their most powerful predator. In the past, the importance of these reptiles within the Everglades was neglected when the focus became the enormous profit from made selling their skin. It was not until 1961 that a law was passed to ban alligator hunting. Since they have become a protected species, the number of alligators in Florida has grown significantly and they are no longer considered at risk.

Myriads of birds crowd around the alligators pits during the winter: pelicans, egrets, moorhens, ibises and storks are usually trustful that they can be observed up close. The darter is a frequent sight; it uses its pointy beak to spear fish, toss it in the air and then swallow it skillfully. After hunting and lunch, the darter stretches out for a long rest with its wings outspread to let them dry. The snail falcon, one of America's rarest birds, flies over the grass river, looking down attentively to find its only

food, the Pomacea snail.

As the rainy summer season approaches, aggressive armies of fauna that are far smaller than alligators—but far more fearful—make their appearance. These are the mosquitoes that as many know, lay their eggs in stagnant water. Even with a good dose of repellent, it is impossible to avoid the attack of these insatiable insects. The frogs are quite happy with their presence, however, as their meals are assured for the entire summer. The evenings are filled with their croaking, and the "lowing" of the alligators joins in so that the entire park becomes the stage for a great concert.

The Everglades are also important because they represent the last refuge for various animals that were once widespread throughout North America: the Florida puma or panther, for example, is present only here—and there are very few specimens. Likewise, the Florida manatee, a peaceful sea mammal weighing a whopping ton, is at very great risk. This is due in part to water pollution, but also caused by the fact that this animal is often mortally wounded by boat propellers, as it moves lazily around the bay and estuaries to nibble on the algae. Fortunately, inside the park there are very strict rules to prevent this magnificent animal from disappearing. Serious protection programs are the only assurance for a better future for the park and its inhabitants, allowing many other visitors to explore its natural charm. (C.P.)

SOUTH AMERICA
INTRODUCTION

S outh America presents a compact and very simple shape, a triangle whose base faces north and whose vertex extends to the Antarctic. Its coastal shapes are not very articulated, without any great peninsulas or inlets and with few islands. Morphologically as well, it can be divided into just a few basic units: the Cordillera of the Andes, the central plains and the eastern highlands.

The eastern highlands include the plateaus of Guyana and Brazil, which are separated from each other by the Amazon Basin; these are Archeozoic and Paleozoic massifs that are composed of crystalline schist on the bottom and many layers of sandstone above this. Intense erosion has dismembered these structures into numerous elements,

separated from each other by deep valleys. The low central lands, composed of Cenozoic and Neozoic sediment, are divided into three great basins: the Orinoco, the Amazon and the Paranà-Uruguay, which then extends to the Pampas and Patagonia. Lastly, the Andes comprise a tall range of rugged mountains that formed recently and show an alpine orogenesis. The mountains—often volcanic—of Central America have the same origin. This long and narrow isthmus, together with the islands of the Antilles, links North and

South America. Expansion in a latitudinal direction and the presence of the soaring cordillera that blocks the ocean winds is the reason there is such great climatic differentiation here. From the Sonora desert to the Strait of Magellan, fifty-six biogeographic provinces can be identified, most of which belong to the neotropical zone. The result is an incredibly rich variety of nature.

The Andes range holds the largest number of volcanoes in the world, including Antonfalla in Argentina, the tallest active volcano (21,156 feet), and Aconcagua, the tallest inactive one (22,828 feet). With a basin covering over 2,702,700 square miles (the largest in the world) and an infinite number of affluents, the colossal Amazon is the river with the largest flow. Lake Titicaca, located between Bolivia and Peru, at an altitude of 12,464 feet, is the tallest navigable lake; Salto Angel in Venezuela is the tallest waterfall (3211 feet); Argentina's Los Glaciares National Park has the most extensive perennial snowcap on the planet. Alongside these records are treasures that are just as priceless; foremost is the Amazon rainforest, whose secrets have yet to be unfolded. But there are also the splendid cataracts of the Iguazù River, the spectacular Cuernos and Torres that soar over the crystal-clear lakes of the Paine River, the characteristic Tepuis, the Pantanal, the Pampas, the Cerrados, the Llanos and the Gran Sabana, the

274 left Lake Llanganuco, with its gray waters of molten ice, anticipates the north face of Huascaran, visible in the background. The face, 5248 feet high, was scaled for the first time by the Italian mountaineer Renato Casarotto in 1977.

274 right Snowy crests and icy slides cover the slopes of Huascaran, one of the most prestigious and highest (22,199 feet) mountains in South America.

274-275 Colossal glaciers that have shattered into thousands of seracs and crevasses, up to more than 21,320 feet in height. For this subgroup of the Peruvian Andes the name Cordillera Blanca seems more appropriate than ever.

275 bottom left Huascaran, the main summit of the Peruvian Cordillera Blanca, rises to a height of 22,200 feet.

275 bottom right The condor of the Andes, with its three-meter wing span, is the largest diurnal bird of prey. The surface of its wings allows it to glide interminably without beating them.

276 bottom right The large Ara parrots, despite their size, are good fliers partly due to their long pointed wings. Although heavy in flight, they can cope with remarkable distances. The picture shows an Ara chloroptera.

277 bottom left An egret, one of the most commonly found birds in the marshes of Pantanal, uses the agility of its long wader legs to move rapidly when hunting fish and amphibians.

276-277 The hyacinth macaw, the largest parrot in the world, shows off its magnificent cobalt blue plumage. Its size and beauty have made it a valuable trading commodity, with grave consequences for the species.

276 bottom left The enormous but very light beak of the toucans, birds of the South American forests, is not only a precious tool. Its glowing colors play an important role in mutual recognition and courting.

INTRODUCTION

Caribbean coral reef; the white beaches of Costa Rica and the paradise of the Galapagos archipelago.

The uniqueness of some of these places led to the UNESCO's decision to catalog some of these national parks as the World Heritage or as Reserves of the Biosphere. Many efforts have been made so far to maintain these natural treasures, and practically all Latin American countries have officially appointed organizations to supervise and manage the conservation areas. However, many hurdles still need to be overcome. There are few funds available to hire enough competent personnel and often there are no infrastructures to guarantee the influx of tourism, the means of support for most of the world parks. The only exceptions are the exemplary protected areas of Costa Rica and several Brazilian or Argentine parks.

As often occurs elsewhere, endemic plants and animals are threatened by poachers. What was once used by the Indios only as food or to produce everyday clothing is now gathered, captured or killed to sell to zoos, for research, for land use and for the fur trade, thus inexorably upsetting the natural balance. Many species are included on the so-called Red List of the Washington Convention of 1973, which bans or limits the international trade of species of wild flora and fauna threatened with extinction; but on the black market, there are orchids, jaguar and caiman hides that sell for astronomical prices. Forests are also at risk—the desire to create new agricultural land, obtain precious wood for foreign multinationals and prospect for oil, is quickly leading to the disappearance of the last Amazon Indios.

The great Argentine and Chilean moors, however, are subject to the growing pressure of the colonists' herds. In order to safeguard areas like Torres del Paine, national parks were created only after much land was expropriated. The colonists represent a dual problem: on the one hand cattle and sheep, in enormous herds, destroy much of the vegetation and take away resources from wild herbivores, while the dogs,

abandoned in a semi-wild state, decimate smaller herbivores such as the pudu deer and drive out carnivores like the long-eared fox. Lastly, oil spills threaten the Caribbean coral reefs originally formed in incredibly clear waters. Thus, there is still a long way to go. But a glance at the next few pages will help you understand all the variety of ecosystems, species, and the steps that evolution has taken to adapt to this ever-changing world that sometime threatens nature. (R.M.S.)

277 top right The splendid spotted coat of the jaguar, seemingly very garish, actually camouflages the animal in the forest's play of light and shade.

277 bottom right The grace and delicacy of a flame-colored butterfly contrast with the aggressive

appearance of the caiman, on which the insect has landed. However, this reptile is not considered dangerous for humans.

278-279 A herd of guanacos, ancient ancestors of llamas, roam undisturbed in the silent valleys of the Torres del Paine Park in Patagonia.

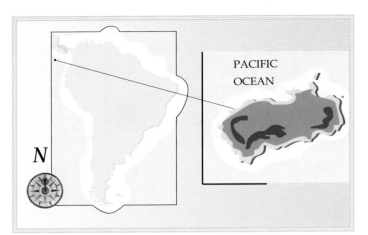

280 bottom left One of the most thrilling encounters: the one with a whale shark. This creature, which boasts the record for being the largest fish in the world, is a harmless filter feeder of microscopic plankton.

280 right A hammer-headed shark clearly shows how it earned its common name. Its small eyes are situated on either side of its mallet-shaped head.

280-281 From the heights of its nest a red-footed gannet seems to scan the horizon. This marine bird has found an ideal spot to reproduce on Coco Island.

COCO ISLAND
NATIONAL PARK

Nowadays a quick glance through an atlas will show an island about 248 miles southwest of Costa Rica. The island is 5 miles long and 2.5 miles wide and it goes by a name that betrays its chief food resource: Isla del Coco, which means Coconut Island. Yet just a few centuries ago this was one of the world's most mysterious places insomuch that many doubted its existence.

This pearl of the tropics was so impenetrable that the imagination of many writers and other artists was piqued. Recently it sprang to the notice of the general public when "Jurassic Park" was filmed there, but as early as the last century it had already acquired literary notoriety. In fact, Coco Island is Robert Stevenson's "Treasure Island," the evergreen backdrop for pirate adventures. It is worth looking

back at the island's fascinating history from the moment of its purely accidental discovery in 1526, when the Spaniard Juan Cabezas spotted this green oasis in an ocean of mist. In the two centuries that followed, the island was used as a supply station for drinking water and fresh fruit by those who navigated these seas: mainly pirates and buccaneers. The island actually had only one landing place—still the case today—the tiny half-moon beach of Chatam Bay. The rest of the territory is composed of extremely dense rain forest, which grows at a rate that, even by today's means, makes it almost impossible to explore.

Coco is a paradise for thirsty tropical vegetation, since annual rainfall is about 23 feet. Obviously, it is not so suitable for human settlement—one or two attempts at colonization in the early 20th century failed quickly and left a heavy bequest of foreign fauna (pigs, mice, cats and goats), which were unfortunately deleterious for local ecosystems.

The reason many courageous colonizers came this far was the mirage of easy wealth; Coco is the legendary location of fabulous treasure (perhaps more than one), hidden by pirates and never recovered. The island was actually the secret hideaway of renowned buccaneers for many years; the most famous was "Benito Bonito," the battle name of Bennett Graham. This English sailor traded his loyalty to Her Majesty the Queen for his ship, the *Jolly Roger*, and became the terror of rich Spanish cargo ships that rode the waves in the 1800s. Graham's most daring feat came at the expense of Lima nobles, who were trying to save their riches from the bloody

281 bottom left On the head of this gray reef shark the nostrils are clearly visible, and are covered by a fold of skin known as the nasal valve. The most developed sense in these fish is the sense of smell.

281 bottom right Numerous hammer-headed sharks hang about offshore in search of prey. Among the sharks found in these waters, the hammer-heads are among the most common.

282 top left A specimen of a sailfish, with its developed dorsal fin, swims placidly satiated just a few feet from the surface. Similar to the swordfish, it too has a pointed rostrum in extension of its upper jaw.

282 top right As in all coral reefs, here there is evidence of enormous biodiversity. The protection of the waters carried out by these national park makes the area extremely rich in fish.

282 bottom Coco Island, still covered with lush forests, was used by sailors and buccaneers in the past as a source of fresh fruit and water.

clashes that wracked Peru, and so decided to entrust their transportation to the British navy. A certain "Admiral Graham" arrived at the appointment and, after loading something like 350 tons of gold, upped anchor, hoisted the *Jolly Roger* and headed for Coco, watched by the flabbergasted Peruvian nobles. Ruthless reprisals followed and the pirates were eventually captured, but there was no trace of the treasure.

Although the growth rate of the vegetation makes it impossible to pinpoint paths or traces of digging, yet this has not discouraged treasure-hunters in search of this gold; the German August Gissler lived (and dug) on Coco for eighteen years before he finally gave up.

Today Coco is little more that an outpost for the Servicio de Parques Nacionales, who will not let tourists stay there. Those who visit the island for several days can do so only if they sleep on the fully-equipped boats that are docked in the bay. Coco is the largest uninhabited island in the world, a fact which makes it even more fascinating. Its isolated geographic position and its climatic zone endow Coco with extensive biological diversity and have made it an exceptional place for the preservation of nature. Its territory is now a complete national park, the pride and joy of Costa Rica, a country that is particularly sensitive to the issue of conservation.

As early as the 1960s Costa Rica set up quite a vast and articulated network of protected areas (today there are sixty parks and reserves), preferring to invest more in safeguarding its small territory than exploiting it. Such forethought is bringing an increasing number of better-informed tourists to Costa Rica—those who are exceptional enough to be truly appreciative of this luxuriant and primordial nature. They are welcomed by excellent organization and efficient structures, and above all by the warmth of a population that is really enamoured of its country. That is why tourists often return and offer valuable economic support to a country that is severly challenged economically.

282-283 The red-lipped bat fish is a rarity. It is, in fact, one of the endemic species that live only in this natural park in Costa Rica.

283 bottom Mistakenly feared for centuries, the manta or devilfish owes its name to two appendages, similar to horns, which it uses to carry to its mouth the plankton on which it feeds.

Isla del Coco is especially interesting for those who enjoy diving; the coastline is a colorful world of tropical fish, sea-turtles and, of course, sharks. There are numerous hammer-fish whose unmistakable silhouette always sends a shiver down the spine of the scuba divers who encounter them.

The importance of this park is its large number of endemic species: about seventy types of animals and just as many plants can be found in no other part of the planet. Coco is a destination coveted by birdwatchers from all over the world; more than eighty species of birdlife nest on the island, including at least three rarities (the Coco chaffinch, the Coco flycatcher, the Coco cuckoo), living examples of evolution's ceaseless industry in generating new varieties of organism. The list of species present on the island grows with each census, not least of all because this is rugged territory with precipices and hills (the tallest is Cerro Iglesias, at 2080 feet) covered with dense, stratified vegetation that does not easily reveal its secrets.

So there really is treasure on Coco Island: its biodiversity. And it is up to us to protect and preserve it (A.S.I.)

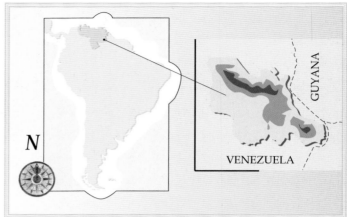

284 top left Similar to the giant anteater but clearly much smaller, the tamandua is essentially arboreal. Its tail, hairless for almost all of its length, is used as a prehensile organ.

284 bottom The Angel Falls plummet for almost a mile. Their name recalls the aviator Jimmy Angel, who discovered it in the thirties. Churùnmeru is the name given to the falls by the Pemón Indians.

GUYANA

VENEZUELA

N

CANAIMA
NATIONAL PARK

Southwest of the Orinoco river, where crocodiles and anacondas reign, Guyana's Tierras Altas can be found, the home of Venezuela's Canaima National Park. The seven and a half million acres that comprise this park are one of South America's most differentiated natural areas.

In the eastern zone of the protected area a vista of grasslands called, the Gran Sabana, forms one of the South America's savannas. The landscape is frequently interrupted not only by tropical river-forests that border and highlight rivers of different sizes, but also by characteristic "tepuis." These are high plateaus that loom brusquely from the plains, whose singular vertical faces are formed by polychrome sandstone. The flat peaks are windswept so dwarf woods grow there: sloping trunk trees that never reach more than thirty-three feet in height and with innumerable interwoven aerial roots.

The area has an equatorial climate, with heavy rain throughout the year; there are many watercourses that flow here, even at the top of the tepuis. When the water abruptly reaches the end of the plateau it plunges down to form foaming cataracts and cascades, such as Salto del Hacha. In 1937, a North American adventurer, called Jimmy Angel, accidentally flew over Auyàn-tepui, which became the most famous of all the tepuis. Jimmy Angel was seeking legendary El Dorado, but instead he found a natural treasure of inestimable value—the world's tallest waterfall, almost a 1000-meter drop—exactly 3,280 feet. The indigenous Pemòn called it Churùnmerù— "water leap"—but nowadays it is called Angel Leap, in honor of its discoverer. Formed by the Rio Carrao, it is a sensational sight: a silver ribbon that contrasts with the grays and reds of the sandstone, gradually increasing its volume and disappearing in a cloud of mist amongst the luxuriant green vegetation.

While the tropical river-forest abounds with "morichales,"

284-285 Rich in water and densely vegetated, the Canaima Park is dominated by the tepuyes. These are characteristic mountains whose vertical walls make the plateaus at their summits almost inaccessible, veritable islands of intriguing biodiversity.

285 bottom left The tapir is a good swimmer that does not hesitate to cross even large water courses, not only as a means of escape but also for its habitual moves from place to place. The first European explorers confused it with the hippopotamus.

285 bottom right A young jaguar follows its mother in the forest. This big cat is the largest South American predator. In admiration of its strength and beauty, the pre-Columbian civilizations made it their god.

which are plant linkages typical to very damp habitats, as well as a predominance of Buriti palms (*Mauritia flexuosa*), the plateaus comprise isolated systems with numerous endemic species. These true natural botanical gardens proliferate with Bromeliaceae such as Ayensua, Ericacea such as Tepuia and Compositae such as Achnopogon, all unique. The western region of the park is called Escudo Guayanés: thousands of acres of impenetrable rain forest, where one special inhabitant is the endemic orchid genus, the Donstervillea. The presence of numerous ecotonal bands (which are points of encounter between different ecosystems) intensifies the extensive equatorial biodiversity, giving the possibility a large number of animals finding food and shelter.

The splendid jaguar here is a silent lord, squat-pawed but so light of foot as to walk on brushwood without snapping a twig, strong enough to carry with ease over 400 lbs, a fine swimmer and climber, a symbol of strength, and for the Indios, of evil. Whether speckled or melanic (the American panther), it is able to capture the most unlikely prey; it will use its tail to hook Pirarocu, enormous grayish fish, or its sharp claws to pierce even the tough squama of a caiman. Only the giant anteater is able to instill fear in the jaguar, as its robust talons can inflict mortal wounds.

Another feline, the ocelot, is much smaller: a clever hunter amidst the tall grass, it often catches a nap on tree branches. Alongside these species, also included in UICN's Red List of animals in danger of extinction, are armadillos and giant otters. There are also numerous types of monkey, all cebids. It is not unusual to see some acrobatics—a monkey hooked tail and paws to a hanging branch and skimming the surface of the river below.

Danger also lurks when the Orinoco crocodiles and spectacled caymans are on the lookout for lunch; even on dry land extreme care is required. Here, anacondas sometimes abandon the water where they are excellent hunters, or there may be a more arboreal boa constrictor, whose splendid livery coils over eight feet, especially active in the hours from sunset to nightfall. The visitor will be especially entranced by the incredible shapes and intense colors that are everywhere, to the point that it may be difficult to actually "see" what is around.

Two tiny sparkling eyes gaze from the heart of a bromelia: a yellow and black frog (*Dendrobates leucomeles*) warns that it is poisonous amongst these garish colors, whilst a cock-of-the-rock uses the self-same colors for his courting rituals, boasting his courage to the females. Another hubbub to be heard is that of countless, kaleidoscopic parrots while the scarlet ibis and the pink spoonbill are not quite so noisy. There are the funny hoazin with golden head plumes like Mohicans, and so adapted to the forest environment that their young have small hooks on the upper wing surface so they can clamber up the trees when they are not yet able to fly.

Last but not least in this unique kaleidoscope, the disproportionate toucans that often seem unreal. Then there are colibris—incredible butterflies and other insects—which are the most populous of the fauna, even though they are so well camouflaged that they are often almost invisible. If we want to experience an extraordinary weath of color, scents and sensation that cannot be found anywhere else, we must go to the Canaima National Park where its isolation has entailed the evolution of a peculiar flora and fauna that do not exist in any other part of the world. (R.M.S.)

286 top   The ocelot, an excellent climber, is one of the best-known of the various species of South American cats. This notoriety comes mostly as the result of the beauty of its spotted coat, which has made it the object of ruthless hunting.

286 bottom   The waters that plummet from the rocky walls create environments suitable for a flora made up of countless species of hydric plants. Mosses and ferns create elegant green gardens.

286-287   Invisible from the surface, a caiman lies in wait for its prey. Since it does not reach the large dimensions of the crocodiles, it feeds off modest-sized prey, predominantly fish and aquatic birds.

287 bottom left The piranhas are legendary fish about whose voracity much has been said, and often exaggerated. However, they are still dangerous predators with powerful and very sharp teeth, which live in large shoals.

287 bottom right The mata-mata turtle lies in ambush in a pond. Camouflaging itself on the bottom, it waits for small prey to pass near it. It will swallow them with a very rapid movement of its long neck and by widening its enormous mouth.

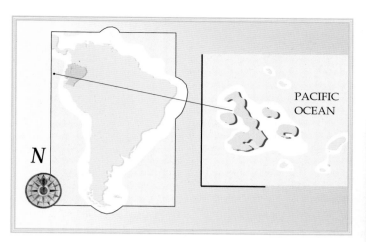

288 bottom The lava rocks and the protuberances of conical shapes leave no doubt as to the volcanic origin of the Galapagos Islands. They are of geologically recent origin, as Charles Darwin noted in his travel diaries.

289 On the island of San Cristobal, in the archipelago of the Galapagos, a group of sea lions takes a rest. Their small beach is hidden between rocky coasts, which were not very attractive to the eyes of the first explorers.

288 top right The archaic appearance and unusual size of the giant tortoises make these reptiles indisputably fascinating. Yet for a long time, man was only concerned with the edibility of their meat.

288 center A male frigate bird exhibits its strange red balloon, which is swollen to attract the attention of a potential companion. In view of its lack of bright plumage and melodious song, this is the large sea bird's strategy.

GALÁPAGOS
NATIONAL PARK

In 1535, Fray Tomás de Berlanga discovered a group of uninhabited and inhospitable-looking islands as he sailed along the western coast of South America. He merely took note of their position, which was level with the Equator, about 620 miles from the continent, and wrote a short report that the King of Spain did not even bother to read.

They were initially called "Enchanted Islands" because of their uncertain position, for the dense sea fog often made

them difficult to sight at all. Between the 1600 and 1700s the archipelago was a haven for English pirates, one of whom, William Dampier, wrote: "…there are great tortoises, with a delicious meat that is tastier even than chicken…" At that time the Tortoise Islands seemed to offer little else of interest. Yet, the Galapagos (a Spanish word that means "tortoise") Islands are now one of the best known places in the world amongst those who are familiar with the Earth's beauty and with natural history.

When Charles Darwin, the great naturalist, visited this archipelago in 1835, he made it a site of exceptional importance for studying the mechanisms of biological evolution, since it was populated by unique animals and plants. Here, Darwin performed studies that led him to perfect his theory of natural selection, the key for interpreting modern biology. Immediately understanding the origins of the archipelago, Darwin wrote: "Seeing every high mountain occupied by its own crater and the edges of lava flows still easily discernible, we have to believe that in a recent geological period the ocean covered everything here."

The park was founded in 1959, and the Charles Darwin Research Station, housed on the island Saint Cruz, began its activities in the early 1960s. The Station is actively involved in scientific research regarding the protection of this unique archipelago that was placed at risk for serious damage because of a shipwrecked oil tanker in early 2001.

The Galapagos are a place where it is easy to see the effect of volcanic phenomena on the landscape. The most ancient rocks are no older than five million years, which is nothing in comparison to the age of the planet Earth. The dark solidified lava that forms the ground is colonized by

pioneer organisms, including lava cactus (*Brachycereus nesioticus*). Much of the territory, however, especially at lower quotas and on more recent lava flow, is desolately bare; but in higher zones, where humidity is high, there are actual forests.

Nevertheless, it is possible to see on the coast some of the Enchanted Islands' more typical inhabitants, such as the sea iguana. These great saurians, which grow to over three feet long, crowd at the coastline in numerous groups. Not even Charles Darwin was able to declare them attractive, but the

290-291 Although its appearance is hardly reassuring, the land iguana is a peaceful vegetarian, particularly fond of cactus fruit. There are two species, but there is little difference between them.

290 bottom left A land iguana moves across the dark volcanic rocks. Charles Darwin said that these creatures were so numerous that they made it difficult to find a place to pitch camp.

290 bottom right The sea iguanas gather in large groups on the coasts. The white incrustations on their heads are the consequence of the excretion of salt, accumulated in excess whilst diving in search of algae.

291 top left Among the many species of crustaceans on the Galapagos Islands, the red crabs are particularly admired and photographed. Thanks to the rapidity of their movements, they are nicknamed "Sally light foot".

Galapagos sea iguana has the most unique habits of all this species. It feeds on algae that it picks up on cliffs and submerged rocks, some of which are over 32 feet below the surface. Another typical coastal inhabitant is the *Grapsus grapsus* crab, also called "Sally lightfoot" for the rapidity of its movements. This crustacean's most striking feature is its bright red color.

Indigenous animals are usually quite confident, as they have evolved in a habitat where there is a substantial lack of predators, so they allow themselves to be approached even at very close quarters. The introduction of rats, dogs, cats and goats, by early western-settlers have endangered autochthonous fauna and flora. Even today, the non-endemic animals create problems for environmental management.

The largest of the nineteen principal islands is Isabela (or Albemarle), constituted by five main volcanic cones, including the volcano Alcedo, one of the archipelago's most impressive sights, with a crater diameter of approximately 4.34 miles where several active fumaroles can be found. It is also one of the places where the giant tortoise (*Geochelone elephantopus*) can be seen in liberty. Once numerous, these great reptiles have been decimated by humans in the past, who exploited them for supplies of fresh meat on board ship, and introduced animals that were not native to the area.

Santa Fe (or Barrington) is one of the smallest of the archipelago's main islands, but it hosts a special kind of land iguana (*Conolophus pallidus*) that differs from iguanas present on the other islands (*Conolophus subcristatus*), since it feeds off plants, including prickly pears. During Darwin's time, these reptiles were so numerous that one of the researchers said it was "almost impossible to set up our tents because of the number of lairs dug in the ground."

Small Seymour island, only slightly above sea level, is one of the best places for birdwatching. The most typical are the hurricane birds (*Fregata magnificens*), whose black males exhibit a vivacious red skin blown up with air during courting. They are also spectacular to observe because of their acrobatic flight, possible because of their long, narrow wings that make the hurricane bird an unmistakable silhouette against the sky. Another of Seymour's inhabitants is the blue-footed booby (*Sula nebouxii excisa*), who executes a funny little dance as part of its courting rite, showing off its blue webbed feet.

291 top right A sea iguana warms itself in the sun, as all reptiles are wont to do. The males, especially those of certain islands in the archipelago, exhibit rather vivid colors.

291 bottom A small lava lizard has climbed onto the head of a sea iguana, giving rise to a curious scene. The iguana, with its tranquil disposition, does not seem particularly bothered.

The Galapagos Islands also have particular climatic characteristics. Since they are at equatorial level, one might expect a hot and damp climate, but this is not the case. During certain parts of year, the waters are decidedly cold, a result of the Humboldt Current coming from the Antarctic. During the austral winter, air temperature does not rise above 77°F, and higher parts of the islands are often immersed in deep fog. In December the flow of hot air from the north is dominant, bringing with it rain that lasts until May.

The Antarctic effect on the climate of the Galapagos also influences the unusual fauna present on the islands, which includes penguins. These seabirds are certainly an unusual presence on the Equator, and belong to a species similar to that found along the coasts of Peru and Chile.

This is a particularly delicate habitat, where fauna are particularly vulnerable, so visits are organized in long itineraries led by Galapagos National Park guides.

Since 1989 the protected area has been extended to include the Galapagos seas, no less fascinating than what emerges above the surface of the water. Swept by both the cold waters of Antarctica and warm currents from the tropical Pacific, Galapagos' colorful marine life is a bizarre mixture of species. Almost one quarter of the marine life in Galapagos is endemic to this archipelago: 17% of its fish and 35% of its marine invertebrates are found nowhere else in the world. Let's visit these two worlds exotic outside the water as well as inside! (G.G.B.)

292 A male sea lion seems to be posing for the photographer. Sociable and playful, they are among the most lively and loveable creatures on the Galapagos Islands.

293 top The sea around the Galapagos is home to both tropical species and species belonging to temperate or cold seas, thanks to its diverse geographical situation. Diving provides many surprises, such as this large shoal of rays.

293 center A group of hammer-headed sharks, with their unmistakable features, moves quickly in the waters of the archipelago. The sea creatures of the Galapagos are no less interesting than their land counterparts, even though it takes a skilled diver to observe them.

293 bottom In the water, the environment they find the most congenial, the sea lions demonstrate their agility to the full. Their acrobatics do not always have an apparent motive and are often just a case of playful behavior.

294-295 A giant tortoise on the island of Santa Cruz. The differences between the fourteen subspecies of tortoises particularly struck Charles Darwin, who from these observations drew important deductions regarding the evolution of the species.

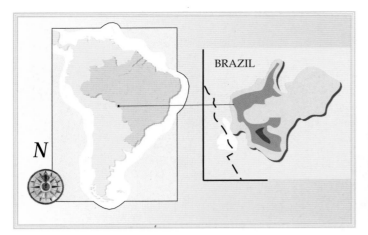

296 top After a gestation period of more than six months, the female giant anteater gives birth to just one baby. It is transported for a long time on her back, and left only when she begins a new pregnancy.

296-297 In the wet season the river Paraguay floods tracts of the plain, at the borders between Brazil, Paraguay and Bolivia.

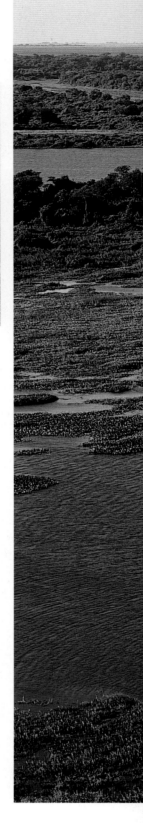

PANTANAL MATOGROSSENSE
NATIONAL PARK

There is a very special place in the middle of the South American continent where the great Paraguay River crosses enormous stretches of territory in its exhausting drive toward the ocean, winding its way and changing direction innumerable times, or stopping, uncertain, about which way to go. This is the Pantanal, a name that literally means "swamplands."

Swamps are generally considered unhealthy places to be and difficult to explore, but they are also among the natural environments with the most life. Since this is the largest wet zone in the world, as well as an extraordinary mosaic of prairies, savannahs and brush, the Pantanal hosts an incredible number of living species that authoritative scholars have estimated to be at 150,000.

But this area of 88,000 square miles is not the perennial kingdom of stagnant water. It is only with the rainy season, from October to April, that the Paraguay and its affluents flow onto the large plain, covering it with a layer of water ranging in depth from a few inches to several feet. The highest areas of land are thus transformed into islands of vegetation that shelter land animals, composed mainly of unique species.

An odd tubular head sticking out its worm-like tongue that is 24 centimeters long, powerful hooves that can dig even the most compact soil and a huge tail covered with bristles half a meter long are just a few traits of the giant anteaters. Only here will you find the elegant Pantanal deer (*Blastoceros dichotomus*), which, thanks to its hooves that can split open and are joined together by a membrane, can move about freely without sinking into the muddy soil. Smelling the air and grasping leaves with it small proboscis, the massive tapir circles about, unaware that it has relatives in far-off Asia. Traditionally associated with the gods of life, strength and power, the jaguar still asks itself why hunters love its spotted coat so much, but today it may feel safer than it did a few years ago, in spite of the fact that it must travel farther to meet one of its brothers.

The immense wetlands are populated by aquatic animals, including the fascinating and repulsive caiman and the large anaconda snake, known here as the sucurì. Also among mammals, there are species that have adapted to a lifestyle halfway between land and water, like the capybara (*Hydrochoerus hydrochaeris*). This is the largest rodent in the world, a sort of gigantic mouse virtually without a tail but weighing 110 lbs. "If these animals also live in the water, it means they're like fish. And so they can also be eaten during Lent": this was consideration made by some European missionaries in the seventeenth century, based on the animal's way of life. Despite its size, however it is also the prey of the legendary anaconda, which never gives up even against caimans, which in turn do not snub piranhas, whose voracity is the subject of many tales, some of which are exaggerated.

But in nature it is often the less-showy species that contribute most to determining the characteristics of an ecosystem, and this also holds true for the Pantanal, where

297 bottom left One of the most extraordinary plants in the blooded habitats of South America is the giant water lily, Victoria cruziana. Its gigantic floating leaves, more than three feet wide, are so robust that they can support several lbs of weight.

297 bottom right A jaguar rests among the vegetation, in the Brazilian Pantanal; despite its size it can easily climb trees. In the periods when the rivers flood most intensely, it can be forced to retreat to the branches for days.

298-299 Despite its threatening appearance, the caiman is not considered dangerous to man because it does not grow to a great size. It prefers stagnant waters to fast-flowing rivers.

298 bottom left The caimans are often found in numerous groups, crowding the places best suited to basking in the sun. Despite having been intensively hunted for their skin, these reptiles are still quite common.

298 bottom right Thanks to the tapered shape of its body and its webbed feet, the giant otter moves in the water with the agility of a seal. It can weigh up to sixty-six lbs and lives in slow-flowing rivers in much of South America.

certain large and seemingly insignificant water snails represent a basic link in the chain of relations that binds the inhabitants of the swamplands. The large snail, present everywhere, ceaselessly devours the vegetation, keeping its proliferation under control. This facilitates the flow of water and prevents the swamps from filling up with soil. The mollusk in turn represents an important source of nutrition for countless other species, such as the jabiru (*Jabiru mycteria*). Known as tuiuiù in the Indios dialect – "driven by the wind" – this large stork with a wingspan of nine feet has been chosen as the symbol of the Pantanal.

When the rains stop in April, the water begins to withdraw, returning to the proper bounds of a normal river, conventional lakes and ordinary ponds. The dissolving layer of water in the residual pools and ever narrower canals leads to a concentration into small areas an enormous number of fish that, during the wet seasons, were spread over a vast area. Many animals thus realize that they have a large quantity of food available for themselves and their young, and they begin their reproduction phase. As a result, you'll see treetops literally covered with colored birds, so many that they look like spectacular blossoms from a distance. The birds, with over 650 species, make the Pantanal one of the most spectacular spots for ornithologists. Different species of herons, pink spoonbills with their unmistakable beaks, parrots like the hyacinth macaw—the largest in the world—ibises, and cormorants are truly marvelous to watch.

The first Spanish and Portuguese adventurers who began to explore the area in the 1500s reported that it was an impassable and hostile area, "an immense area of lakes, swamps and impenetrable reed thickets, with a large number of caimans, enormous snakes, mosquitoes and other dangerous animals." This did not keep slave traders and gold diggers from wiping out the local Indios, the Guatos, in the 1600s.

In the nineteenth century, cattle breeders were the ones to discover that the grassy stretches of the Pantanal were perfect for open-pasture breeding. Millions of cattle wander here today, mainly small and frugal "tucura" cows that get lost on the lands of fazendas as large as 247,100 acres. As long as animal husbandry is practiced extensively and not with the intention of exploiting the full production potential of the ecosystem, however, this will not cause particular damage.

Located mainly in Brazil, in the state of Mato Grosso, the Pantanal extends into Paraguay and Bolivia. Little known until the 1980s, this natural treasure became famous in Brazil in a rather unusual way: the biggest television hit of 1990 was a soap

A UNIVERSE OF WATER

299 bottom left In Pantanal, bodies of water and submerged areas of land have no precise borders. The seasonal floods of the Paraguay River constantly alter the details of an environment that is quite unique.

299 top right The water hyacinth, with its large pink flowers, is a typical plant of tropical wetlands. The petioles of its leaves, inflated and full of air, allow it to float.

299 bottom right Two capybaras splash about in a sea of water hyacinth, a typical tropical floating plant. These enormous rodents frequent the wet areas in family groups or in bands that can sometimes contain even dozens of specimens.

opera entitled "Pantanal," about the lives and loves of a family of cattle breeders from a local fazenda. Many Brazilians thus discovered that right in their own country they had a wildly beautiful region that was still virtually intact—the perfect destination for naturalistic tourism—and they began to come here to see it in person. Since them, many fazenderos have started to charge visitors for a place to stay, thus supplementing their income and allowing an ever greater number of people to get to know this environment.

The dry season, from April until the beginning of October, is the best time to visit the Pantanal: it's hot, it doesn't rain and you can get around in a jeep, a boat or on horseback, and there are many opportunities to observe the fauna, particularly the bird life. But it is the last part of the rainy season offers the most spectacular flowering.

Pantanal Matogrossense National Park, covering 137,000

hectares, was established in 1981 and includes the old biological reserve of Cará Cará. It is located at the confluence of the Paraguay River with Rio Cuiabá and the San Lorenzo. Despite its vastness, the park represents only a small portion of the enormous territory known as the Pantanal. Another national park, Chapada dos Guimarães, protects a beautiful and important zone on the plateau that surrounds part of the Pantanal, the so-called Planalto, the location of the sources of many of the affluents of the Paraguay River.

These protective measures seem to be necessary in light of the recent history of the Pantanal which, in spite of the fact that even the Brazilian constitution has defined it as worth safeguarding, has had to deal with serious problems. The biggest one arose at the end of the 1980s with the "Proyecto Hidrovìa," promoted by Argentina, Brazil, Bolivia, Paraguay and Uruguay. The goal of the project was to create a link that could be navigated by large ships, going from the center of the continent to the Atlantic. The Pantanal would have been devastated, but in 1995 the promoting countries, pressured by those who feared for the fate of the great swampland, reviewed their stands.

It seems that the danger is now past, but this fact shows that even a large and seemingly inviolable environment must be protected carefully. Nevertheless, as the great Brazilian poet Manoel de Barros claimed, "the Pantanal cannot be measured with any meter: it is boundless." (G.G.B)

IGUAZÙ
NATIONAL PARK

Only an airplane flight will allow you to appreciate in its entirety what might be defined as the most beautiful border in the world: the waterfalls, or rather the cataracts, of the river Iguazù, which in Guaranì means "big water." Located between Argentina and Brazil, not far from Paraguay, they extend for a length of approximately 8,528 feet. This river, which has its source in the Serra do Mar, then runs into a narrow gully between steep slopes before finally flowing into the state of Paraná, just a few miles before the confluence that this marvelous natural spectacle originates.

Easy to reach, each year hundreds of tourists come to admire and gaze enraptured at the great precipice with between 160 and 260 drops, depending on the flow of the river, whose principal course plunges into the Garganta del Diablo (Devil's Throat), with a fall of more than 230 feet. Higher than Niagara Falls and

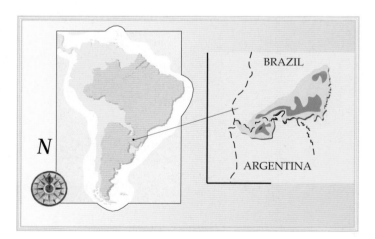

second only in width to Victoria Falls, in the wet season (in reality the annual rainfall is around 79 inches and fairly evenly distributed) the waterfalls look like a wall of around three miles of silvery foam, which can be heard miles away, bouncing off the rocks below before dissolving into a thousand rainbows. This colossal natural monument has led to Argentina and Brazil's undertaking to safeguard it and to protect the surrounding area; it was, in fact, in 1928 that Argentina founded Iguazù National Park, which covers around 123,550 acres of forest, followed by the Brazilian Iguaçu National Park, with 420,070 acres.

Along the banks of the river there is an interesting plant combination in the shape of the gigantic peroba rosa (*Aspidosperma polyneuron*), in whose shade grow groves of palms (*Euterpe edulis*). These palms have slender trunks (they can reach 65.6 feet in height with a trunk 8 inches in diameter) ending in a

bud that is highly valued as food. Removal of this palm heart causes the tree to die, which is why a sin of gluttony has led to the disappearance of this species in many areas outside the park.

Take a look in the river water and you will catch sight of countless species now in danger of extinction; you may spot the giant otter hunting fish and crustaceans, and the curious yapok (*Chirinectes minimus*), a small marsupial that is another excellent underwater swimmer, or perhaps the Brazilian merganser. In addition, even though it generally catches small-size prey, a close lookout has to be kept for the broad-snouted caiman (*Caiman latirostris*) that, despite being chiefly adapted to marshes, does not scorn this environment with its ample vegetation.

All around is the Paranaense Forest, which appears to embrace and protect the river and its spectacular cataract. A lush mass of green, it is compact and impenetrable, with an altitude of sixty-six to ninety-eight feet, from which every now and again there emerge the even taller tops of incense-trees and the ybiràpyta.

The birds that circle above the water in search of fish and the gaily-colored butterflies that approach visitors seem to be extending an invitation to explore the rainforest, but the tangle of around two thousand vascular plants and the presence of barriers of bamboo thirty to fifty feet high provide an immediate deterrent. The few who succeed in the venture find themselves in an Eden of a thousand colors with bromeliads and all orchids proliferating everywhere, as well as twelve species of humming birds with metallic glints, five species of toucans with their incredible beaks, and amphibians and reptiles so brightly colored they do not look real. Worthy of particular mention among the reptiles is the famous coral snake, whose gaudy livery is in reality a signal of danger; in fact it possesses one of the most powerful venoms in the animal kingdom, even though, given that it has a good-natured disposition and a very small mouth, it never attacks humans.

In this jungle the comical American tapir finds huge amounts of fruit, flowers, buds and insects, while in the trees opossums, arboreal anteaters and various types of primates, including the capuchin monkey and howler monkeys, go from one branch to another. Finally, among the great variety of bats that find an endless source of food here, is the legendary vampire bat (*Desmodus rotundus*): a small and almost inoffensive creature, which surely has no idea to what extent its eating habits have gripped the human imagination. (R.M.S.)

302 top In the flood season the Iguazù River has a flow seven times greater than the famous Niagara Falls, situated between Canada and the United States.

302-303 On the border between Brazil and Argentina is one of the most spectacular natural phenomena in the world, the falls of Iguazù. Nearby stretches one of the last strips of Brazilian Atlantic forest.

303 bottom left The islands of vegetation that break up the great waterfall at numerous points provide an ecosystem of great interest. Unusual aquatic plants withstand the force of the water thanks to sucker-like structures.

303 bottom right The terrible roar of the waters, the incessant shaking of the vegetation, the rainbows that form as a result of the vaporization produced in a drop of almost a 500 feet, accentuate the majesty of the spectacle.

THE WALL OF WATER

304-305 The impressive façade of the Perito Moreno Glacier immersed in the Gran Lago Argentino; this is the only glacier on the Pacific side that is not affected by phenomena of regression.

304 bottom The Fitz-Roy massif, so called in honor of the captain who "made known to geographical science the coasts of southern America." Also traveling on the English brig The Beagle, commanded by Fitz-Roy in his trip round the world, was the young naturalist Charles Darwin.

305 top right This is what Lake
Viedma looks like from a satellite;
set between impervious ice-covered
crests it is difficult to reach for
anyone who is not an expert trekker.

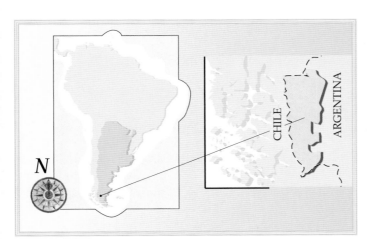

LOS GLACIARES
NATIONAL PARK

Where the desert and desolate Patagonian plateau unexpectedly rises, almost shattering against the Andean cordillera, from an imposing granite colossus soar the legendary Cerro Torre (10,280 feet) and Mount Fitz Roy (12,710 feet), permanently crowned with clouds like fumes that rise out of a crater (which is why it was for a long time mistakenly thought to be a volcano).

Although barely reaching 13,000 feet above sea level, these mountains are a destination coveted by the world's greatest mountaineers and are considered to be the most inaccessible mountains on earth. They have only been conquered on very few occasions and at a high price: it was a French expedition that was the first to conquer Fitz Roy, although not until 1952, while it was the Italian Cesare Maestri and the Austrian Toni Egger, who unfortunately lost his life during the descent, who conquered Cerro Torre. Scaling these practically vertical walls is made highly demanding not only by the technical difficulties involved, but by particularly adverse climatic conditions, including the conflict between great masses of air in the east from the Atlantic Ocean and in the west from the Pacific Ocean, which do in fact trigger sudden and very violent blizzards.

Since 1937, these two legendary mountains have been part of the Parque Nacional Los Glaciares, included in 1981 by UNESCO in the list of the world's natural patrimony. With an area of 1,482,000 acres, the park also contains the spectacular lakes Argentino and Viedma, and includes a large portion of the famous glacier Hielo Patagonico Continental Sur, a reminder of the vast Pleistocene mantle that covered the whole of Patagonia during the Ice Age. The Hielo Continental is constantly fed by the blizzards that rage all year round on the highest peaks of the cordillera.

On the Pacific side, where the snowfall is abundant and constant, the glaciers remain stationary, while on the eastern side the increase in average temperatures and a drop in precipitation is causing their regression; the only exception is the Perito Moreno, the most popular tourist destination. To reach the lookout point ("mirador"), which gives an extraordinary view of the glacier front, an immense white wall rising from the milky waters of the large Lago Argentino, the best base is without doubt the pleasant El Calafate, the park's main entranceway. Established on the shores of the lake, it enjoys a particularly favorable microclimate and is equipped with every tourist facility, as well as with fabulous "Hosterìas" where you can try the gastronomic specialties of Patagonia and, to wind up the evening, take part in the "mate de yerba" ritual, a concoction that must be drunk by all those present from the same cup.

The name of the El Calafate derives from the word for Magellan barberry (*Berberis buxifolia*), a shrub with thorny

branches, which produces bluish berries (with a bittersweet taste) capable of withstanding the winter. A Tehuelche legend, passed down from father to son, tells of an ancient shaman who, because he was slow on the march, was abandoned by his tribe, who were taken by surprise by an early winter while they were still in the summer hunting grounds. When the birds returned from their migration in spring they saw that the old man had survived, and in autumn he shared with them the juice of the berries that had kept him alive. From that time, the greediest birds decided never again to abandon this place, and others stayed at least

until the arrival of the first snow so they could enjoy the delicious fruit of the Magellan barberry, the plant that became the symbol of Patagonia.

In the calm Laguna de los Cisnes, numerous lovely black-necked swans find refuge, together with common flamingos and countless varieties of ducks. As early as August, on the small islands in the midst of the water, where it lives and feeds off algae and invertebrates, it is possible to observe the nesting of this splendid swan with its characteristic plumage: white all over the body and black on the neck and head, where a sort of pale crown seems to highlight its regality, and a flaming red beak as a final touch.

Between the sheer rock and wind-eroded walls of the south shore of the Lago Argentino, open the Cuevas del Gualicho, caves inside which one can admire Patagonian rock paintings with abstract figures, geometric designs and classic handprints in negative. Now less well-known than the Cuevas de las Manos, they were actually the first to be discovered and provide information on the peoples that settled in Patagonia immediately following the last Ice Age. It is truly thrilling to enter these places and perceive the sacredness ascribed to them by ancient artists, and to admire the brilliancy of colors that are thousands of years old (at least 7,000), created with a special technique used only here and in the Algerian Maghreb.

Still following the southern shore of the Lago Argentino, we reach the little port of Puerto Bandera, from where trips on the lake depart. Navigating amidst icebergs the launch approaches the immense wall of the Glaciar Perito Moreno, whose altitude exceeds the water level by almost sixty feet. The dramatic sound of blocks of ice which, as they become detached, plummet into the lake is reminiscent of an artillery battle. Since 1988, there has been no reoccurrence of a phenomenon that has made this glacier famous from 1947 onwards. Every three or four years the glacier would advance until it joined up with the Magellan peninsula opposite, blocking the drainage of the Brazo Rico river and forming a dam. The water would therefore flood the valleys until the pressure of the column of water (about sixty-six feet above normal) reached such a force it would cause the ice dam to explode.

Another thrilling walk is without doubt the one that leads to Lago Roca, south of the Magellan Peninsula: a ring of some 5.5 miles that allows you to enjoy splendid views of the Lago Argentino, the Brazo Rico and the Glaciar Perito Moreno and, above all, to appreciate the region's various ecological habitats, ranging from beechwood to prairie. On a walk in the woods containing beeches such as the nire, the lenga and the cohiue, evergreen trees that exceed a height of 115 feet and whose trunks reach seven feet in diameter, you often hear the drumming of the Patagonian black woodpecker and, if you look carefully you will see the tracks of countless foxes.

Higher up, amidst the Magellan barberry bushes and the notro, with its splendid red flowers, several varieties of wild orchid peep out from a blanket of moss, lichen and the very widespread topa-topa; here it is not at all difficult to spot guanacos, which venture as far as the slopes of the glaciers, where the arvejilla (*Lathyrus nervosus*), a carnivorous plant, covers the terrain with a blue carpet. It takes more luck, however, to come across a piche, a small armadillo.

A road that runs along the northern shore of the Lago Viedma leads to El Chaltén, at the foot of Fitz Roy; only trekking enthusiasts will be able to access the park from here though. Enchanted woodland settings, where the puma hunts the last huemul deer left in the area, majestic peaks, imposing glaciers and the slow wheeling of the noble condor will certainly reward the exertions of anyone who makes this jaunt. (R.M.S.)

306 and 306-307 The Perito Moreno once again, in a photo that allows you to admire the immensity of the Hielo Patagonico Continental Sur in the background, and the detachment of icebergs from the glacial wall.

307 bottom The Cerro Torre glacier in the valley that has been dug out in the course of thousands of years. This impressive massif was scaled by the Italian Cesare Maestri and the Austrian Toni Egger, who unfortunately died in the enterprise.

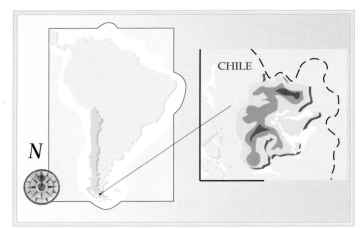

CHILE

N

308 top right This glacier, which extends as far as Lake Pingo, seems to rise out of the clouds, within the territory of the national park.

TORRES DEL PAINE
NATIONAL PARK

The sun's rays have just lit the countryside and two guanacos are chasing each other along the banks of a sky-blue lake whose waters reflect the distinctive triple peaks of Cuernos del Paine: Cuerno Principal, the highest one at 8,528 feet, Cuerno Este and Cuerno Norte, which are slightly lower. This is the first sight to greet visitors, but continuing northeast we reach the pure and crystal-clear blue Lake Sarmiento de Gamboa, looking like a luminous reflection set amidst the yellowish grassy vegetation. Finally, against the background there stand out the three bold

spires of Torres del Paine, after which the park is named: Torre Sur De Agostini, Torre Central and Torre Norte Monzino, all between 8,528 and 8,692 feet.

The Cuernos and the Torres seem to be framed against a third group of mountains, against which stand out the peaks of Cerro Paine Grande, with its altitude of 10,653 feet, and Cerro Fortaleza, which reaches 9,840. These three separate mountain groups form the Massif del Paine, one of the most spectacular orographic systems in the world, with its tumultuous rivers, high-altitude lakes, frothy waterfalls and above all unique array of colors. In fact, it is mainly at sunrise that we can best appreciate the grayish-blue tones that dissolve into purple on the mountain faces, contrasting with the pink vermilion reflected by the granite of the mountaintops.

The hues described here are the result of a particular geological formation of the following complex: an upper layer of sedimentary rock that is dark in color, dating to the Cretaceous, covers the granitic rock beneath it, which dates to the lower Triassic period. During the last Ice Age, the glaciers eroded the entire sedimentary mantle for a thickness of over three thousand feet and today, the dark color of the schist that escaped the erosive action is what creates the particular chromatic association with the granite that is present.

In 1925, the Chilean government issued the first decree to safeguard the nature of this vast territory, which is located between the eastern slopes of the Cordillera of the Andes and the Patagonian steppe, a little less than 186 miles from the Parque Nacional Los Glaciares. Later, in 1970 the Parque Nacional Torres Del Paine was created and then expanded a few years later when Italian mountain-climber Guido Monzino donated the land of his Estansia Rìo Paine to the park. Because of its great importance from a naturalistic standpoint, the park, which now covers an area of more than 494,200 acres, was declared a Reserve of the Biosphere by UNESCO in 1978.

308 bottom Highly alert for the least sign of danger, two young guanacos, known as chulengos, find time to "smile" at the photographer. The guanacos are the wild ancestors of llamas.

308-309 In the golden light of a southern dawn, the Cuernos del Paine seem so close you could touch them, whilst Lake Pehoe has not yet been reached by the rays of the sun.

309 bottom A particularly clear picture of the Fitz-Roy massif: usually the peak of Fitz-Roy is enveloped in clouds, so much so that for a long time it was mistakenly thought to be a volcano.

310-311 Almost as if they want to imitate the long-limbed shape of the Torres del Paine, which visible in the background, the elongated inflorescences of the lupine flowers fill the Chilean plateau with color.

The course of the Rio Paine is quite unique, in that it drains a complex hydrographic system fed by melting glaciers and frequent rains. The river originates from the Dickson Glacier, becomes Lake Dickson and then, as it gradually descends in altitude, forms spectacular waterfalls like Cascada del Rio Paine and Salto Grande Rio Paine. It then goes through the splendid and pristine lakes Paine, Nordenskiöld, Pehoé and Toro, one of the largest basins in this region. After leaving the basin, named Rio Serrano, and collecting the waters of the torrent Grey from the glacier by the same name, it flows into Seno Ultima Speranza.

The presence of mountainous massifs, broad lakes and glaciers determines a notable climatic variation within the territory, with autumn fog and summer temperatures that reach 86°F near Lake Paine, strong summer winds and mild temperatures at Lake Toro and cool summers and winters hovering at 24°F at Lake Grey. As a result, different areas of vegetation have also developed. At the lower altitudes, the

WHERE CONDORS DARE

flightless birds resembling ostriches that reach a height of a meter and a half. The guanaco, a member of the camelide species from which the domestic llama was selected, has a soft thick coat and is the only large herbivore that has spread from the Peruvian Andes to Tierra del Fuego. As a result, it has been the main resource of the indigenous populations for thousands of years, who use its meat as food, its hide and wool for clothing and shelter, its tendons as ropes and its bones as tools and weapons.

In the historic age, these areas were used as summer hunting grounds by the Tehuelche (Patagonia's indigenous population); this is demonstrated by some of the place names, including "Paine," which means "blue" and refers to the numerous bodies of water. One of these is the lagoon Laguna Amarga, suggestive of the colonies of flamingoes found there. It is demarcated by a whitish encrustation along all its banks, caused by a very high concentration of mineral salts that, as its the name suggests, give the water its bitter taste.

Here and in the other wet areas it is also possible to see many of the migrant geese of the Strait of Magellan and a few bandurrias (*Theristicus caudatus*), an odd ibis that is always searching for invertebrates and plants for food. There are also anatids like the Chilean baldpate and the small screaming duck. Another extravagant specimen is the marsupial frog with its pointed face; a number of males take care of the eggs laid by one female and when the embryos start to move, each male takes some of them into its own vocal sac, where they well remain until they have completed their metamorphosis.

In areas where the water conditions of the soil are good, the slopes are colonized by the deciduous Magellanic forest. The dominant species here is the lenga (*Nothofagus pumilio*), splendid in the autumn because of the reddish color of its leaves. The panoramic trails through the woods start from Lake Grey. The icebergs that drop from the glacier over it get beached on its shores. This silvery blue wall—200 feet high—can be reached using a special trimaran. If you pay close attention, you might see some scarlet-crowned hummingbirds agilely crossing through the branches, since this species can fly up to 5,000 feet.

At higher altitudes is the Magellanic tundra, which then turns into a full-fledged high-altitude desert where the last shrubs gradually give way to moss—sphagnum dominates—and lichen. In the bogs that form here, you can also see the small Drosera, a carnivorous plant also found in Europe. From here, you can easily see the flying shapes or the nests of numerous birds of prey such as sparrowhawks, eagles and the undisputed lord of the Andean skies: the condor. This outstanding glider has a wingspan of over nine feet and can smell an animal carcass miles away. However, it can also wound and kill cattle. This greedy bird can eat from 11 to 15 lbs of meat a day—stuffing itself to the point where it can longer fly! (R.M.S.)

Patagonian Steppe alternates with xerophytic pre-Andean brush. The shrubs growing on the dense carpet of grasses, with a predominance of straw, are often thorny, like "mata guanaco" (*Anarthrophyllum desideratum*), "mata negra" (*Verbena tridens*) and barberries (*Berberis buxifolia*). Bright colors liven the landscape in every season: yellow grasses and poacea are dotted with showy flowers like "Don Diego de Noche" (*Oenothera stricta*), violets, primroses and marvelous wild orchids—splendid miniature jewels.

In these wide-open spaces, you can easily observe whole family groups of guanacos, which have a large enough territory in the park for their seasonal migration, as well as Darwin's rheas,

312 *A southern dwarf owl* (Glaucidium nanum), *perfectly camouflaged in the undergrowth and in the light of dusk, prepares for a night of hunting.*

312-313 *The majestic flight of the Andean condor, notwithstanding the size of the creature, is not very laborious; instead, the condor, master of these lands, is highly skilled at exploiting to its best advantage the winds and currents, thus reducing to a minimum the beating of its wings.*

313 bottom left *Four cubs to take care of! This gray fox of Patagonia divides her time between feeding, supervision, playing and searching for food.*

313 bottom right *Cerro Paine Grande, with its blanket of perennial ice, gets ready for its morning awakening in a light that makes it seem unreal. Its peak reaches an altitude of 10,653 feet.*

314-315 *The massive bulk of Mount Almirante, in the foreground, seems to be preventing the clouds from passing, and instead they form a compact cap for the Torres del Paine, which looms in the background.*

INDEX

PHOTOGRAPHIC CREDITS

ANTONIO ATTINI/ARCHIVIO WHITE STAR: pages 12 bottom, 14 bottom right, 144 bottom right, 145 bottom right, 226 left, 227 top right, 228 bottom right, 228-229, 246 top, 247 bottom left, 247 bottom right, 249 bottom left, 249 bottom right, 256 top, 257 bottom right, 260, 261 top, 262 left, 263 bottom left, 263 in basso a destra, 264 top, 264 bottom, 264-265, 267 left, 267 right, 265 bottom right, 268-269, 267 left, 267 right, 268-269.

MARCELLO BERTINETTI/ARCHIVIO WHITE STAR: pages 66 bottom, 78 top left, 78 top right, 80 bottom right, 81 left, 81 right, 88 bottom left, 88 bottom right, 88-89, 89 left, 90 top right, 90 bottom, 92-93, 94, 95 left, 95 right, 102 top left, 102 top right, 102 bottom, 105 left, 105 top right, 105 center top right, 105 center bottom right, 105 bottom right, 108 top, 108 bottom, 127 bottom right, 144 bottom left, 144-145, 145 top right, 146 bottom, 148 bottom right, 150 top left, 151 bottom right, 176 top, 176 bottom, 177 bottom left, 177 bottom right, 178 bottom, 178-179, 179 top left, 179 top right, 179 bottom, 180 top left, 180 top right, 180 center, 180 bottom, 181, 227 bottom right, 233 bottom left, 234 top, 234 bottom, 235 bottom left, 238, 239 bottom right, 254 top, 269 right, 270 bottom left, 271 left, 271 right, 274 left, 274 right, 274-275, 275 bottom left.

MASSIMO BORCHI/ARCHIVIO WHITE STAR: pages 12 top, 228 bottom left, 248 bottom.

ALFIO GAROZZO/ARCHIVIO WHITE STAR: pages 302, 302-303, 303 bottom left, 303 bottom right, 304 top, 306.

LUCIANO RAMIRES/ARCHIVIO WHITE STAR: pages 56 top, 56 bottom, 56-57, 57 bottom left, 57 bottom right, 68 top right, 70 bottom right.

GIULIO VEGGI/ARCHIVIO WHITE STAR: pages 68 top left, 68 bottom, 70 top, 70 bottom left.

LUIGI ACCUSANI: page 155 left, 239 bottom center, 243 left, 248 top, 251 top.

LUIGI ACCUSANI/PANDA PHOTO: page 245 top.

K. AITKEN/PANDA PHOTO: page 199 bottom left.

AISA: pages 74, 75 bottom left, 76-77, 77 top left, 77 top right, 77 bottom.

ALLOFS/ZEFA: pages 126 left, 188 top right, 213 top, 213 bottom.

KURT AMSLER: pages 48 top right, 48 bottom, 49, 50-51, 51 top left, 51 top right, 51 bottom.

ARDEA LONDON LTD: pages 46 bottom right, 47.

KATHIE ATKINSON/OXFORD SCIENTIFIC FILMS: page 187 bottom left.

ADRIAN BAILEY/OXFORD SCIENTIFIC FILMS: pages 125 bottom, 133 left.

CHRIS MARTIN BAHR/ARDEA LONDON LTD: page 44 bottom left.

DARYL BALFOUR/GALLO IMAGES: pages 108-109, 110 bottom left, 110 top right, 110-111, 111, 122-123.

DARYL BALFOUR/NHPA: page 108 center

top, 121 bottom left.

FRANCO BANFI: page 148 bottom left.

ANTONY BANNISTER/NHPA: pages 124-125, 129 bottom left.

A. P. BARNES/NHPA: page 45.

SHAUN BARNETT/HEDGEHOG HOUSE NEW ZELAND: page 218.

DES E JEN BARTLETT/BRUCE COLEMAN COLLECTION: page 120 bottom.

DES E JEN BARTLETT/OXFORD SCIENTIFIC FILMS: page 202.

F. BELTRANDO/PANDA PHOTO: page 14 bottom left.

D.BENSON/MASTERFILE/ZEFA: page 129 bottom right.

CLAUDIO BERTASINI: pages 147 bottom, 150 top right.

M. BIANCARELLI/PANDA PHOTO: page 39 bottom.

BOEHNKE/ZEFA: page 9 bottom.

OLIVER BOLCH/AGENTUR REGINA MARIA ANZEMBERGER: pages 138 center, 186-187, 240-241.

FABIO BOURBON: pages 28 bottom left, 28 bottom right, 254 center, 254 bottom, 257 bottom left.

CHARLES BOWMAN/SCOPE: pages 284 bottom, 284-285.

M. BRANCHI/PANDA PHOTO: pages 42-43.

STANLEY BREEDEN/HÉMISPHÈRE: pages 206-207.

G. CAMMERINI/PANDA PHOTO: page 299 top.

JOHN CANCALOSI/BRUCE COLEMAN COLLECTION: pages 204-205.

CLAUDIO CANGINI: pages 146 top, 149 top, 150 bottom, 293 bottom.

L. CAPPELLI: pages 23, 46 bottom left.

ALAN AND SANDY CAREY/OXFORD SCIENTIFIC FILMS: pages 248-249.

R. CARNE/ZEFA: page 189.

G. CARRARA/PANDA PHOTO: pages 65 bottom, 65 center.

CHRIS CATTON/OXFORD SCIENTIFIC FILMS: page 168 bottom.

PIERS CAVENDISH/ARDEA LONDON LTD: page 44 bottom right.

E. COPPOLA/PANDA PHOTO: page 163 right.

DANIEL J. COX/OXFORD SCIENTIFIC FILMS: page 165 bottom right.

JULES COWAN/BRUCE COLEMAN COLLECTION: pages 262-263.

GERARD S. CUBITT/BRUCE COLEMAN COLLECTION: pages 216-217, 217 bottom right.

G. CUBITT/PANDA PHOTO: page 161 bottom.

SOPHIE AND MICHAEL DAY/BRUCE COLEMAN COLLECTION: page 139.

F. DAMM/SIMEPHOTO: pages 118-119, 304 bottom, 306-307, 309 bottom.

F. DAMM/ZEFA: page 198 top.

MARK DEEBLE E VICTORIA STONE/OXFORD SCIENTIFIC FILMS: page 84 bottom.

M. AND C. DENIS HUOT: pages 2, 8, 9 top right, 14 bottom center, 79, 80 bottom left, 90 top left, 91, 96-97, 97 bottom left, 97 bottom

right, 98, 99 top left, 99 top right, 99 bottom right, 104, 110 top left, 112-113, 113 top, 114 top, 128.

NIGEL J. DENNIS/GALLO IMAGES: pages 119 bottom, 121 bottom right, 130 bottom right.

NIGEL J. DENNIS/NHPA: page 123 bottom right.

NIGEL J. DENNIS/PANDA PHOTO: pages 122 top, 126 right, 126-127, 127 bottom left, 129 top, 129 top left, 133 right center, 133 bottom right.

GRANT DIXON/HEDGEHOG HOUSE NEW ZELAND: pages 166-167.

ERIC DRAGESCO/ARDEA LONDON LTD: pages 54-55.

ERIC DRAGESCO/PANDA PHOTO: pages 24 bottom, 25 top, 26-27, 31 bottom right.

JEAN PAUL FERRERO/ARDEA LONDON LTD: pages 168-169, 169 bottom, 170-171, 171 left, 171 right, 171 bottom, 173 center, 174-175, 175 bottom, 182-183, 198-199.

DAVID B. FLEETHAM/OXFORD SCIENTIFIC FILMS: page 186.

FOCUS TEAM: page 219 top left.

MICHEAL FOGDEN/OXFORD SCIENTIFIC FILMS: page 118 bottom.

DAVID FOODWALL/NHPA: page 165.

J. FOOT/PANDA PHOTO: pages 164-165, 165 bottom left, 241 bottom left, 262 right.

STÉPHANE FRANCES/HÉMISPHÈRE: page 123 bottom left.

CHRISTER FREDRIKKSON/BRUCE COLEMAN COLLECTION: pages 163 left, 240 left.

GALLO IMAGES: pages 130-131.

ANGELO GANDOLFI: pages 68-69, 72-73.

MARTIN GARWOOD/NHPA: pages 52-53.

GEOIMAGE PTY ltd: page 192.

GIEL/SIMEPHOTO: page 226-227.

LAUREN GIRAUDOU/HÉMISPHÈRE: page 160 bottom.

GRZEGORZ GLAZEK: pages 30 bottom, 30-31, 33 center, 33 bottom.

A. GOGNA/K3 PHOTO AGENCY: pages 11 bottom, 58-59, 59 bottom left, 59 bottom right.

FRANÇOIS GOHIER/ARDEA LONDON LTD: pages 174 left, 284 top, 285 bottom left.

NICK GORDON/ARDEA LONDON LTD: page 285 bottom right.

HAMOR GRINBERG: pages 150-151.

P. GRIVA AND N. SANTONA/PANDA PHOTO: page 25 bottom.

JACQUES GUILLARD/SCOPE: pages 48 top left, 50 bottom.

TORE HAGMAN/BRUCE COLEMAN COLLECTION: page 118 center.

MARTIN HARVEY/GALLO IMAGES: page 115 bottom.

MARTIN HARVEY/PANDA PHOTO: pages 99 bottom left, 114 bottom, 116, 125 top left.

PHILIPPE HENRY/OXFORD SCIENTIFIC FILMS: pages 22 bottom, 40 bottom.

MIKE HILL/OXFORD SCIENTIFIC FILMS: page 291 top right.

DAVID HOSKING/PANDA PHOTO: page 277 bottom left.

HPH PHOTOGRAPHY/BRUCE COLEMAN:page 133 top left.

JOHANNA HUBER/SIMEPHOTO: pages 188 bottom, 201 bottom.
MASAHIRO IIJINA/ARDEA LONDON LTD: pages 160-161, 162-163, 172, 173 top, 173 bottom, 174 right.
F. JACK JACKSON: page 183 top left.
TIM JACKSON/GALLO IMAGES: page 132.
TIM JACKSON/OXFORD SCIENTIFIC FILMS: page 130 bottom left.
JOHNNY JOHNSON/BRUCE COLEMAN COLLECTION: pages 232 top, 232 bottom.
B. JONES AND M. SHIMLOCK/NHPA: pages 176-177.
MIKAAII KAVANAGH/OXFORD SCIENTIFIC FILMS: pages 156 bottom left, 159 top.
AVI KLAPFER/JEFF ROTMAN PHOTOGRAPHY: pages 282 top left, 282-283, 283 bottom.
KRAHMER/ZEFA: pages 232-233.
MIKE LANE/NHPA: page 208 bottom.
M. LANINI/PANDA PHOTO: page 40 top right.
CHARLES LÉNARS: page 198 bottom.
G. BRAD LEWIS/INNERSPACE VISION: pages 222 right, 222-223, 224 bottom, 224-225.
STEVE LITTLEWOOD/OXFORD SCIENTIFIC FILMS: page 22 top right.
JOE MCDONALD/BRUCE COLEMAN COLLECTION: page 203 bottom right.
G. MARCOALDI/PANDA PHOTO: pages 24-25, 32, 33 top, 40-41, 64.
MASTERFILE/ZEFA: page 129 bottom right.
MASSIMO MASTRORILLO/SIE: pages 4-7, 205 bottom, 252-253.
WOLFGAN MAYR/AGENTUR REGINA MARIA ANZEMBERGER: pages 256-257.
TED MEAD/OXFORD SCIENTIFIC FILMS: page 217 bottom left.
L. MEIER/ZEFA : pages 199 bottom right, 201 top.
F. MERCAY/PANDA PHOTO: page 203 bottom left.
STEFAN MEYERS/ARDEA LONDON LTD: page 52 right.
STEFAN MEYERS/PANDA PHOTO: pages 31 bottom left, 38-39, 227 top left.
MARCO MILANI/K3 PHOTO AGENCY: page 307 bottom, 314-315.
COLIN MONTEATH/OXFORD SCIENTIFIC FILMS: pages 308-309.
J. C. MUNOZ/PANDA PHOTO: page 138 bottom.
NASA: pages 89 right, 122 bottom, 261 bottom, 305.
R. OGGIONI/PANDA PHOTO: page 200 bottom.
LUIS ORTEO/HÉMISPHÈRES: page 243 right.
STAN OSOLINSKI/OXFORD SCIENTIFIC FILMS: page 155 right.
R. PACELLI/PANDA PHOTO: page 268 bottom right.
VINCENZO PAOLILLO: pages 134 bottom

left, 134 bottom right, 134-135, 135 left, 135 right, 136 top left, 136 top right, 136 bottom, 136-137, 137 bottom, 146-147, 151 bottom left, 282 top right, 282 bottom, 288 top, 290-291.
VINCENZO PAOLILLO AND GIANFRANCO D'AMATO: pages 286 bottom, 286-287, 287 left, 287 right.
D. PARER AND E. PARER-COOK/ARDEA LONDON LTD: pages 116-117.
DOUG PERRINE/INNERSPACE VISION: pages 221 bottom, 222 left, 223 bottom, 224 top.
A. PETRETTI/PANDA PHOTO: pages 53 bottom right, 55 top.
SERGIO PITAMITZ/SIE: page 215 left.
FRITZ POLKING/PANDA PHOTO: page 277 bottom right.
FEDERICO RAISER/K3 PHOTO AGENCY: pages 235 bottom right, 236-237.
LUCIANO RAMIRES: pages 10 top right, 10-11, 22 top left, 38 bottom, 40 top left, 52 top left, 53 bottom left, 54 bottom left, 54 bottom right, 55 bottom, 62, 62-63, 63 bottom left, 63 bottom right, 65 top left, 65 top right, 66 top, 67, 70 bottom right, 71.
Y.J. REY-MILLET/PANDA PHOTO: page 277 top right.
ROBERTO RINALDI: pages 20-21, 146 center, 148-149, 149 bottom, 193 left, 193 right, 194 top, 194 center, 194 bottom, 195, 196-197.
M. RIPANI/SIMEPHOTO: pages 44-45, 46-47.
GORDON ROBERTS/HEDGEHOG HOUSE NEW ZELAND: page 216.
JEFF ROTMAN: pages 280 left, 280 right, 280-281, 281 bottom left, 281 bottom right, 292, 293 top, 293 bottom.
ANDY ROUSE/NHPA: pages 298-299.
GALEN ROWELL: pages 1, 13, 9 top left, 18-19, 160 top, 162 bottom, 166-167, 220 bottom, 233 bottom right, 246 bottom, 246-247, 258-259, 262-263, 268 bottom left, 270 bottom right, 270-271, 278-279, 288 bottom, 289, 230-231, 234-235, 255, 272-273, 310-311.
GALEN ROWELL/FRANCA SPERANZA: page 256 bottom.
F. SAVIGNY/PANDA PHOTO: pages 120-121, 154 top, 154-155.
KEVIN SHAFER/NHPA: pages 101, 125 top right.
A. SHAH/PANDA PHOTO: pages 78 bottom, 82-83, 100 top left, 102-103, 103 bottom, 108 center bottom, 113 bottom, 117 bottom right.
JOHN SHAW/BRUCE COLEMAN COLLECTION: pages 238-239, 242-243.
JOHN SHAW/NHPA: page 229.
DAVID SHEN/INNERSPACE VISION: page 225 bottom.
SILVESTRIS FOTOSERVICE: pages 58 top, 58 bottom, 59 top, 60 top, 60 bottom left, 60 bottom right, 60-61, 61 bottom left, 61 bottom right, 74-75, 75 bottom right, 76 top.
GIOVANNI SIMEONE/SIMEPHOTO: pages 24 bottom, 25 top, 28-29, 244-245, 250-251, 251

center, 251 bottom.
G. SUNDBERG/PANDA PHOTO: page 29.
G. TOGNON/PANDA PHOTO: page 299 bottom left.
DAVID TOMLINSON/BRUCE COLEMAN COLLECTION: pages 266-267.
L.TREVERTON/ZEFA-APL: page 201 top.
TUI-DE-ROY/HEDGEHOG HOUSE NEW ZELAND: page 219 right.
TUI-DE-ROY/OXFORD SCIENTIFIC FILMS: page 288 center.
STEVE TURNER/OXFORD SCIENTIFIC FILMS: page 117 bottom left.
STEFANO UNTERTHINER: pages 239 bottom left, 269 left.
MASA USHIODA/INNERSPACE VISION: page 220 top.
T. VAILO/PANDAPHOTO: page 10 bottom.
DRIES VAN ZYL/BRUCE COLEMAN COLLECTION: page 131.
UWE WALZ/BRUCE COLEMAN COLLECTION: page 244 bottom left.
M. WATSON/ARDEA LONDON LTD: pages 138 top, 168 top, 184-185, 286 top.
JAMES D. WATT/INNERSPACE VISION: pages 187 bottom right, 220-221.
DAVID WRIGGLESWORTH/OXFORD SCIENTIFIC FILMS: page 242 bottom.
KONRAD WHOTE/OXFORD SCIENTIFIC FILMS: pages 114-115, 244 bottom right.
DAVID WOODFALL/NHPA: pages 142-143, 164 bottom.
ZEFA/POWERSTOCK: pages 202-203.
GÜNTER ZIESLER: pages 10 top left, 16-17, 34 bottom, 34-35, 35 top, 35 bottom, 36 bottom, 36-37, 37 top, 37 bottom, 38 top, 80-81, 84-85, 85 bottom, 86 bottom, 86-87, 87 top, 87 bottom, 96 bottom, 100 center, 100 bottom, 100 right, 106-107, 113 center, 140 bottom, 140-141, 141 top, 141 bottom, 152 top, 152 bottom, 152-153, 153 bottom left, 153 bottom right, 156 top left, 157, 158-159, 159 bottom, 182 top, 182 bottom, 183 top right, 184 bottom, 185 top, 185 bottom, 188 top left, 190-191, 200-201, 204 top, 204 bottom, 208-209, 209 top, 209 bottom, 210 left, 210 right, 210-211, 211 bottom, 212 bottom, 212-213, 214, 215 top, 241 bottom right, 245 bottom, 275 bottom right, 276 bottom left, 276 bottom right, 276-277, 290 bottom left, 290 bottom right, 291 top left, 291 bottom right, 294-295, 296, 296-297, 297 bottom left, 297 bottom right, 298 bottom left, 298 bottom right, 299 bottom left, 299 bottom right, 300 top left, 300 top right, 300 bottom, 300-301, 302, 302-303, 303 bottom left, 303 bottom right, 308 top, 308 bottom, 312, 312-313, 313 bottom left, 313 bottom right.
DANIEL ZUPANC/NHPA: page 215 bottom right.

TRANSLATION
GLOBE, Foligno (PG)